IN SEARCH OF CENTRAL AMERICA AND THE CARIBBEAN

IN SEARCH

OF

CENTRAL

AMERICA

AND THE

CARIBBEAN

Reader's
Digest

PUBLISHED BY THE READER'S DIGEST ASSOCIATION LIMITED

LONDON   NEW YORK   MONTREAL   SYDNEY   CAPE TOWN

Originally published in partwork form,
Des Pays et des Hommes,
by Librairie Larousse, Paris

A Reader's Digest selection

IN SEARCH OF CENTRAL AMERICA AND THE CARIBBEAN

First English Edition Copyright © 1993
The Reader's Digest Association Limited, Berkeley Square House,
Berkeley Square, London W1X 6AB

Copyright © 1993
Reader's Digest Association Far East Limited
Philippines Copyright 1993
Reader's Digest Association Far East Limited

Originally published in French as a partwork,
Des Pays et des Hommes
Copyright © 1991
Librairie Larousse

Translated and edited by Toucan Books Limited, London
Translated and adapted by Andrew Kerr-Jarrett, Jonathan Mantle

ISBN 0 276 42058 6

Printed by Printer Industria Gráfica S.A., Barcelona

Contents

COVER PICTURES

Top: *A pyramid-temple at Chichen Itza in Mexico's Yucatán peninsula is impressive
testimony to the sophistication of the ancient Maya civilisation.*
Bottom: *Extravagant costumes such as this make Trinidad's pre-Lenten carnival one of the region's most colourful celebrations.*

The Cockpit of the Americas

Christianity and ancient Indian beliefs share the honours in the church of St Thomas which rises at the centre of Chichicastenango, a town in Guatemala's western highlands. The church itself was built in 1540 by Spanish missionaries, who simply placed it on top of a temple erected centuries earlier by the Mayan people, creators of one of the most sophisticated civilisations of the ancient Americas. Inside, the church is neatly divided in two. To the left, facing the main altar, are several lesser altars dedicated to traditional Mayan divinities; to the right, the altars are dedicated to Christian saints. Offerings of flower petals, lit candles and alcohol stand before the altars – Mayan and Catholic alike – and the air is thick with incense burnt by local worshippers, the direct descendants of the Maya of old. The steps of the former temple, leading up to the church, are black with the remains of burnt offerings, some left in honour of St Thomas (the local patron saint), some in honour of the gods of the Maya.

Religions, cultures and races mingle and co-exist in intriguing patterns in Central America and the Caribbean. When, in 1492, Christopher Columbus made his first landfall in the Americas in what are now known as the Bahamas, he opened the gates to a flood of immigrants coming from the far corners of the earth. Over the centuries that followed, Spanish *conquistadores* ('conquerors'), British and French buccaneers and sugar-cane planters, Dutch traders, African slaves, Jews escaping persecution in Europe, indentured labourers from the Indian sub-continent, Chinese, Lebanese and Syrians (many of whom arrived as peddlers and ended up as substantial businessmen) – all made their way (voluntarily or involuntarily) across the seas to the Caribbean. One testimony to the resulting mix is the Papiamento language spoken in the Dutch West Indian island of Curaçao. This was originally a dialect of Portuguese used by Jewish settlers in the 17th century. But, in the centuries since then, it has gathered elements of grammar and vocabulary from Dutch, Spanish, French and English, as well as the various African languages of the former slaves whose descendants now form the bulk of the Caribbean's population. The mingling has produced one of the most fascinating of the region's many 'creole' (or patois) tongues.

Meanwhile, the native Indian inhabitants – themselves descended from peoples who had crossed the Bering Straits from Asia around 50,000 BC – survived as best they could. In the islands of the Caribbean, most of them died out, due to overwork on plantations, or from unknown diseases brought by their European conquerors. On the mainland, they survived in greater numbers, despite numerous barbarities committed against them. Some intermarried with the Spanish, and their *mestizo* (mixed-race) descendants adopted many Spanish ways. Others retreated into remote jungles and mountain *sierras* (ranges), where in places their lifestyles have continued comparatively little changed to this day. They include such groups as the Huichol Indians living in the Sierra Huichol of north-western Mexico, whose traditions include a 250-mile annual pilgrimage across mountains and deserts in search of the sacred (and hallucinogenic) *peyotl* plant. Farther south in Mexico, in the mountains of Chiapas, are the Tzotzil Indians. The centre of their scattered community is San Juan Chamula, which outsiders are allowed to visit only when accompanied by a Tzotzil official carrying a mahogany baton as his wand of office.

Elsewhere are groups of more recent date. Among the Caribbean islands, Jamaica has the Maroons, descended from escaped slaves who kept up a successful guerrilla warfare against the British colonial authorities in the 17th and 18th centuries. They were never defeated and still form a kind of state within the state, with their own system of justice and an elected 'colonel' as leader. The French islands include the tiny Iles des Saintes, lying off Guadeloupe's southern tip. The ancestors of their inhabitants came from Brittany, Normandy and the region around Poitiers in central France in the 17th century. They still form a closely knit, 'poor white' community, living as their ancestors did from fishing. Lying south of Les Saintes is Dominica which, like many of its neighbours, changed hands several times between the French and British, but ended up as a British colony from 1805 until its independence in 1978. Living in a 'reservation' in the east of the island are the last 2000 or so Carib Indians, whose warlike ancestors once dominated the whole of the eastern Caribbean and gave the sea its name.

The region's geography is scarcely less varied than its racial and cultural mix. Running down Central America's western, Pacific side is a chain of volcanic mountains linking the Californian Coast Ranges to the north with the Andes of South America. Many of the volcanoes are still active, including Tajumulco in Guatemala – 13,810 feet above sea level and Central America's highest point. Mexico has high inland plateaus stretched out between the different branches of the Sierra Madre. Spread across one of them is the huge sprawl of Mexico City, one of the most populous cities on earth; its centre occupies the site of the former capital of the Aztec empire, overthrown by the *conquistador* Hernán Cortés and a handful of followers in an astonishing campaign starting in 1519. Elsewhere are the survivors of the gold and silver mines that enticed the Spanish in the first place. Towards the Caribbean coast are very different regions of lowland tropical jungle: Mexico's Yucatán peninsula and the Petén region of northern Guatemala. Sheltering among them are the remains of large temples built by the Maya from around 250 BC onwards.

The Caribbean islands encompass equal variety. In size, the inhabited islands range from Cuba – covering 44,218 square miles and only a little smaller than England – to tiny dots on the map, such as the Dutch island of Saba, an extinct volcano rising sheer from the sea and covering just 5 square miles. Trinidad in the south-east lies at the foot of the arc of smaller islands running down the Caribbean's eastern rim and known as the Lesser Antilles. It is essentially a detached piece of the South American mainland and has an exceptionally rich wildlife. Together with Tobago – the two islands form a single state within the Commonwealth – it is home to more bird species than any other Caribbean island, including 41 different kinds of hummingbird. Another of Trinidad's marvels is the strange oozing mass of the Pitch Lake. It was formed by crude oil seeping through porous rocks from an underground reservoir, and is 285 feet deep in the middle and nearly a mile around the edge. Glorious beaches abound throughout the Caribbean (giving rise to one of its most profitable modern industries, tourism). The larger islands of the west, known as the Greater Antilles, also have impressive mountain ranges. In Hispaniola – shared between Haiti and the Dominican Republic – these rise to Pico Duarte (10,417 feet), the highest point in the islands.

The islands and their mainland neighbours have not always found it easy to come to terms with their geography and history. History has bequeathed them the heritage of resentments lingering on from the times of slavery and colonial domination, and economies that were often more geared to the benefit of a 'mother country' than the long-term good of the local people. Geography has blessed places such as Mexico and Trinidad with oil and almost all the countries with rich tourist potential in spectacular beaches, lakes or mountains. On the other hand, the islands in particular have to contend with problems such as their fragmentation into tiny states or territories, some French-speaking, some English-speaking, some Spanish-speaking, some Dutch-speaking – or sometimes speaking more than one language.

Even the more stable and prosperous of these nations (such as Barbados or the Bahamas) find it comparatively hard to hold their own. Others have been less fortunate. Haiti started off with high hopes when its black slaves threw off the French colonial yoke at the beginning of the 19th century. Since then, its history has been dominated by chronic political instability (it had 20 different rulers between 1843 and 1915) and acute poverty – it is by far the poorest country in the western hemisphere. On the mainland, Guatemala has suffered numerous brutal dictators since it first became an independent republic of its own in 1839 – it still has a poor human rights record. Since 1959, Fidel Castro's Cuba has doggedly pursued its own Marxist course, with the collapse of Communism in Eastern Europe seeming only to increase its leader's determination to stay true to his ideology. Even so, inevitable question marks hang over the future of a regime that demands continuing sacrifices of a people, many of whom long for the consumer delights of capitalism.

For many of the Central American and Caribbean peoples, life is unlikely to get much easier in the foreseeable future. However, they possess resources of less tangible kinds. In religion, these encompass almost every conceivable brand of Protestantism as well as Catholicism, the surviving religious beliefs of the native Indians of Central America and African-based religions such as Voodoo in Haiti. In music and dance, popular traditions range from the *mariachi* bands of Mexico to the sensous *biguine* and *calinda* dances of the French West Indies. In recent times, Jamaica has produced the vibrant rhythms of reggae. Among painters and artists are the great muralists of 20th-century Mexico, notably Diego Rivera, and Haiti's 'naive' school of painters. Writers include Nobel prize-winners such as Guatemala's Miguel Angel Asturias and, most recently, the poet Derek Walcott from St Lucia in the Lesser Antilles. The search for an identity is an almost obsessive priority for the region's nations, large and small alike. In many cases, the material resources for the quest are scarce; culturally, however, most have an abundance to draw on.

Mexico

With some 24 million inhabitants, Mexico City is the second-largest city on earth and may soon become the largest. The country as a whole is as spectacular as its capital: in its extremes of poverty and wealth, the mingling of its 'three cultures' (Indian, Spanish and modern), and its landscapes of high plateaus and volcanic peaks. In its mountain heartland, the Toltec and Aztec empires rose and fell. Along its Caribbean shore flourished the gentler civilisation of the Maya. Mexico has also given birth to some of the most original of modern artists and writers – such as the muralist Diego Rivera and the man of letters Octavio Paz.

Previous page:
A charro *(cowboy) from the western state of Jalisco around Guadalajara wears the traditional sombrero of the men who work the ranches there. Jalisco is a state of cattle, large estates, rodeos and bullfights.*

Sparkling mosaics decorate the outside walls of Mexico City's university library. The work of Juan O'Gorman, they depict the march of science from a Mexican perspective: from the times of the Aztecs (and their skilled astronomers) to the discoveries of modern international science.

Multicoloured concrete pillars mark the approaches to one of Mexico City's modern workers' suburbs. From a distance, they look like blocks of flats. In fact, they are there for ornament, reflecting a Mexican delight in decorative architecture.

Heartlands of the Aztec Empire

Mexico City, lying over 7000 feet above sea level, has long struck visitors with awe. For the Spanish chronicler Bernal Díaz reaching the region with his fellow *conquistadores* in 1519, it looked 'like an enchanted vision … Indeed, some of our soldiers asked whether it was not all a dream.'

Nearly 500 years later, the city has changed beyond all recognition from that discovered by the Spanish, with stately palaces and sweet-smelling cedar groves rising majestically from islands in large expanses of lake. The heart of the Aztec empire, which since the early 13th century had spread to control much of modern Mexico, is now one of the largest, and fastest growing, cities on earth, best known for its pollution, smog and the poverty of many of its citizens. It also hit the world headlines in 1985 when it was shaken by an earthquake, which took at least 7000 lives. Mexico City is still, however, a place of awesome beauty alongside the grime and misery.

Travelling overland like the *conquistadores* from the Caribbean coast to the east, the first glimpses of what lies in store come near the city of Puebla. Rising 177 feet into the air above Cholula, just 5 miles west of Puebla, is the great pyramid of Quetzalcóatl, the plumed serpent god of the Aztecs and of their predecessors the Toltecs. It is the largest pyramid in the world, far surpassing those of the ancient Egyptians; its base covers nearly 45 acres.

The Spanish lost little time in trying to sanitise its pagan past and built the Chapel of Los Remedios on its summit. Even so, as the setting sun silhouettes the twin volcanic cones of Ixtaccíhuatl and Popocatépetl to the west, the presence of an older, more mysterious world is apparent. A local legend tells the story of a couple whose names the two volcanoes bear. Popocatépetl was a mighty Aztec warrior who was falsely reported killed in battle. Hearing the news, his lover Ixtaccihuatl died of a broken heart. Popocatépetl came home to find her dead, and pined over her body until he too died and they were reunited in heaven.

Night falls over Cholula, and out of sight beyond the two peaks are the sprawling lights of the capital itself. 'It is not surprising … that I should write in this vein,' commented Díaz. 'It was so wonderful that I do not know how to describe this first glimpse of things never heard of, seen or dreamed of before.'

The rest of the country is as majestic as the region around its capital. A land of volcanic mountain ranges and high plateaus, Mexico has lowlands only along its Pacific coastline in the west, along the Gulf of Mexico and on the Yucatán peninsula which pokes into the Caribbean in the east. Its highest peak, Citlaltéptl, rises to 18,855 feet in the eastern state of Veracruz and is perpetually snow-capped; Popocatépetl looming over the capital reaches 17,887 feet.

Some 70 per cent of the country lies over 1600 feet above sea level. The central plateau is a region of high plains and great deserts, merging into broad valleys, lakes and dormant volcanoes towards the south. In the north-west, the mountains of the Sierra Madre Occidental form a huge barrier between the plateau and the Pacific coast. In the east rise the peaks of the Sierra Madre Oriental. South of Mexico City, the Sierra Madre del Sur extends towards the Guatemalan border, until broken at the narrow isthmus of Tehuantepec.

Mexico of the Indians

Mexico is still strongly Indian. In 1519, the Spaniard Hernán Cortés, with 16 horses and 588 soldiers (including the chronicler Díaz), landed on its eastern coast and, against considerable odds, defeated the Aztec emperor Moctezuma. Within a few years the *conquistadores* had pillaged the entire empire. From the very first, however, there were a few Spaniards, such as the Dominican priest Bartolomé de las Casas, who shrank from the attempts to eliminate the Indian cultures and values that had underpinned the former empire. Despite the widespread greed for gold and a determination to impose Spanish ways and the Catholic creed on this 'new world', there was also something about the Indian world that fascinated some of the new conquerors.

Modern Mexico is a result of conflicting historical influences. When the Mexicans of today seek to understand who they are and what makes them distinctive, they find themselves drawn irresistibly towards their past. Testimonies to this cult of history abound across the country. They can be seen in the statues on Mexico City's central Paseo de la Reforma: of Christopher Columbus and Charles IV of Spain, representing one side of the equation; and of Cuauhtémoc, Moctezuma's nephew and the last reigning Aztec emperor, representing the other. Cuauhtémoc led the final resistance to the Spanish, until

Etècatl, the god of wind, was one of many divinities worshipped by the Aztecs. Although ruthless conquerors, the Aztecs were always remarkably hospitable towards the gods of the peoples they subdued, often building new temples for them. Alternatively, the conquered peoples could come to Tenochtitlán, the Aztec capital, to worship at the Temple of All the Gods.

Mexico City's many museums and galleries are popular places, with ample explanations of the various works of art and well-planned layouts. Here, a pair of visitors sit in front of one of the more gory works of the frescoist José Clemente Orozco in the Museum of Fine Arts.

Balloon and toy sellers add colour in Mexico City's northern suburbs. Life for Mexican children is punctuated by a succession of festivals, though here at Guadalupe the festive spirit lasts most of the year. The original basilica was built where the Virgin appeared to an Aztec Indian shepherd Juan Diego in 1531, but has been closed by subsidence and is now a museum. Instead, pilgrims pay their homage to the Virgin in the futuristic edifice directly opposite.

Humility and religious fervour mark the face of this Indian woman, shuffling on her knees across the square at Guadalupe. The Indians have adopted the Virgin of Guadalupe as their patroness, and no effort is too much for pilgrims. They put on their best clothes and buy the most elaborate candles they can afford. Only their prayers they keep to themselves.

captured in 1521 at the end of a four-month siege of his capital Tenochtitlán (roughly the site occupied by central Mexico City today). His subsequent refusal under torture to reveal the whereabouts of hidden Aztec treasure made him a hero of stoic defiance.

Such monuments are not confined to the capital. Throughout the country, towns and villages have statues to figures such as Miguel Hidalgo (the country priest who in 1810 triggered Mexico's struggle for independence from Spain – a freedom which the country finally won 11 years later in 1821); Benito Juárez (a Zapotec Indian from the south who was twice president in the 1860s, and a hero of the Mexican struggle against foreign, particularly French, interference); and to the two revolutionary leaders of the turn of the century, Emiliano Zapata and Pancho Villa. Hotels, schools, universities and public buildings are all festooned with immense paintings, mosaics or murals depicting dramatic moments from the past.

The mingling of Spanish and Indian is evident elsewhere: in the country's folklore, in its succession of colourful festivals, even in the names and mottoes daubed in large letters on the front bumpers of trucks – *El Tigre loco* (The Mad Tiger), *En Dios solo confío* (In God alone I trust), and so on. In Mexico City, the morbid side of the culture is all too apparent in a quick glance at the cinema listings. Horror films outnumber others, while out on the streets lurid posters invite you to a gruesome feast of flesh-creeping drama.

The Mexican capacity for hanging on and surviving is evident in the number of Indian peasants who, after centuries as refugees in the relative safety of the remoter mountain regions, are now pouring into the country's cities. The official policy is to integrate them into a

Mexico City – the veneer of prosperity

The capital is monstrous – in its appeal, as well as in its poverty and sheer sprawling size. Its two main axes are the Avenida de los Insurgentes running roughly north-south for 16 miles (it is one of the world's longest thoroughfares) and the Paseo de la Reforma, extending for a more modest 9 miles. Both arteries are noticeably European; it was the Austrian Archduke Maximilian – briefly and disastrously imposed on the Mexicans as emperor by an alliance of the French and local conservatives in 1864–67 – who decided the route of the Paseo de la Reforma and commissioned plans for many of its buildings.

Appearances are deceptive, however. Only yards behind the prestigious office blocks of the great thoroughfares are narrow streets and alleys, haunted by beggars and street-sellers (most of them with precious little to sell), who settle themselves here in the early morning, anxious not to miss the first passers-by. The streets do not get busy until nine o'clock when many people eat breakfast on the street. This is the most profitable part of the day for the small shops and stalls selling fruit juices: mango, pineapple, pawpaw, orange and puréed banana – often laced with raw egg.

For the more wealthy, breakfast can mean a trip to the local Sanborn's, a chainstore-cum-restaurant. The style here is very different from the streets – and distinctly international. Waitresses in music-hall interpretations of traditional Indian or Spanish dress whizz past with trays of tortillas, tacos, American-style hamburgers and glasses of Coca-Cola. Some Sanborn's occupy important historical sites, such as the beautiful 16th-century Casa de los Azulejos (House of the Tiles), covered with blue and white tiles, near Mexico City's historic centre, the Zócalo. Inside are frescoes by the early 20th-century artist José Clemente Orozco.

A contrast to the expensively dressed businessmen in Sanborn's lies north along the Paseo de la Reforma in

The modern world mingles with the old as an Indian mother and child pose for the camera in front of an image of the Virgin. The photographer provides the sombreros, and the resulting picture will be a treasured memento.

national Mexican culture – an approach that is well summed up in the words inscribed on a memorial in Mexico City's Plaza de las Tres Culturas (Square of the Three Cultures): 'On August 13, 1521 fell Tlatelolco [a city adjoining Tenochtitlán, where the Aztecs made their last stand] heroically defended by Cuauhtémoc. It was neither triumph nor disaster, but the painful birth of the *mestizo* [mixed-race] people that is the Mexico of today.'

The reality is, of course, less tidy. The waves of people converging on the cities inevitably suffer on two sides. As country people, they have little in common with the established city-dwellers. But then, neither do they belong any longer to the cultures of their ancestors. For them, the grim reality of Mexico's *mestizo* culture lies in the shantytowns that surround the capital and other cities.

the district known as Guadalupe. Here, an annual pilgrimage is held in honour of Our Lady of Guadalupe, the best-loved of the Mexican Virgins. According to legend, she appeared to an Indian convert and shepherd, Juan Diego, on a December morning in 1531, just over a decade after the Spanish first arrived, and left her image imprinted on his roughly woven cape.

She has a further significance. The story has it that she appeared to Diego in the dress of an Aztec princess, and thus in some way redeemed the treachery of another Aztec princess, known to the Spanish as Doña Marina. Doña Marina was captured by the *conquistadores* soon after they arrived on Mexican soil, but far from resenting her capturers she rapidly became their confidante. She advised Cortés on the Aztec empire, interpreted for him, and later became his mistress and bore him a child. She was a woman of remarkable intelligence, but for the Aztecs and their descendants, *La Malinche* – as they know her – is a supreme example of betrayal.

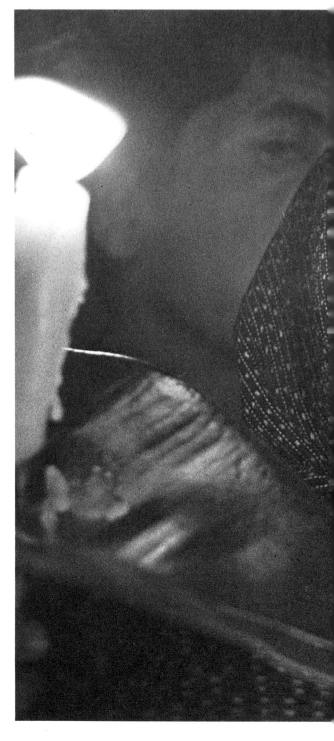

A mask hides the identity of a 'penitent' taking part in the ceremonies of Holy Week. Such people aspire to share in some of the sufferings of Christ – a sacrifice that will in some cases help to take their minds off their own struggle for survival.

Our Lady of Guadalupe has more devoted followers than any other figure of worship in Mexico. To capture the real feel of the depths of piety, faith and hope she arouses in people, you have to mingle with the men and women, young and old, who come to her shrine each year with their children and grandchildren.

They shuffle forward on their knees, their arms filled with flowers, while they hold candles and offerings for the Virgin in their hands. Some come alone, and are soon lost in the throng outside the immense modern basilica which was completed in 1976; the original church built in honour of the Virgin in 1533 had long since become inadequate for the millions of pilgrims who arrived each year. Others are more organised. One woman has a fleece which she uses as a cushion, and which a companion drags forwards each time she shuffles a little closer to the front. Local children stand around with heaps of newspapers that can be used in similar fashion – they offer them to pilgrims in return for a few centavos.

Inside the basilica, the crowd is huge, and everyone wants to get as close as possible to Diego's cloak with its image of the Virgin. Many miraculous healings have been attributed to the cloak, whose preservation over the centuries is itself something of a miracle. To keep things moving the authorities have even installed a moving walkway to transport people. Even so, the atmosphere is suffocating.

Our Lady of Guadalupe is not alone, of course. From the time when Spanish priests first brought Christianity to the country, its people have shown a taste for the

An Indian woman keeps her rebozo (shawl) wrapped tightly about her face during an act of worship. The Indians put all their religious fervour into the events of Holy Week, much as their ancestors did during the celebrations in honour of the gods of the sun and moon, of fertility, spring and rain. The offerings of fruit and vegetables that they still bring to church on festival days are a reminder of those much older rites.

The flame of a candle symbolises the light of hope; a burden of spiny cactus branches represents the sufferings of Christ. This 'penitent' takes the celebration of Holy Week to its limits.

saints of the Catholic church and all the different 'incarnations' or images of Christ and the Virgin. Theirs is an all-embracing spirituality which delights in worshipping the Virgin of Los Remedios, the Virgin of Solitude, Our Lord of Chalma (in a village church west of Mexico City), the Virgin of Zapopán at Guadalajara and a host of saints.

Each region, town, village, and even household professes a special reverence for a particular saint or Virgin. Over the centuries, many of these have acquired qualities that were formerly attributed to the gods worshipped before Cortés reached Mexico. The 'gods' of today no longer need to be propitiated with human sacrifices – though animal sacrifice is still widespread among rural Indians. What the Mexicans of today do offer, however, is an intense religious fervour, seen most vividly in the festivals – carefree or mournful, or both at the same time – that sprinkle the calendar.

Inside their baskets, the women have piles of tortillas – the thick Mexican pancake made from maize flour. The cooking pans contain a variety of fillings, meats and vegetables, mostly generously spiced with chilli. A tortilla with a filling makes a cheap and nutritious meal.

Flower sellers prepare for the market at Chalco. Mexican gardens and the Mexican countryside abound in flowers, and they are popular offerings on festival days.

The sacrifice now is financial. Many Indian families will dig deep into their meagre resources, to celebrate each festival in fitting style.

Although December 12 is the special day for worshippers of Our Lady of Guadalupe, a festival atmosphere fills the basilica and its square for most of the year. Many faces of Mexico mingle here, from the cheerful shoe-shine boy dressed in rags, to the lady of Spanish descent, clad in elegantly tailored suit and black mantilla. The smell of fried food drifts across the square from the stalls of food sellers. Music from transistor radios blends with the laments of devout pilgrims, and then suddenly a troupe of dancers, in feathered costumes, bells on their ankles and ribbons floating in the wind, come bounding along the esplanade. Past and present come face to face and blend together in a strangely moving fashion.

It seems as if only the image they worship has changed over the centuries. The Indians of old honoured Tláloc, god of rain and water, and thus lord of the harvest. They gave him thanks at the end of a drought, and when the floods receded. His monumental stone figure still adorns the fronts of many of the most beautiful modern buildings in Mexico (bringing back memories of the 'great towers and buildings' which so impressed Bernal Díaz). Tláloc took a multitude of forms, and was constantly reborn – he was also the god Chac of the Maya of the south during the pre-Columbian ages.

Similarly, the god Quetzalcóatl, the plumed serpent and opponent of human sacrifices, kept reappearing. God of peace and life, he was the product of the civilisation of Teotihuacán, which flourished in the uplands north-east of Mexico City until around AD 900, long predating the Aztecs. He re-emerged with the Toltecs, who sacked the capital of the Teotihuacán empire in about AD 900 and survived as the region's dominant power until the 12th century. However, a priestly caste dedicated to human sacrifice objected to the bloodless worship he inspired. The story goes that he fled into exile in the Yucatán, before finally disappearing 'towards the east', from where he was supposed to return one day. He thus inadvertently played a crucial role in the defeat of the Aztecs: when the Spanish landed in April 1519, Moctezuma and his advisers thought that they were the fulfilment of this ancient prophecy.

There were many lesser Indian deities whose secrets still lie hidden under the pavements of Mexico City.

Some of these were discovered after work on a tunnel not far from the city's cathedral in 1978 unearthed Aztec remains – including an 8-ton stone disk depicting the moon goddess Coyolxauhqui. Nearby, archaeologists excavated all that was left of the Templo Mayor (Great Temple), whose centrepiece in the days of the Aztecs had been a 150-foot-high pyramid in honour of the redoubtable god of war Huitzilopochtli.

Businessmen and mediums

A meeting with a fairly typical Mexican businessman reveals a lot about the country. He is dynamic and knowledgeable about the latest developments in agricultural technology and marketing systems, and speaks fluently about them all, while through the office

Below left: The death's-head cartoons of the engraver José Guadalupe Posada summed up the spirit of those who resisted the dictatorship of General Porfirio Díaz, ruler of Mexico for three and a half decades from 1876. The revolution that ousted him in 1910 is one of the great landmarks of Mexican history – comparable with 1821 when the country finally won independence from Spain.

As in other Latin countries, street life is relaxed in Mexico. People chat in doorways or while waiting for a bus; others settle down on the pavement for a quick snack.

An Indian woman sits in one of the punt-like craft of Lake Xochimilco, and prepares cobs of maize for boiling and then roasting. She will sell them to the pleasure-seekers who converge on Xochimilco every Sunday.

window comes the endless rumble of traffic on the Paseo de la Reforma below. It is definitely the 20th century. Our Lady of Guadalupe, Quetzalcóatl and the *conquistadores*, all seem a thousand miles away.

But again, appearances are deceptive. When friends meet the tone of the conversation changes. *'Hola*, little brother, how's my godmother, Doña Lolita?' the businessman cries, and suddenly the Mexican in them

both has resurfaced. The few words of English which spatter their conversation (*¿Quieres un drink?* – Do you want a drink?) serve only to emphasise just how Mexican they really are.

The inquiry after Doña Lolita leads them on to tell her story. One day, the godmother went to pray to the Virgin de los Remedios, in an effort to get rid of some of her many aches and pains. Disdaining the good

offices of the Catholic church, however, she went to the Obra Espiritual, a popular church which mixes a few basic Christian forms with spiritualism and other practices from the Mexican Indian past. With the help of a medium, she entered into conversation with the Virgin, who then introduced – or re-introduced – her to Dolores, Doña Lolita's late mother. Dolores duly assured her daughter of her protection, but also

informed her that her various ills had a purifying value. The next day, Doña Lolita felt a lot better, and was able to cope calmly with the vehement reproaches of her Catholic confessor.

Her story illustrates the contradictions in a people who are by nature profoundly religious but who have often rebelled against the Catholic church and its opposition to social or economic change. At a time when the poor of Mexico started to hope for a better life, the church – with the exception of a few radical priests – stood for the preservation of the status quo.

City without limits

The statistics speak for themselves. In 1970, Mexico City had 8.5 million inhabitants. By 1990, it had about 24 million, and experts predict that by the year 2000 its population will have soared to 35 million.

The network of streets in central Mexico City alone stretches roughly 25 miles from north to south and from east to west. Everything about it is gigantic. To get around this sprawling mass, there are various means of transport. First, the Metro, which is fast, efficient, but still totally inadequate for the pressure of people using it. Alternatively, there are buses or *camiones*, which are scarcely more comfortable. The danger here is the hasty scramble on board at stops where no one is quite sure how long the bus is going to wait. The third option comes in the form of communal taxis which are the most enjoyable and economical way of getting around.

Inside the taxi, passengers come under the protection of the Virgin of Guadalupe. Almost invariably, her image stands up from a tiny, gilded altar on the dashboard, decorated with flowers. It is a minor work of art, typical of Latin America's passion for religious ornamentation. The most surprising thing is the way in which it has emerged as a kind of pop art – spontaneous, original and entirely authentic. In most cases, the taxi-owner will have employed a local craftsman or artist to make his altar, but his own taste is

Teresita and Conchita are among the names given to the restaurant-boats that do a brisk trade on Lake Xochimilco on Sundays. They are decorated with flowers and designs that reveal the continuing influence of Aztec art.

usually imprinted on it as well. He will often have added a picture of his wife or girlfriend, or a bootee belonging to one of his babies.

As the driver eases his way through the crowded streets, the markets are probably the first thing to attract attention. A swirl of colour, noise and endless movement, the markets are another institution that mingles several traditions. In the days before the Spanish arrived, the Indians regularly set out on long journeys to sell their wares in other regions. Then, after the *conquistadores* had seized the country, Indian traders moved into their new towns, most of them laid out on rigid grid plans. They would find some corner of a square to lay out on the bare paving or a mat their vegetables, fruits, rolls of cloth, pottery or lucky charms.

Over the centuries, these impromptu markets became more organised. Sometimes the Indians would be chased away by the authorities, but they always came back. They learnt a few of the basic rules of Spanish-style commerce, but to this day the markets are filled with more or less the same brightly coloured woollen materials and pottery with the same shapes and patterns that the Indians have traded for generations. The dignified, somewhat impassive faces of the traders squatting behind their stalls still display that quality of endurance – waiting patiently for a better future – that features so often in the tales of Mexico's mythology.

Mexico's three cultures

A good place to linger is near the heart of the city: the Plaza de las Tres Culturas. It is easy to see why it was given that name. On one side are the ruins of an Aztec pyramid; on another the imposing walls of the 16th-century convent of Santiago Tlatelolco; on the next rises the Ministry of Foreign Affairs. Mexico's three cultures, Indian, Spanish and modern, stand face to face in the symbolism of stone. The eye roams from the basrelief carvings of the Aztec ruins, to the rounded arches of the convent, to the starker lines of the modern buildings.

A building fever gripped Mexico City throughout the 16th, 17th and 18th centuries. The Zócalo, a few blocks south of the Plaza de las Tres Culturas, is where the different styles of these three centuries blend most harmoniously. Here rises the cathedral – the oldest and largest in Latin America, started in 1525 and completed only in 1813 – and the National Palace, the former seat of the Spanish Viceroys, which was rebuilt in 1692 on the site of Moctezuma's palace. Over its main entrance hangs the so-called Liberty Bell – once the church bell of Miguel Hidalgo's country parish on the plateau north-west of Mexico City, which he rang in 1810 to signal the start of his armed insurrection. This event is celebrated each year, an hour before midnight on September 15, when the President rings the bell (now rather prosaically controlled by electricity) and, before assembled crowds, gives the republican *grito* or cry: *¡Mexicanos, Viva México!*

Elsewhere in the capital, the juxtaposition of different architectural styles can be more startling: the remains of an Aztec temple in a Metro station; a superb baroque church rising above the shacks of a shanty town; dilapidated houses with cracked walls just a few paces from the fashionable Zona Rosa.

The people of Mexico City are particularly proud of their university, which has some superb examples of modern Mexican architecture and ornament. Brightly coloured mosaics on the library tower illustrate the history of science, from the findings of Aztec astronomers to the latest molecular theory. The most famous of all 20th-century Mexican artists, Diego Rivera, contributed a series of basrelief sculptures depicting the history of Mexican sport for the University City's Olympic stadium.

The Plaza de las Tres Culturas displays a similar sense of national ambition. The Mexicans know that theirs is a country with proud traditions, but whose identity is still evolving, and whose future depends on how successfully they construct that identity.

The Mexicans are obsessed with culture. They are, for example, voracious readers, devouring the printed word everywhere and all the time. From early morning, children squat in front of stalls where they sell nuts or ready-peeled figs or key-rings with figures of the Virgin dangling from them … and pore over dog-eared paperbacks or photo-strips with titles that range from the alluring to the melodramatic, the subtly erotic to the more light-heartedly romantic. Often you see six or seven people squeezed onto a bench in a park or square, each of them deaf to the hubbub as they study the newspaper or lose themselves in a novel. They have an astonishing ability to become wrapped in words. They walk along the street reading; they eat reading. Occasionally, people shaking hands with friends will scarcely lift their eyes from the page in front of them. This is one place in the world where the gift of literacy is never wasted.

If reading is one way of escaping the harsh realities of everyday life, the promenade or stroll is another. Sunday is the day for taking the air, and for the people of Mexico City the lake of Xochimilco, to the south, is a favourite spot. It is steeped in memories, for it is all that remains of the immense lake with bays, spits and

The charro *(cowboy) is the epitome of everything to which the traditional Mexican male aspires. But the rituals that surround public displays of the* charro's *art have room for women, too. Girls from the cattle-raising areas of the west learn to ride from childhood, and their traditional finery is no less elaborate than that of the men.*

Cowboy displays – charreadas – compete with bullfights. They give cowboys a chance to show off their riding skills and their dexterity with the lasso, and provide an exciting spectacle for the often highly critical crowd.

A taste for bright colours is a Mexican characteristic. These girls come from the north, and the influence of Andalusia in southern Spain – the original home of many of the region's early colonists – can be seen in the high collars and long sleeves of their dresses.

islands on which the Aztec capital Tenochtitlán was built. Here, for one day of blissful peace, people escape the noise and pollution of the city. Boats decorated with scented, brightly coloured flowers drift lazily amidst the *chinampas* (these were once nursery beds perched on top of soil-filled wooden rafts and anchored to the shore, but gradually they put their roots down to the lake floor to form clusters of tiny islands). The music of *mariachi* bands wafts over the waters, with the distinctive sound of trumpets accompanied by guitars and violins, their players traditionally clothed in the *charro* (cowboy) dress of the state of Jalisco, west of Mexico City. There are also boat-restaurants which tie up alongside and serve a full meal.

From here, it is a far cry to the bustle and heat of the market of La Merced back in the centre of Mexico City. This covers a vast area in the heart of the city, and sells just about every imaginable household item. It is divided into different areas, each specialising in different products. Shoes, for example, are big business in La Merced and take up several bays, though food is not surprisingly the most important commodity. There is also a 'fringe' market in the streets and squares outside the market place, where business is equally brisk, though less organised.

Near the market are sordid alleys, sheltering many *pulquerías*. These are drinking houses where *pulque*, a fermented drink extracted from the fibrous maguey plant, offers temporary oblivion to the down and out. Prostitutes and their pimps wander up and down the streets. Marijuana passes from hand to hand. And yet, even here, the contrasts persist. For, only a few blocks away, there are neighbourhoods which, though poor, have pretensions to respectability. Woe betide young couples who are too overtly amorous in the streets: the police here are on the look out for just such offences, and in accordance with local by-laws can impose substantial fines.

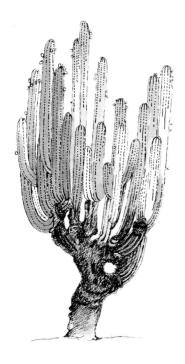

Cactuses grow across much of Mexico, and are one of the most characteristic features of the landscape. Some, such as the aptly named organ pipe cactuses (above) and the various torch cactuses, are used to make garden hedges. The extremely hard wood of their trunks makes an excellent fuel and is often used to fire potters' kilns.

Battered cars, a boy on horseback and a donkey carrying a bundle of wood reveal rural Mexico at its most basic. Life is hard and often lonely for village people, enlivened only by the religious festivals which offer an opportunity to dance, dress up and feast.

The arts of good living

Just about everywhere, in the market and in the narrow streets surrounding it, women carry little bundles of white cloth, inside which are piles of tortillas. These thick pancakes serve as edible plates for the rich fillings poured over them. They are simple to make: maize flour is the basic ingredient, but a pinch of powdered lime is added, to give them a bitter taste.

Traditionally, the dough is kneaded with the palms of the hands, until it reaches just the right texture. Nowadays many of the tortilla stalls in the market are equipped with huge machines that knead several enormous heaps of dough at a time. Fillings are varied: well-cooked, spicy mince; pork; turkey; fish, and vegetables, notably *frijoles* (beans).

In the west of the city, the Paseo de la Reforma emerges from dusty streets of dilapidated houses into the Zona Rosa, a district of large hotels, elegant shops and smart night spots. This is a favourite meeting place for the city's financial elite, and is where most of the foreign embassies and many large businesses are situated. Farther on again, the Reforma leads into the park of Chapultepec. On the left, near a lake, rises the rococo palace where the ill-fated Emperor Maximilian lived. On the right is another fine specimen of modern Mexican architecture: the Museum of Anthropology, built by Pedro Ramírez Vásquez. It includes a huge patio sheltered by a vast concrete mushroom, measuring over 45,000 square feet.

Hills surround most of the city; in the west these include the district of Lomas, which enjoys stunning views of the capital. Among the pine trees that clothe much of the hillsides are the homes of the very rich. Their owners include American and Mexican business-men, a few Europeans, politicians and diplomats. Life in Lomas is aloof. Its residents do not mix much with outsiders, and there is none of the street bustle of central Mexico City. People here prefer to live off the costly products of luxury stores.

Heading west from the city, motorists reach a region of peaks which reach nearly 10,000 feet above sea level. Huge forests of firs cover the mountainsides. Once the haunt of hermits, these are today the favourite pleasure-

A farm worker 'milks' the spiny leaves of a maguey plant. This versatile plant is grown in long rows in many parts of Mexico – rather like potatoes or beets elsewhere in the world. Its 'milk' is used to make the potent alcoholic drink pulque, *its fibres for coarse cloth or matting, and brushes.*

The native Mexicans were the first people to domesticate the common turkey (Maleagris gallopavo) for the table. The Spanish introduced it to Europe in the early 16th century, and the English to North America. Chicken has largely replaced turkey in the Mexican diet, but it remains the essential ingredient of the dish mole poblano, *where it is served with a chocolate sauce.*

grounds for *chilangos* – people from Mexico City who at weekends search out fresh air and peace. There is plenty, too, for the sightseer. Beyond Toluca – famous for its crafts market on Fridays – rises the round pyramid of Calixtlahuaca, dedicated to Quetzalcóatl. South is the site of another Aztec temple at Malinalco, with magnificent carvings of eagles and jaguars, and beyond that the church of Chalma. The Christ of Chalma is the country's most popular statue of Our Lord, whom the Mexicans refer to as the 'Son of Mary' – thus indicating their sense of heavenly priorities.

Just over 60 miles south of Mexico City is a summer resort with ancient lineage. The Aztec emperors used to winter in the place now known as Cuernavaca, fleeing the bitter cold of the central plateau in favour of the gentler climate which earned it the nickname 'City of Eternal Spring'. Cuernavaca is still a pleasant resort city, where the rich of the capital come to relax in their luxurious homes and spectacular gardens.

From Mexico City towards the east, the road heads for Izúcar de Matamoros, a large industrial town on the way to Puebla. In the villages lining the road are some masterpieces of Indian decorative art – usually in Christian churches. The church of Santa María Tonantzintla is a fine example of ornate baroque splendour. Its gilded cherubs with multi-coloured headdresses, some of them holding cobs of maize between their teeth, probably give a better impression of what pre-Columbian temples were really like than the

ruins of today which have long since had the colour washed out of them.

On festival days, the church echoes to the sounds of the parish orchestra. Throughout the day, violins keep tune with guitars, and the voices of worshippers sing out the refrains of religious chants. The monotonous, melancholy tinkle of the triangle marks the time. Village women come timidly to the front to leave offerings of apples, oranges and flowers. With the tips of their fingers, they lightly touch the bottom of the mantle covering the image of the Virgin, and then turn back furtively to kneel in the shadow of a pillar.

The mixture of influences is intoxicating: Catholic rites, Indian decorative styles (though they were strongly influenced by colonial Spanish forms, as well), Christian liturgical chants and music that probably has its roots as much in the fertility worship of Xipe Totec, the pre-Columbian god of spring and new vegetation, as of Mary.

Several Indian peoples, the Nahuas, Totonacs and Otomis, live in the *sierra* of Puebla, and celebrate with spectacular pageantry a string of religious festivals in honour of their favourite *santitos*. The church of Cuetzalán has a statue of Christ with a plumed headdress of brilliant bronze-green and red feathers from the *quetzal* bird (native to southern Mexico), similar to those worn by the Aztec emperors of old. On festival days, the women still deck themselves out with *quexquemitls*, shawls of transparent embroidered gauze.

Two Indian women chat under the church walls of Santa María Tonantzintla. Though dilapidated at the back, the church is a marvel of Mexican baroque architecture. It is notable especially for the stucco-work and carvings of its interior by 16th-century Indian craftsmen.

A Nahua Indian baby sleeps peacefully in its wickerwork carry cot, tied in with a piece of string and a tiny sheet. In this way its mother or an elder sister can safely take it with her to market or about her daily chores.

Where the sun was born

North of Mexico City thousands of acres of whitish soil support pallid, fleshy-leaved maguey plants. They are 'milked' when the maguey reaches maturity, about five to seven years after planting. The juice is extracted – and afterwards fermented to make *pulque* – after which the plant dies. In common with other members of the American *Agave* genus, the maguey's fibres can be made into coarse cloth, brooms and brushes, and in some places roofing.

North-east of the capital, in the ceremonial centre of the Teotihuacán culture, there are yet more remains of the Indian past. It was here, according to myth, that the gods met to create the sun. The site of Teotihuacán bears awesome testimony to the spirit and power of the

Traditional pot-bellied storage silos can still be seen in the remoter parts of the Mexican countryside. Their walls are made of baked earth, and small thatched roofs are perched on top. To reach the maize or other crops stored inside, the farmer uses a rickety ladder.

civilisation that produced it. A sense of brooding religious mystery still clings to the immense pyramids dedicated to the moon and sun and to the monumental alleys bordered with temples and stairways linking them. The rigorous geometry of the groundplan and the ornaments on its buildings is a reminder of the strict sense of hierarchy that accompanied the culture's religious ceremonies. This overriding sense of solemnity is echoed a little farther to the west in the later, Toltec site of Tula. Here again, awesome masses of grey stone dominate the surrounding countryside, conjuring up the fears and hopes of ancient worshippers.

Very different, too – though in a bleaker sense – are the modern counterparts to these menacing giants from the past: the sprawling shanty towns that spread out north and east of Mexico City. Here, in places such as Netzahualcoyotl, bare-footed children wandering between the most primitive of huts create an overwhelming sense of poverty without hope.

Yet even here the monasteries of Tepotzotlán and Actopán are havens of graceful architecture and richly gilded interiors, fronting onto quiet squares. Climbing roses clamber over stone balustrades. Homesick for their native land, the missionaries constructed these retreats from the world of 'barbaric' gods they had so brutally dethroned. Their spirit still lives in the atmosphere of meditative calm, the flower-filled patios and the elegant lines of the architecture. Today, most such monasteries are empty, but their calm survives, while outside in the square children read, do their homework or play with that quiet gravity that is so typically Mexican.

Cattle were unknown in the Americas until the Spanish arrived, but are now one of the pillars of Mexican agriculture. Although most rural Indians remain fairly indifferent to red meat, the people of the cities are big beef-eaters and represent a growing market.

In the Footsteps of the Maya

'On our continent, or even perhaps our planet, there is no more deeply human country than Mexico. Shining through its luminous successes, but also through its gigantic errors, one sees the same links of grandiose generosity, profound vitality, inexhaustible history, and a capacity for continual rebirth.' It was not a Mexican who wrote these words, but Pablo Neruda, the 20th-century Chilean poet, for whom Mexico represented a sort of epic summing up of the destiny and potential of Latin America as a whole.

Exploring the coastlands of the Gulf of Mexico is a particularly rich experience. Here, you find the remains of the first of Central America's succession of great civilisations: that of the Olmecs, who traded, built cities, carved awesome sculptures and devised the earliest calendar in the western hemisphere between around 1500 BC and AD 300 – thus laying the foundations on which their various successors, from the Maya to the Aztecs, would later construct their own societies. Here, too, you follow in the footsteps of the *conquistadores* disembarking at Veracruz on Good Friday, April 21, 1519. In the Yucatán peninsula you meet Mayan Indians, who in appearance and language, preserve much that is recognisable from the culture of their ancestors in its heyday during the 4th to 10th centuries AD. You also encounter the most important source of contemporary Mexico's prosperity and economic independence: oil.

Finally, it is in the byways of the countryside, far from the bustle of the capital, that you meet some of Mexico's most rugged characters – people whose entire history has been a struggle to maintain their rights to the soil they have tilled for hundreds of generations.

Land and liberty

'Land and liberty!' This was the rallying cry adopted by the followers of the guerrilla leader Emiliano Zapata in the early 20th century, but it expresses the hopes of millions of rural Mexicans at almost any time in the country's recent history. Although Mexico is now overwhelmingly urban (with more than 70 per cent of the population living in the towns and cities), its heroes traditionally emerged from the countryside, most of them closely identified with the struggle for freedom and a more equitable distribution of farming land.

In 1542, Spain promulgated its 'New Laws', which released the Indians from slavery and gave them the

Chac-Mool, the Maya god of rain, turns his back firmly on the pleasures of sea and sand on the island of Cancún. Until recently, Cancún was a near-desert; now it rivals Mexico's famous Pacific coast resort, Acapulco.

rights of free subjects of the crown. But it proved, by and large, to be a theoretical rather than a practical freedom. At best, Spanish rule was – for the Indians – paternalistic; at its worst, downright brutal. For nearly 300 years after the Spanish conquest, the Indians suffered at the hands of semi-religious orders such as the Holy Brotherhood and the Acordada, which were guilty on occasions of horrific massacres. They also perished from malnutrition and diseases the Spanish brought with them, to which the native Mexicans had no natural immunity. When the *conquistadores* arrived in what

Fishermen draw in their nets on Mexico's Gulf coast. It was on this coast that Cortés and his followers landed in 1519. Nowadays, it is the centre of the country's oil industry.

became New Spain (that is, modern Mexico, plus the territories that became part of the United States in the 19th century – Texas, Arizona, New Mexico, California, Nevada, Utah and parts of Colorado and Wyoming), its Indian population numbered between 12 and 15 million people. A century later, only a million survived. This was the background against which the struggle for independence from Spain would later be fought.

The battlecry for that long struggle was first sounded at dawn on September 16, 1810. The setting was the small village of Dolores (now Dolores Hidalgo), in the central highlands north-west of Mexico City, peopled mostly by impoverished Indian and *mestizo* (mixed-race) workers on the huge estates of the surrounding countryside. For some time, the village priest, Father Miguel Hidalgo y Costilla (an impassioned champion of the rights of his peasant parishioners), had been planning an armed uprising against Spanish rule. The night before, Hidalgo and his fellow plotters had received word that the authorities had got wind of their plans. Precipitated into action, the priest rang the church bell at first light to call his parishioners together and delivered a passionate speech, spurring them on for the fight ahead. He finished his address with the now famous *grito* or cry: '*¡Mexicanos, Viva México!*'

The insurrection soon spread, and Dolores became a potent symbol of the strength of ordinary Mexican people determined to win back their rights and freedom. But Hidalgo never lived to see their eventual triumph. By the spring of 1811, he had gathered a large but poorly disciplined army of about 20,000 soldiers, seized several important towns and cities north of Mexico City and was heading for the capital. At a vital moment, however, he hesitated and withdrew. His forces lost heart and many deserted. Within a few months, Hidalgo had been captured and executed at Chihuahua in the north-west. His head was taken to the garrison town of Guanajuato, not far from Dolores, where it was exposed on the walls of the military fort – as a warning to others.

Nevertheless, the struggle continued under other leaders, and bore fruit in 1821 when the Spanish finally surrendered. A long and chaotic period of successive coups and rebellions then followed. Popular discontent remained, and there were always plenty of people ready to enlist under a new banner, when it became clear that existing regimes were either unwilling or unable to offer substantial improvements in their living conditions. Conflicting political, economic and religious currents created a situation of baffling complexity, which only the maverick General Antonio López de Santa Anna seemed able to turn to any advantage, though even his career was distinctly turbulent. He was president from 1833 to 1836, made a comeback as dictator in 1841, was temporarily ousted in 1845–46 and again in 1848, and finally returned as president in 1853–55. He was then ousted once more, and died in poverty in 1874.

It was also during this period – between 1836 and 1848 – that Mexico lost more than 40 per cent of its territory to the United States. This process culminated in the Mexican–American War of 1846–48, when Mexico City itself was captured by US forces, despite the heroic last-ditch resistance of a handful of military cadets – commemorated as the *Niños Héroes* (Child Heroes).

Only when Santa Anna's successor, the liberal Benito Juárez, came to power in 1855 did things begin to settle down somewhat – although even then there were several years of bloody turmoil. Juárez was a Zapotec Indian, who had been adopted and educated as a child by a wealthy priest from Oaxaca in the south. One of his measures as President was to confiscate the immense estates owned by the Catholic church and redistribute them among smaller farmers – though this brought only limited benefits to most rural Indians.

Even so, Mexico was still not free from foreign interference. Between 1861 and 1867, Napoleon III of France became involved in a contest that (for France, at least) was to prove disastrous. At first, he was allied with Britain and Spain, and all three powers sent in troops on the pretext that Juárez had suspended payments on foreign debts. The British and Spanish withdrew when they were repaid, but Napoleon had dreams of a greater role for France in the affairs of the New World and his troops remained. They occupied Mexico City where, with French backing, local conservatives invited the Habsburg Archduke Maximilian to become their emperor. Maximilian proved to be much more liberal in his politics than his backers had suspected. He lost the support of the conservatives, but failed to win support elsewhere. When Napoleon was obliged to bring his troops back to France to meet a threat from Prussia,

Maximilian found himself helpless against local rebels. He ended his life in front of a Mexican firing squad after a catastrophic four-year reign.

Within ten years, another dictator had emerged: the redoubtable Porfirio Díaz, with the cynical motto, *Pan o palo* – literally, 'bread or rod', meaning that where he could not buy the people off, he would beat them into submission. He remained more or less continuously in power until 1910. It was a hard time for the Indians who were once again reduced to little more than slavery and deprived of much of their land. They seemed in no condition to rise up against their oppressor, and yet a new generation of revolutionary leaders did appear. These ranged from the wealthy landowner Francisco Madero to the guerrilla leaders Pancho Villa in the north and Emiliano Zapata in the south. The revolution of 1910 – one of the landmarks of modern Mexican history – finally ousted the aging Díaz, though fighting among revolutionary factions lasted into the early 1920s.

Memories that live on

Memories of these armed bands and of the great deeds of the Mexican revolution are recaptured all over Mexico on its public buildings. José Clemente Orozco, Diego Rivera and David Siquieros were the three great

A new breed of men has emerged on the Gulf coast: the petroleros. *The saying goes that they use up their lives faster than their other countrymen – and there may well be some truth in it. On average, they earn 12 times as much as ordinary farm workers, but their pay is soon spent on luxuries such as huge American cars which they drive at breakneck speed along the roads of Tabasco state.*

masters of the country's modern tradition of historically inspired mural painting; their frescoes are among the boldest and most grandiose works of art the Mexicans have produced since the time of the Spanish conquest. They also contain the most revolutionary of utterances, often in the most unlikely of places. 'God does not exist' proclaims a fresco tracing the history of Mexico in one of the capital's largest hotels. Others include startling juxtapositions: Karl Marx haranguing a crowd of Mexican *campesinos* (peasants); 'Uncle Sam' complete with top hat stuffing his pockets with loot, before fleeing from a jeering mob; Catholic prelates represented as creatures of grotesque rapaciousness.

The Mexican revolution was also in many ways a state of mind as well, and as such has lasted in modified form to this day – indeed, the official Mexican line is that the events of 1910 were the start only of a continuing revolution. In the words of the writer Octavio Paz, it was, and is, the 'painful and creative drama' of a people in search of its identity, ready to suffer most things in order to assert its rights. The spirit of the revolution has thus become absorbed into the mainstream of political life – a process that is encapsulated in the curiously named Institutional Revolutionary Party, which is still in power. Not that the revolutionary

The guayabera *is still worn in much of southern Mexico. It is white, with pleats and an embroidered front, and is usually worn with white trousers.*

This man's job is to deliver tortillas to various local clients. His balancing abilities are by no means unique in Mexico. Wherever you go, you see people precariously balancing huge piles of newspapers on handcarts; parents and children wobbling along on the same bicycle; or women who are scarcely visible beneath a mountain of bundles strapped to their backs and perched on their heads.

spirit has kept its original purity. Since the mid-1980s, in particular, the government has shed much of its fiercely nationalistic fervour, espousing a more pro-American approach along with free-market economics.

Blue seas off tropic shores

Whichever way you strike out from the high plateaus of the interior for the Gulf of Mexico coastlands, you have to cross mountain barriers – and these journeys, more than anything else, bring home the extraordinary contrasts of the Mexican landscape. Within a few hours, everything changes: temperature, climate, vegetation and way of life. Crossing the sierras is no longer the feat it was in the days of the *conquistadores*, and takes less time than it did then. But this simply makes the changes around you all the more striking.

From Mexico City to the port city of Veracruz, the main road crosses high mountain passes, and then descends in a series of tight hairpin bends to the plains

Music – especially the characteristic son jarocho – is an essential part of life in Veracruz on the Gulf coast. Veracruz was also the place where the slow, voluptuous danzón (originating in Cuba) first took root in Mexico. It is particularly popular in the nightclubs of the resort Villa del Mar.

Horse-drawn cabs still ply the narrow streets of Mérida on the Yucatán peninsula. For the many tourists who now visit the city, the best time to take a cab ride is at sunset, when the city's white walls reflect the sun's last rays in a myriad different shades of red and orange. It is the perfect prelude to an evening meal of barbecued chicken done in the local pibil style.

below. The speed of the descent can be dizzying. In little more than half-an-hour, you pass from a region of cold mists and pine forests to another, completely different world of stifling humidity and lush tropical vegetation. Just to remind you of the contrasts, you look back and see rising far above the permanently snow-capped volcanic cone of Mount Citlaltéptl.

Even before you leave the mists, you begin to see a few odd palms and banana trees mingling with the last straggling stands of pine. Then the vegetation runs riot. Near Fortín de las Flores, one of the first *pueblos* (villages) you cross after leaving the pine forests, a rocky track – degenerating into a slipway of pure mud during the rainy season – branches off the road and plunges down towards a deep ravine, the Barranco de Matalarga. At its bottom, the waters of a small torrent run red with the soil they carry down from the heights above. On either side are huge stretches of coffee and banana plantations, sheltering a busy world of noisy, chirruping animal and bird-life. Flowers in a range of brilliant hues cover the ground, and many-coloured hibiscuses droop over a network of narrow paths – used by the estate workers, mostly Indians dressed in white with machetes at their sides. Strange sack-like 'growths' hang down from some of the trees. At first sight, they look like a kind of tropical parasite – in fact, they are birds' nests. A flash of colour marks the quiet passage of a humming bird, or the noisier one of a parakeet.

From north to south, and along the fertile horn of plenty of the Yucatán peninsula, the coast passes through a series of different landscapes. In the far north, in the state of Tamaulipas, Nuevo Laredo (Mexico) faces Laredo (Texas) on the other side of the river that marks the Mexican-American frontier – the Río Grande for the Americans, the Río Bravo for the Mexicans. This whole region of the north-east was once a near-desert, due to its low rainfall. Now, it has become the principal cotton-growing area in Mexico, thanks to irrigation systems established here in the 1930s.

A little farther south, the vast plains of Tampico in the hinterlands behind the coast are livestock-raising country. The traditional dress of the local women – waistcoat, skirt and leather boots – bears elegant witness to that long tradition. On the coast, citrus-growing is one of the chief sources of wealth. Inland and farther south again, around Ciudad Mante, huge sugar-cane estates dominate the landscape.

In the coastal city of Tampico, all the region's various activities come together. Oil and natural gas pipelines link it with Mexico City, while the harbour is busy with cargo ships loading with fruit, cotton and textiles for export. Tampico is also an important fishing port, famous for the abundance and variety of its seafood. Indeed, fishing is important all along this coast. In Tuxpan, south of Tampico, fishermen use river nets to bring in huge catches of pike and tarpon, known here as 'silver king'. Sea fishing in the clear waters of the Gulf is equally good: more tarpon just offshore and, farther out to sea, barracuda, marlin, shark and tuna fish, all provide a living for communities of small fishermen.

Early morning beams of sunlight catch the faces of market women at Muna in the Yucatán peninsula. The natural elegance with which they wear their head and neck scarves contrasts with the scanty products they have to offer: oranges, apples and a few knobbly sweetsop fruit.

The cheerful grin of a market woman reveals the good humour for which the Maya are famous. Except during festivals, most Mexicans are relatively grave in their dealings with one another. The Maya, however, generally have a boisterous sense of humour and a refreshing streak of irony.

Veracruz: where the new world met the old

'Veracruz alone is beautiful!' is the proud boast of the city's inhabitants. 'Come quickly, and visit Tampico,' reply the inhabitants of the other port, no less confident of their city's charms. 'That will soon shut you up!' Despite all this, most visitors will probably feel that Veracruz wins the day. Tampico cannot really compete with the indolent, southern charm of the great port that now stands where Cortés disembarked in 1519. Four-and-a-half centuries of close contact with Europe have left the people of La Rica Villa de la Vera Cruz – 'The Rich Town of the True Cross', to use the full name Cortés originally gave it – with an open, jovial character that nowhere else in Mexico matches. By origin, they are Spanish, Indian and African, all so mixed together that few people fit into any clearly definable racial group.

The *jarochos* – people of Veracruz – are also famous for their music, the *son jarocho* (literally, '*jarocho* sound'). Wherever you go, it seems, you encounter musicians serenading passers-by on street corners or outside shady cafés, hopeful of a few coins for their reward. The range of styles and instruments is impressive: the *marimba* (a sort of wooden xylophone on legs, played by three or four musicians); harp and guitar quartets and trumpet-players.

The Zócalo – the name means 'pedestal', and comes from Mexico City's Plaza de la Constitución (or Zócalo) where for a long time there was a pedestal without a statue – is lined with terrace cafés. Here, clients sit and while the time away as they sip delicious Mexican beers – Bohemia, Superior or Noche Buena – or drinks such as tequila or *rompope* (a tasty cocktail of egg yolks, milk, rum and cinnamon). The Café de la Parroquia is especially popular, notably with business-men, who come here to savour one of a number of local coffees. Custom demands that you attract the waiter's attention by striking the side of your cup or glass with a spoon. He then rushes up with more coffee and a jug of milk to add to it.

On one side of the square, the Banda de Marinas (Marine Band) – its players are all veterans of the Mexican Navy – alternates popular classics with more lively Latin American dances such as the *mambo*. As night begins to fall, men in red neck-ties and elegant white shirts (*guayaberas*) escort ladies in light dresses to a square dance floor, and there they dance face to face to the slow, sensual melodies of the *danzón*, a dance originating in Cuba, and perfectly attuned to the voluptuous warmth of the Veracruz dusk.

The people of Veracruz celebrate the pre-Lenten carnival as passionately as anywhere in Mexico. But for

them it unleashes their natural gaiety, rather than the painful sense of tragedy displayed elsewhere in Mexico. Groups of young people, or *comparsas*, move happily through the city's streets and squares, performing local dances such as the *cumbia,* which they have been rehearsing for months in advance. There are processions of brightly decorated carts and floats, and the air is thick with the loud bangs of crackers, fireworks and pistols fired into the skies above. The festival reaches its peak as darkness falls, when the fronds of palm trees along the sea front begin to flutter in the cooling night breeze blowing in from the sea, and the velvet-fingered moon-light strokes the ocean waves.

Tree branches tied together with string and rope form the grandstand for this village bullring. Women, children and teenagers are among the keenest spectators.

From Olmec warriors to oil rigs

From the United States' frontier down the Gulf coast as far as the Yucatán, oil is hard to escape. This new 'black gold' has given birth to industrial developments, one of the largest of which is Coatzacoalcos-Minatitlán, at the mouth of the River Coatzacoalcos. This is a flat, somewhat bleak region of lagoons and salt marshes, sprouting the metal superstructures of oil rigs, and crisscrossed by long, straight roads used chiefly by enormous trucks.

These signs of modern life apart, the atmosphere of the place seems more like that of some prehistoric landscape – where *zopilotes* (vultures) wheel far overhead, and rivers reach the sea in a maze of marshes and narrow channels sheltering caymans (American crocodiles) and many species of waterfowl.

Ancient and modern mingle in extraordinarily close proximity along the Gulf coast. To the north of the city of Veracruz, an oil refinery at Poza Rica lies immediately across a short stretch of jungle from the ruins of El Tajin, a city dating from the Teotihuacán era around AD 600–900. El Tajín's most famous and impressive feature is the mysterious Pyramid of the Niches, whose various tiers are punctuated by 365 niches – they may have held offerings for each day of the year.

In similar fashion, the industrial complex at Coatzocoalcos lies at the heart of the region where the Olmec's civilisation sprang up. Some of the huge basalt heads that appear to have been one of the signatures of Olmec culture have been transferred to an open-air museum in La Venta Park in Villahermosa. Others can be seen – more unexpectedly, and in a way more movingly – in the *zócalos*, or main squares, of some of the region's towns.

A pair of turkeys strut across the dirt patch in front of an Indian hut on the Yucatán peninsula. These homes are almost exactly the same as those described by 16th-century Spanish chroniclers. They are rectangular with an alcove at each end. At the front, the thatched roof often juts out over a shady verandah.

Towards the Yucatán peninsula, small coastal roads, usually keeping their distance from the actual shoreline, are lined with villages where everyone – whether at work or play – lives out of doors. Homes, for the most part, are simple huts of wood or mud walls, with roofs of palm thatch or corrugated iron, all opening onto the road. It does not matter whether an icy wind is blowing from the north, or rain is falling in terrifying tropical downpours, or the midday sun is burning overhead: you never feel alone on these friendly byways. There are always villagers walking home from their fields or the nearest town, or men on horseback emerging suddenly from sunken side lanes or from gaps in the roadside vegetation which immediately closes up behind them. Sometimes, you pass whole families piled onto one bicycle – the father pedalling, the mother with a baby tied up securely in her *rebozo* (shawl), clinging on behind, riding side-saddle above the rear wheel.

The decorative instinct is still strong among the Indians of the Yucatán. Doors are often painted in bold primary colours, and the more spacious homes have stone walls around them, ornamented with carved stones and ceramic jars placed on top of them. This home (above) also enjoys the luxury of electricity. Often (left) the outside walls are daubed with whitewash (or tan in the Mayan language, which is still spoken by the Indians). Representations of local Mayan sites are sketched over them – frequently, no doubt, for the benefit of the tourists who now swarm over much of the peninsula.

Peninsula of mystery

River deltas and marshes for a long time kept the Yucatán largely isolated from the rest of the country, and even today, arriving from the tropical regions of the Gulf, you still feel a strange sense of disorientation. The feeling of having entered a slightly magical world grows even stronger when you discover the origin of the name Yucatán. The invading Spanish apparently asked a group of Maya what they called the peninsula. One of the Maya, lacking an interpreter, replied reasonably enough in his own language, 'I don't understand' – which the Spanish took to be the name of the place … or, at least, so the story goes.

What is beyond doubt is that, around AD 1000, the Yucatán – a land of dusty savannah pastures, scrubby bushlands and dense jungles – was home to a remarkable civilisation. The Maya people were experts in mathematics, astronomy and the art of writing – a skill that was by no means universal in the pre-Columbian civilisations of Central and South America. In both the jungles of the peninsula's southern regions and the arid lands of the north, they also left eloquent testimony of their talents as architects, sculptors and painters. The north, in particular, has the temple complexes of Chichén Itzá and Uxmal, founded around the 5th to 7th centuries AD after the Maya had abandoned – no one knows why – their earlier centres at Copán, Palenque, Bonampak and other sites in the jungles of the south.

These northern sites also reveal a strong influence from the Toltecs, whose contacts with the peninsula are associated – in legend, at least – with the flight from their own lands in the central highlands of Mexico of the god Quetzalcóatl, whom they called Kukulrán. The Toltecs in the Yucatán may have come as conquerors. Or they may have been refugees from their own people, who remained loyal to Quetzalcóatl and also helped to breathe new life into the old civilisation of the Maya.

Farm workers sort sisal leaves before they are sent off to have their fibres extracted. According to Indian tradition, the cultivation of sisal dates from the time of the Toltec king Zama, who cut himself one day on the spiky tip of a sisal leaf. Angrily, he tore the whole leaf out and crushed it on a rock. He then noticed the fibres inside, and realised some of the uses to which they could be put.

Whatever the case, even the sites at Chichén Itzá and Uxmal had been long abandoned by the time the Spanish arrived, and mystery shrouds the last great days of the Mayan culture.

Yet the day-to-day life of the Maya does not seem so very far removed today from what it was before the Spanish arrived. The invaders brought with them their new ways and religion and, in the 19th and 20th centuries, put Maya *peones* (farm workers) to the back-breaking, ill-paid labour of the *chicle* plantations – *chicle* is the coagulated juice of the sapodilla tree (*chicle zapote*) and is the main ingredient in chewing gum. But, despite this, Mayan life and ways still bear a remarkable resemblance to those described by the 16th-century Spanish chronicler Diego de Landa in his *Relation of the Things of the Yucatán*.

The style of homes he described, for instance, are unmistakably those still found in villages throughout the peninsula today. To build them, a series of tree trunks are rammed into the soil around a carefully marked-out rectangular space, with a rounded alcove at each end. Bamboo stems fill the gaps between the trunks, and the steep roof is covered with palm fronds. Inside, there is no furniture or only very little: a few mats for sitting on during the day, and hammocks, hung from the beams, for sleeping in at night – safe from scorpions or other dangerous creatures. In one corner is a *metate*, a sort of stone tripod, on which the women grind the maize with a large stone rolling pin. A wooden box contains their pots and other cooking utensils.

The villages of the Yucatán seem like small oases of luxuriant vegetation in what are often arid surroundings. Most are built near a natural well, one of the *cenotes* of pre-Columbian times (wells were sacred to the Maya, who usually built their temples near them). Even where the soil is relatively poor, a little bit of irrigation from a well yields astonishing results, and smallholders are able to raise a variety of rich crops, which grow so fast 'it makes you frightened to see', in the words of Diego de Landa. Among their products are beans, maize, tomatoes (which, like the domesticated turkey, originated in Mexico, where they were known as *jitomates*), cabbages, flowers and tropical fruit. The fruit includes bananas of all sizes and hues, avocados, pawpaws, guavas and mangoes.

The boom times for sisal production were in the 19th century. That was when sisal replaced hemp as the most common material for making twines, cords and mats. An additional boost came in the 1880s when the development of machines for binding grain created a worldwide demand for cheap twine. Today, local craftsmen also use sisal to make goods, from hammocks to hats.

To extract the fibres, special machines crush the sisal leaves between rollers and scrape off the resulting pulp. The fibres, usually around 4 feet or more long, are then left to dry on wire racks, before being sent off to factories where they are made into twine or matting.

When harvesting sisals, the bottom leaves are always cut out first, allowing the younger leaves on top to grow to maturity. A plant will remain productive for up to 20 years. The sisal plant is a member of the agave family, like the closely related maguey.

the sisal plantations or, in the more southerly Yucatán states of Quitana Roo and Campeche, in the *chicle* plantations, where they gather the precious resin of the sapodilla trees in calabashes.

Tourists and flying dancers

The charms of the Yucatán peninsula are now well known far beyond its confines. Isolated fishing communities survive in the remoter corners of the coastline, living much as their ancestors have done for thousands of years. But for most of its length, the locals now share their territory with new waves of invaders –

This young man (below) is about to perform the dizzying volador *dance. The rituals surrounding the performance start with a forest dance in honour of the tree that will be felled to provide the tall pole needed for it (far left). Once the pole has been erected, four dancers – under the supervision of a leader who perches at the summit – tie themselves to ropes that have been wrapped around it. The main performance begins at last with the dancers flying alarmingly through space as the ropes unwind (left).*

You will find all these products in the local markets, where their colours mingle with those of the women's traditional *huipils*, long white blouses whose square necklines and hems are decorated with bright embroidered flowers. The men, meanwhile, almost invariably wear white trousers and shirts with pleated fronts – *guayaberas*. On their heads, they wear straw hats, made from palm or sisal leaves, and for shoes they sport *huaraches*, thonged sandals with soles made from leather – or old tyres.

The countryside on the peninsula's northern side is mostly flat, with scarcely any streams or rivers, since any rain is rapidly absorbed by the soil and flows into underground caves and passages. It is these under-ground waters that are tapped in village *cenotes* (wells) and used to irrigate the smallholdings. Elsewhere, the most widely grown crop – and in many places, just about the only one that can be profitably grown in such dry conditions – is sisal, like the maguey plant of the central highlands, a member of the agave family. The fibres in its leaves are processed in local factories into binder twine, and then exported worldwide. Local craftspeople, too, have a long tradition of using sisal. Women, most of them working at home, use it to make hammocks, sandals, baskets, bags and toys.

Women have always played an influential role in Mayan society, and still do. No family decision concerning the purchase of grain, the marriage of a child, or how much to spend on offerings in some religious ceremony is taken without the mother's full agreement. As for the men, they work their small patches of ground or hire themselves out as labourers on

American and European tourists, as well as many Mexicans, who now annually flood the Yucatán and its neighbouring islands such as Cancún.

Far from the luxury hotels, however, there is a very different world where festivals and holidays provide relief from an otherwise harsh existence. For many Mexicans, these festivities have a mystical importance that reaches far back into their past. Processions, dances and gymnastic displays were all essential parts of the religious ceremonies of the Americas before the Spanish arrived. Most of them have disappeared or changed beyond recognition, sometimes enriched, sometimes impoverished by contact with Spanish civilisation.

Most of these have their roots in the rituals of warriors and priests, anxious to appease all-powerful deities. In the forms they take today, they perpetuate the Mexican love of colour, movement and athletic skill, but also the need that many local people still feel to propitiate fate with extravagant acts of devotion. These traditions find their most notable expression in the dance of the *volador*, a veritable challenge to death.

The Totonac Indians of Papantla north of Veracruz are the chief exponents of the *volador*, which also once formed part of the worship of Xipe Totec, god of the spring and of nature. His festival came close in the calendar to the Christian feast of Corpus Christi – which took over some of its rituals. The modern festival lasts for a week, usually around the end of May.

The dance of the *volador* is by far its most gripping spectacle. Performing it involves five men: a leader who directs proceedings with a small flute and drum, and four dancers, or *voladores*, all wearing red trousers, white shirts and strange conical caps decorated with brightly coloured ribbons. They scale a wooden pole, about 100 feet high, which has previously been wrapped around with ropes. Near the top is a narrow platform called the *tecomate*. The leader takes his post on this alarmingly narrow ledge. His first act, which reveals his own considerable balancing skills and announces that the 'sacred flight' of the *voladores* is about to begin, is to turn towards each of the four points of the compass in turn, all the time playing his flute with one hand, and waving a bunch of ribbons in the other.

Then comes the flight itself. While the leader has been performing, the four *voladores* have each knotted one of the ropes around the pole about their ankles. On a signal from the leader, they launch themselves head first into space, whirling out in dizzying arcs as the ropes gradually unwind. The leader continues on flute and drum, and the dancers swing out in ever-increasing circles as they approach the ground. At the last minute, just as they seem about to dash themselves to death on the hard soil beneath, they flip themselves upright, landing nimbly and unharmed before an awestruck audience. It is an extraordinary sight – and one towards which no man or god could possibly remain indifferent.

A battered jeep is one of the few signs that this forest home belongs to the 20th century. Idyllic though it may appear on the surface, life in the lowland forests of Mexico has many dangers. The climate is extreme, droughts alternating with periods of torrential rain in summer. Work is hard and tourists, though they bring a welcome, alternative source of income, are also increasingly intrusive. Small wonder that the towns and cities, and the supposedly easy money to be made there, exercise a powerful lure for many young people.

Rambles through the South

Pachucos, braceros, nacos, indios, gachupines, gringos … The Mexicans use a host of different terms to describe the different groups within their society. Some, simplifying things to their most basic level, talk of the rich and the poor. For others, the great contrast is between urban Mexico and the Mexico of the countryside – by which they mean, the Mexico of the Indians. Others again speak in terms of 'races': *gachupines* (Spanish people living in Mexico), creoles (Mexicans of European descent), *mestizos* (mixed-race Mexicans) and the various Indian groups.

But strongest of all in such classifications is the notion of belonging to a particular region, village or piece of territory, and to the traditions of that territory. According to this way of seeing things, people change the moment they leave their home and lands. As a result, the Indians who now populate the shantytowns around the big cities are no longer truly part of the life of their home villages – and consequently feel a strong sense of alienation. Arriving in the cities, they become part of another group and take on the ways of another culture. The expression in their eyes becomes hardier and more aggressive. Living on the margins of two worlds, those of the city and of the countryside, they no longer belong to either, and thus add yet another layer to Mexican society.

A passion for tradition

The *indio* is the Mexican who has stayed on his home lands. It is the *indios* you meet throughout the mountain regions of the south, pushed ever farther and higher into these relatively safe havens during the long centuries of Spanish rule. Trapped on barren soils – to which they have become passionately devoted and which link them with the cherished traditions of their ancestors – the Indians take refuge in a stubborn worship of ancient ways and loyalty to their village communities.

They need all the consolation they can get, for life while it lasts is usually hard for them and the surroundings are scarcely friendly. High on the mountainsides of Mexico's far south-eastern state Chiapas – notable for an extreme climate of icy cold nights and broiling midday sun – you often see tiny plots of maize tucked between rocky ledges and surrounded by tracts of forest. Slash and burn is the method most often used here. Farmers make a clearing in the forest, and then, after a period of years, abandon it, in favour of another patch farther away and higher up. They also have an unusual way of dealing with the shortage of cultivable soil. For generations, they have planted more than one kind of seed in the same hole: maize plants sprout as best they can between the rocks, and beans sown in the same holes use their stems to support their climbing tendrils.

The vegetation covering the mountains is dense; often you can scarcely make out the thatched roof of a hut lost among the trees. Yet, remote though they are, these forests are remarkably well populated, and there are always plenty of people on the move, trudging along mountain tracks to their fields in the heights above or making their way to the nearest market town. Market trips can become veritable expeditions. People can, of course, always hail a passing truck, whose driver will usually take them part of the way for a few pesos. But many prefer to save the money and walk.

Night and day, men, women and children stride across the mountains of Chiapas, laden with heavy burdens, which they often carry in large pouches on their chests just as their ancestors did in the times of the Mayan empire. Back packs are common, too – and you frequently see women bent almost double under the weight of a sack of maize or beans. They may also have

The Tzotzil-speaking Chamulas live in small, widely scattered communities among the mountains of Chiapas state. They are fiercely independent, and visitors are allowed only limited access to their 'capital', the village of San Juan Chamula.

Three donkeys nose around for meagre pickings outside the church of Chenalo in Chiapas. The people of Chenalo are Chamulas and organise their own religious rites. Each year, they choose an official, advised by a council of elders, to be their religious leader. Only rarely do they ask for the services of the nearest Catholic priest.

a baby tied to their back with one of their indispensable, multi-purpose *rebozo* shawls. One hand helps to support the load on their back, while in the other they carry a huge basket.

Foreigners driving around Chiapas after dark are often astonished at the number of people they pick out in the beams of their headlights, walking along the roads at all hours of the night. Where do they come from? And where are they going? The answer is usually to or from market, which may be a good five-hour trek from their mountain villages or huts. The next day, you may well meet the same people squatting behind piles

of goods in the nearest town looking as calm and impassive as if they had enjoyed a full night's sleep in their beds. The children (*niños*) are usually in on it all as well, trotting docilely behind their parents, an elder sister helping out by carrying one of the babies. The children also take an active part in the business of selling. In village schools, when the teacher takes the roll call in the morning, there are often almost as many absentees as children present.

The best-known of the Indian markets is the one at San Cristóbal de las Casas, toward the Guatemalan border. It is also one of the most attractive, and among

the most popular with tourists, because most of the market people are Tzotzil Indians who come down from the nearby mountain villages of San Juan Chamula and Zinacantán. Even by Indian standards, the Tzotzils are exceptionally loyal to their traditions. Most of them still wear the full finery of their traditional costumes, even for everyday use, while their craftsmen and women keep alive the full range of their ancestral skills. Tzotzil women wear long skirts of coarse black wool and woollen *rebozos* of vivid blue. Women from Zinacantán cover their shoulders with a kind of white cape edged with thick pink or blue borders. The men wear *chamarros* (similar to ponchos), their costumes differing slightly according to their position in the community or marital status – unmarried men, for example, go around bare-legged.

The Tzotzils make a striking picture as the brilliant midday sun beats down on the market place, and for a moment you almost forget their poverty. The costumes are repeated in a variety of different sizes on grandmothers, mothers and little girls – and even smaller, when girls come up to you with arrays of dolls, all clad in replicas of the same outfit. The stalls, meanwhile, display fruit and vegetables arranged in neat pyramids on top of mats or pieces of cloth spread out on the bare ground. The products sold are all almost exactly the same, so that the sellers, in their efforts to draw buyers' attention, have to compete with each other in the skill

Tzotzil Indians rest a while on steps in one of San Cristóbal de las Casas's squares. San Cristóbal is the chief town in the region, and this is where they come to sell their vegetables, fruit and craft products in the tiangui *or market.*

The main item of traditional dress for Zinacantec or Tzotzil men is a pink cotton chamarro, or blanket, which is worn rather like a poncho. On their heads, they wear straw hats decorated with coloured ribbons. Their sandals or huaraches *have a piece of leather rising high at the back of the ankle, which makes it more comfortable for walking long distances.*

with which they arrange their wares and the eye-catching combinations of colour they create.

A little to one side in the market is the stall of a man who is half seller, half *ilol* (traditional healer). Among his wares are iguana and cayman skins, anatomical engravings (the idea is that you point out the place where you have a pain), and flasks and sachets of magic powders. If these healers' claims are to be believed, you can be cured of just about any ailment, or obtain just about anything, so long as you obey the instructions written on the side of the packet and read out the spells or incantations that go with them. A compliant and attractive wife, accommodating neighbours, longed-for revenge, fame and fortune – all are available.

The family altar is the centrepiece of most peasant homes. It has an image of the Virgin or a favourite saint, and is always ornamented with flowers, tinsel and brightly coloured cloths. Flowers are also the most popular offerings people present to the local patron saint in the village church.

A Tzotzil girl combs her younger sister's hair. According to Tzotzil mythology, every time a baby is born, so too is its animal soul, living on a sacred mountain. These animal souls watch over human beings from birth to death, when the soul is given a higher or lower place on the mountain according to how faithfully the human has lived by the community's rules.

Loyalty to your roots

The Tzotzil community of San Juan Chamula is particularly interesting for having organised itself against yearly invasions of tourists – without completely shutting the door on visitors bearing much-appreciated foreign currency.

The way in which the local communities organise themselves – not many of them are 'villages' in the normal sense of the word, since many of the Chamula people live up to 10 or 15 miles away from the church of San Juan – is extremely hierarchical. As in most Indian communities, power is shared between three different sets of authorities: the religious authorities (headed by the local 'wise men'); the political authorities (in other words, the municipal council); and the economic and judicial authorities, who consist of local people appointed to the task by their fellows for a year at a time. The ceremonies in which powers are passed

on from one set of people to another are grand affairs, reflecting the importance attached to them. To become a community leader is to accomplish one of the highest duties in a society where the idea of individual profit is still totally rejected, and where everyone is meant to strive for the good of the community as a whole.

These are the authorities whose permission you need as an outsider if you wish to visit San Juan Chamula and its church. First of all, you have to buy a permit; then an official, carrying a mahogany baton (his wand of office), will escort you to the church – a wonderful building of dazzling white, picked out with ornamentation of red and green. And woe betide anyone who pulls out a camera – reactions are often hostile.

Inside the church, some kind of service seems to be going on most of the time. Families wander in and out at all hours of the day, and settle themselves on floors strewn with hay. They stick candles of varying sizes directly onto the paving. Some pray silently; others chant out loud; or alternate silent prayer with chants. Some even leave libations of Coca-Cola. Statues of the saints are attired in rich garments, which are washed every year for their feast days. One saint, Santa Rosa, is looking particularly resplendent in pink satin robes. Tomorrow is her feast day, and she will be carried in procession through the surrounding district.

The winds of the isthmus

Heading west out of the Chiapas highlands, the main road is bordered on either side by dense banks of forest vegetation, studded here and there with brilliantly coloured flowers, orchids, birds and even monkeys. Slowly, you come down towards the Isthmus of Tehuantepec and the Pacific coastline. Around Tuxtla Gutiérrez (capital of Chiapas) the landscape opens out in large sugar, coffee and tobacco plantations. Nearby is El Sumidero, Mexico's most impressive canyon, up to a mile deep in places – where, according to local legends, 16th-century Indian warriors threw themselves over the

Tzotzil-speaking Indians sell the fruit and vegetables grown on their tiny mountain plots at the market of San Cristóbal de las Casas. Despite their ingenuity in finding land to cultivate, many of them live in extreme poverty. It is not uncommon for women to go round the restaurants in San Cristóbal, begging for bones from the kitchens, which they will use to make soup for their families.

edge rather than surrender to the Spanish. After that comes the plain and the constant buffeting winds of the isthmus. The beach of La Ventosa ('the windy'), near Salina Cruz, is particularly well named, its coconut palms swaying almost unceasingly in the turbulent air. Inland is an arid landscape of thorn bushes and cactuses.

In the lively port town of Tehuantepec, traditional colour is mingled with a more modern feel. The saying goes that the women of Tehuantepec are the most beautiful in Mexico. Certainly, their traditional costume is impressive: a short *huipil* embroidered with gold and silver thread, over a flounced satin skirt. The origins of the costume are probably as mixed as those of the people of Tehuantepec, whose ancestors included sailors and traders from all over the world. They have a reputation as shrewd business people, and in the market – a lot noisier than those of the high *sierras* – you have to be prepared for hard bargaining.

After Salina Cruz, the road continues along the coast – the Costa Chica – with more mountains rising only a short distance inland. The beaches here are magnificent, bathed by the bright blue waters of the Pacific – and almost completely deserted. On the face of it, this is a wilderness region. Yet it also manages to shelter a multitude of small Indian villages, scattered over the mountainsides or at the ends of rocky paths.

It is just over 400 miles from Tehuantepec to Acapulco. Between the two places, the landscape is touched by modern development only in the small ports

The Lacandon Indians of the Mexican-Guatemalan border have mostly avoided contact with the outside world. They live in clearings in the jungle where they erect a carribal or group of huts (right); then, when the soil is exhausted, they move on to make another clearing. Men have several wives (left), and children learn from an early age how to handle canoes on the River Usumacinta (below). Despite their success in withstanding the advances of Western-style civilisation, the Lacandons are a dwindling people, numbering no more than some 300 in all.

Iguanas are common throughout tropical Mexico. They eat flowers, fruit and insects, and can reach lengths of around 3 feet. Their flesh is considered a great delicacy.

of Puerto Angel and Puerto Escondido. Both are emerging as tourist resorts, though both have traditionally relied on fishing as their chief industry.

Acapulco is a different world again – a Pacific paradise for the wealthy, a place of luxury hotels and shops, and long sandy beaches stretched out at the feet of a majestic mountain backdrop. In the past, it was also one of the most important ports on the Americas' Pacific coastline, where Spanish treasure fleets set sail for Manila in the Philippines carrying Mexican silver which they would exchange for the porcelain, silks and spices of the Orient. Among its most spectacular modern sights is the much-photographed 'death leap' from the 140-foot cliffs of La Quebrada. Here, local divers (holding lighted torches at night) time their plunge into a narrow creek below so that they hit the waters of an incoming wave – the only moment when there is enough water in the creek to prevent them from being dashed to death. The port's inland fringe presents a very different face, however: a series of shantytowns, home to many of the workers who service the hotels and villas of the rich.

The road linking Acapulco with Mexico City passes through another fabled spot: Taxco, the great silver boom-town of the 18th century. Its streets and houses rise in terraces across the mountainside, topped by the pink-stoned baroque splendour of the church of Santa Prisca. This was built, in the 18th century, by the Frenchman José de la Borda (originally called Joseph Laborde) who made a fortune from the local silver mines. The exterior of the church is a riot of carved stone, matched only by the extravagant stucco and gilt-work of the interior. Silver is still Taxco's lifeblood. Its narrow streets are lined with the workshops – *platerías* – of jewellers and silversmiths, doing a brisk trade with the tourists who are now drawn here each year in their thousands, creating yet another Mexican mix of wealth, easy-going charm and dire poverty.

In the mountains of the Mixtecs

Mountains in Mexico are often known by the names of the Indian peoples who live in them: around Acapulco, the Mixtecs. North-east of Acapulco, the coastal Mixtec lands give way to the lush tropical vegetation of the Mixtec hills, a series of low plateaus grooved by fertile valleys. Then come the Mixtec highlands, a mountain region lying at the meeting point of the twin ranges of the Sierra Madre Oriental and Sierra Madre Occidental. The inhabitants of the highlands have to make do with arid lands, which bristle with the strange, slightly fantastic profiles of *mezquite* plants, their weirdly twisting trunks sprouting tufts of stiff leaves.

Here, the Mixtecs live in widely scattered communities, eeking a meagre subsistence from the poor soil. Maize, beans and gourds, grown in tiny barren pockets of land, are the staples of their diet. Throughout the

year, men, women and children supplement family incomes by plaiting straw hats, which they sell for a few derisory pesos to middlemen from the more prosperous coastal region. During the coffee harvest, the men go down to the coast to work on the plantations. Some also venture into the far north-western state of Sonora where they work as tomato pickers.

For the Mixtecs, as for the Tzotzils of Chiapas, the community is everything. They live according to a kind of primitive communism, which is dominated by a sense of shared responsibility and extends even to the business of marriage, always a community affair. Since marriages are often arranged soon after birth, unmarried people are extremely rare. Throughout their lives, the fate of an individual is subordinated to the interests of the community as a whole, as is the destiny of his or her soul. Everybody is under the protection of an *ilol* (healer) whose job it is to watch over the person's *chulel*, a kind of animal companion spirit which accompanies people throughout their lives, sharing their various ups and downs. *Chulels* are subject to all kinds of dangers, both natural and supernatural – the supernatural ones coming from *brujos* or wizards. It is therefore most important to be on good terms with your *ilol* – the only person who can save your *chulel* from being bewitched and who can allow your soul to be properly reintegrated with your body.

Treasures of the south

The people of Mixteca – the Mixtec highlands – also produce some of southern Mexico's most intriguing pottery. In the town of Acatlán, local potters lay a whole range of shapes out to dry in the sun: goats, mermaids, frogs, suns, moons, tortoises and rabbits. They also hang them in fantastic jumbles on the branches of trees, the resulting profusion looking like some weird form of

Brightly painted fishing boats are drawn up on a beach at Acapulco. On the far side of the bay rise towering tourist hotels. With the sparkling waters of the Pacific before it and the mountains looming behind, Acapulco deserves its reputation as an earthly paradise – although the contrast between the wealth of the holidaymakers and the poverty of some of the inhabitants somewhat tarnishes the lustre.

Tourists relax in the shade of beach shacks, while Indian women try their hardest to sell them bits and pieces of local craftsmanship. As the tourist guidebooks warn you, there is little point in visiting the shops in Acapulco – sooner or later, most of the goods on sale in them will be brought to you on the beach.

A woman from the more fertile Mixtec lowlands uses a large round stone to shape an earthenware bowl. The women here often wear no more than a waistcloth like this, decorated with simple geometric patterns.

tropical vegetation – or like the huge organ cactuses which provide an equally extravagant touch to the surrounding valleys.

Just outside many villages, a piece of ground is set aside, which offers the slightly surprising spectacle of young Indian men, in caps with long eye-shades, playing baseball under a blazing sun. A Coca-Cola sign hangs outside the village shop: another reminder of

Mexico's influential neighbour to the north. Throughout the region, in the remotest mountain communities, Fanta, Coca-Cola and Pepsi-Cola have become favourite drinks, almost dethroning *atole* and *pinole*, their traditional Indian counterparts made from maize.

The region's capital, Oaxaca, built at the heart of a fertile valley with a ring of mountains rising all around, owes its charm on the one hand to its superb colonial

architecture, which gives its central Zócalo a noticeably European feel, and to its position as a meeting place for the local Indian peoples, on the other. As a centre of Indian culture and crafts, it rivals San Cristóbal de las Casas – especially in its markets. One of these covers several *cuadras* (blocks) – Oaxaca like most of Mexico's colonial cities was built on a grid plan. But there are two other factors as well: a crafts market in the city centre (now catering mostly for Mexican and foreign tourists) and an enormous produce market (catering for the locals) just outside the city.

The latter swarms with people – much more so than the markets of the centre. Immense stalls, often stretching for 60 feet or more, are covered with piles of *sombreros* (hats) made from straw or plastic, and heaps of rope, string, hammocks and baskets. Mountains of fresh or dried peppers (the dried ones looking like old leather, in rich shades of red and brown) rise so high that the seller is often hidden behind them. Two other specialities abound: bundles of the local vegetable sponges (unbeatable for giving yourself a thorough clean) and, chattering away unceasingly in their cages, rows of parrots and parakeets.

Prickly pears and organ cactuses provide a suitably arid setting for this hut in the Mixtec highlands. Life here is hard and the Mixtecs have to scratch a meagre existence from the few plots of relatively fertile soil.

The name Tehuantepec – given to both Mexico's narrow southern isthmus between the Caribbean and Pacific, and to the isthmus's chief town – means 'hill of the jaguar'. Jaguars still roam the region's tropical jungles. In pre-Columbian times they were considered sacred; the Olmecs often gave human figures the faces of baby jaguars in their carvings.

The crafts market, organised in sections, each dedicated to a different type of goods, is given over to the traditional wares produced by the local Indians: pottery in black clay, made without a wheel; gorgeous embroidered *huipils* from the village of San Antonino; and *sarape* blankets and rugs from Mitla to the southeast and its surrounding villages.

These are the more sophisticated wares. But throughout the market, children also carry around old tin lids covered with crudely fashioned statuettes of onyx or obsidian (a shiny black or banded volcanic glass), while others tease the more credulous tourists with fake antiques. These are remarkably skilful copies of pre-Columbian pots and figures found either at ancient Mixtec sites that have been excavated at Mitla or at Zapotec sites at Monte Albán, to the west of Oaxaca. Also fake, though much more valuable, are the products of local gold and silversmiths who create superb reproductions of pre-Columbian jewellery found in a tomb at Monte Albán.

Matching the glories of the local crafts traditions are the quiet beauty and comfort of Oaxaca's colonial palaces, hotels, museums and convents – all of them with patios brimming over with flowers and lush foliage: hibiscuses, jasmines, banana trees and poinsettias (or *nochebuenas*), whose red topknots last throughout the year here. On the streets, the people of Oaxaca enjoy a seemingly endless succession of festivals, all celebrated with elaborate processions and dances. Some are more or less confined to a particular district; for instance, you may stumble almost by accident on a small square where a group of Indians are performing the 'feather dance' which originated in the Zapotec village of Teotitlán del Valle.

Others – such as the celebrations for Oaxaca's Virgin of La Soledad (one of Mexico's most famous Virgins) – bring whole streets to a halt with torchlit processions starting out from one of the many churches. There are heaped offerings of fruits, too, and children dressed as nuns, singing chants in Latin, Spanish and the various Indian tongues. Often, there are floats depicting scenes from the life of the saint whose festival is being honoured. All these contribute to an overwhelming sense of fantasy, as human actors, heavily made up and in elaborate costumes, hold themselves rigid in postures that are meant to imitate the pale statues inside churches. Inevitably they wobble slightly as they do their best to maintain their frozen gestures on the backs of trucks or ox-drawn carts.

The feast of the dead

Throughout Mexico, the magnificence of the various festivals and the amount of money spent on them (in many cases, using up several years of a family's hard-earned savings) are signs of their importance. They are the times in the year when Mexicans can freely express their deepest feelings, pouring out all the sorrows and joys that have accumulated over the previous months – and that the rigours of everyday life have kept bottled up until then.

The festival in honour of a village's patron saint is, not surprisingly, one of the most important, and is

Needlewomen and weavers in Oaxaca's crafts market put the finishing touches to their richly coloured textiles. Rugs and sarape blankets are a particular speciality of the village of Teotitlán del Valle, some 15 miles outside Oaxaca, where the main street looks more like an open-air workshop than a thoroughfare for traffic.

accompanied by dancing, singing and music performed on a variety of instruments: from fiddles and guitars to trumpets and *tepontzlis*, wooden pipes dating from pre-Columbian times. When night falls, the villagers let off barrages of rockets and flares. It is as if they want the noise and light of their festivities to carry as far as possible, pushing back all that is uncertain and alarming in the world that surrounds them.

But the highlight of the year is undoubtedly the festival in which the living remember the dead, and offer them the comfort of their own flesh-and-blood presence. According to mingled Indian and Catholic traditions, November 2, All Souls' Day (or the Day of the Dead), is when the dead make their way back to their old homes, and when the whole family should be

Doña Rosa (above) from the village of Coyótepec near Oaxaca has an international reputation for her black pottery. She and her fellow potters use no wheel; instead, they make their pots by superimposing thin strips of black clay, one on top of the other. Other local pots are glazed green, the glaze often being decorated with floral patterns (left).

there to greet them. Even people who have left their villages for the bleak life of the city shantytowns often return, anxious not to miss out on the one day in the year when they can re-establish contact with their roots.

The preparations are elaborate, and everyone lends a hand. People buy or sew themselves new clothes, to let their dead relatives know that all is well and that the family is not in need. The impression of material wellbeing is essential, since it is supposed to comfort the dead who have long years ahead of them on their painful voyage through the afterlife or *olontik*, and are largely dependent on the support of their living relatives. Indeed, it is this annual visit home which will give the dead renewed strength with which to face the loneliness of the coming year, and to wait patiently for the moment when they will be allowed once more to live upon the earth.

The festival includes plenty of sustenance for the living, too. People drink chocolate – sometimes the tasty *xocoatl*, in which the chocolate is ground by hand and spiced with cinnamon, though more often nowadays it is simply made from cocoa powder bought in tins. They eat local specialities such as *ajo-comino*, a peppery dish of chicken cooked with garlic and other aromatic herbs and spices. Music is, of course, a key part of the festivities, though once again the modern world often leaves its mark: traditional instruments are sometimes replaced with a radio turned up full blast.

In a corner of most homes, a table is covered with a coloured wax cloth or, better still, a sparkling white table cloth, symbolising purity. On top of that are arranged bunches of flowers, piles of fruit, corn cobs, *pan de hueso* ('bone bread', made in the shape of a shinbone), and skulls made from sugar (produced specially for the Day of the Dead – for the past few weeks, the windows of the local confectionery shops will have been more or less taken over by them).

Drinks include milk, beer, Coca-Cola, *pulque* and *chicha* (an alcoholic drink made from sweetened maize). Incense is burnt before the image of a favourite saint, and the festivities are ready to begin with chants and prayers which mention by name all the dead members of the family. That duty done, people tuck into what are generally referred to as the 'remains' of the feast. 'You have eaten enough,' is the usual refrain addressed to the dead. 'That is good. Now, we will take what you have left …'

In the Tzotzil village of Romerio in Chiapas, the Day of the Dead is celebrated with a pilgrimage to the local cemetery. The village people set out early in the morning, their arms laden with tortillas, fruit and flowers (marigolds or *zempaxochitls* are especially popular for their cheerful orange colour, which is said to please the dead). The atmosphere of the procession is calm and meditative. When they reach the cemetery – a wind-blown hill, topped by a row of huge wooden

Colour is everything at Mexican festivals: red scarves, straw hats with bright ribbons, chamarros *(ponchos) of pale pink. Many of these men come from the Tzotzil-speaking peoples of Chiapas, and can be recognised by the ribbons on their hats.*

These 'bird-men' prepare to dance the feather dance of the Oaxaca valley. They evoke the words of the Aztec prince-poet Ayocuán: 'Must I pass away like flowers that fade? Will anything remain of my name, of my fame upon earth? At least the flowers last! At least the songs!'

One of Oaxaca's most spectacular fiestas – the festival of Guelaguetza – is held on the last two Mondays in July. Groups from all over the neighbouring region come together to perform ritual dances; this girl comes from the Zapotec village of Yalalag.

crosses, as high as the scraggy pine trees that surround them – the Chamulas make first of all for the graves of those unfortunate enough to have no family left to care for them. After that, each family visits the graves of its own relatives. The women lift the plank covering each grave and leave their offerings on the bare earth beneath. Then they light candles and use their *rebozo* shawls to make a kind of tent, covering the flame, the plank and their own faces. This leads to one of the strangest parts of the ceremony, during which they embark on a detailed account – interspersed with ritual chants and lamentations – of all that has happened in the last year. Happinesses and sadnesses, marriages and births, the weather and the harvest – nothing is left out of this recital of the year's events, designed to make the dead person feel that he or she is still a part of it all.

Around midday, the more cheerful part of the proceedings begins. Musicians strike up on their violins and guitars, and people unwrap their provisions. They sing and drink, and some of them dress themselves up for amateur theatricals based partly on Biblical stories, partly on current events – all to amuse and serenade the dead. Things get lively, as more and more alcohol is consumed. Sometimes this leads to trouble as enemies settle long-standing quarrels. Sometimes people lapse into a maudlin despair, marked with piercing cries and bouts of weeping.

Huge bunches of flowers, large family photographs and candles are all part of the festivities for the Day of the Dead on November 2. Village people gather in their local cemeteries and remember their dead relatives.

Death and art

'Our death illuminates our life. If our death lacks any kind of meaning, it is because our life lacked meaning.' This assessment of life and death by the country's best-known contemporary writer Octavio Paz is Mexican through and through.

All of Mexico's Indian traditions of poetry – whether expressed in the Mayan, Otomi, Zapotec or Nahua tongues – have had this same tragic sense of life, which only the arts, including those of war, were able to celebrate in the most appropriate way. In the circumstances, the cult of blood sacrifice and the sumptuous ostentation that surrounded the princes, priests and warriors of pre-Columbian times were scarcely surprising. Nor were the remarkable passion and skill with which Mexico's Indian artists later immersed themselves in the new techniques and styles introduced by their Spanish conquerors. From the wonderful stone mosaics of Mitla near Oaxaca (probably dating from the 13th century) to the delicate embroideries of modern San Antonino and the imposing frescoes of Diego Rivera and David Siquieros, Mexican art reveals the same taste for minutely detailed, patient workmanship. It is worthy of those whom many consider the founders of the whole tradition: the Toltecs of the 10th to 12th centuries AD.

Northern Lands Where the Deserts are Green

A horseman in a wide-brimmed sombrero, a Colt revolver hanging from his belt, makes his way along a narrow, dusty road. Suddenly, a truck appears on the horizon behind him, rushing along at full tilt. Within minutes, it has caught up, hurling itself into a roadside ditch and out again as it overtakes. Painted in bold red letters on its radiator grill are the words: 'Go where your destiny leads you.' The solitary figure on horseback plods on, without batting an eyelid.

Such scenes, seeming to confirm many a Hollywood-style cliché, are common enough in Mexico's northern border lands and encapsulate much that is characteristic of the region. In part, they represent the contrast between the old and the new, but here they are given added point by the parallel contrast between Mexico and the United States. 'Poor Mexico – so far from God, so close to the United States,' runs a well-known saying, attributed by some to the former dictator Porfirio Díaz. It is hard, anywhere in Mexico, not to be aware of its powerful neighbour – reviled, on the one hand, but exercising an undoubted fascination and influence, on the other. And nowhere is this more so than in the north. Not, of course, that Mexico is an economic backwater any longer. Industry thrives all along the border – taking advantage, among other things, of a cheaper workforce. Moves in 1992 to set up a North American Free Trade Agreement between Mexico, the United States and Canada will probably encourage this. Even so, the contrasts are unquestionably there: between horse and horse-power, between the more regimented order to the north and the more carefree Latin and Indian ways of the south.

For the visitor entering Mexico from the north, the contrasts can be as exhilarating as they are striking: to the north, the luxurious homes of Texan millionaires lining the banks of the River Sonora (which also gives its name to the Mexican state of Sonora); to the south, groups such as the nomadic Indian Seri people, 'Children of the Ocean and the Desert', who fish the giant turtles of the Gulf of California and cling firmly to their ancestral ways on the island of Tiburón. Even within northern Mexico, the contrasts continue: between, for example, the commercial and industrial bustle of the border towns Tijuana and Ciudad Juárez, and local Indian groups, such as the Yaquis in southern Sonora state, who keep alive ancient warrior traditions.

Vale of plenty

Farther south, between the Sierra Volcánica and the Sierra Madre Occidental, stretches one of Mexico's most prosperous regions: the fertile plain of the Bajío, the country's wheat basket, which was first developed by the early Spanish colonists.

Three of Mexico's most beautiful colonial cities mark the borders of the Bajío: Querétaro, Guanajuato and Guadalajara. The region between them is rich in history. Here, for example, lies the village of Dolores

Hidalgo, near Querétaro, where the radical priest Father Miguel Hidalgo y Costilla launched Mexico's struggle for independence in 1810. It was also in the Bajío that the Emperor Maximilian met his end. Deserted by all but a handful of supporters, he was captured after a battle at Querétaro in May 1867 and shortly afterwards shot by a firing squad on a nearby hill, the Cerro de Las Campañas. His last words summed up his strangely quixotic career as emperor: 'I am going to die for a just cause, that of the independence and liberty of Mexico.'

In Guanajuato – literally, the 'hill of the frogs' – houses in shades of burnt brown, pink and yellow clamber over the sides of a basin in the mountains, the

Storm clouds mass behind a resting fisherman from Michoacán state in Mexico's central highlands. Michoacán's many lakes explain its name, which means 'land of fishermen' in the local Tarascan language. This man fishes the rich waters of Lake Pátzcuaro.

barren heights above them bristling with cactuses and thorn bushes. Its wealth was built in the 17th century on the neighbouring silver mines. It used to be said that a third of all the silver in circulation in the world came from the mines of Guanajuato – which mostly lie idle now. The city still has the magic charm of its days of glory, with shady squares and streets that are so narrow that in one of them, the Callejón del Beso (Alley of the Kiss), a couple standing on balconies on either side of the street can stretch out and kiss each other. In places, it also has the feel of a city in Andalucía in southern Spain, where many of the early colonists came from. This is especially true during its yearly Cervantes Festival when students from the university turn many of the squares into impromptu open-air theatres and act out *entremeses*, one-act satirical plays inspired by the works of the great Spanish writer Miguel de Cervantes (1547–1616). Singers known as *estudiantinas* serenade

passers-by in costumes of black breeches and pleated neck ruffs, and add to the impression that you have somehow stumbled back in time.

Guadalajara has more bloody associations. It was founded in 1532 by the notorious *conquistador* Nuño Beltrán de Guzmán, whose quest for mythical cities paved with gold led him to commit appalling barbarities against the local Indians – enough to shock even the Spanish authorities who packed him off to Madrid.

Despite its past, Guadalajara – Mexico's second-largest city – now has a distinctly relaxed atmosphere and is now better known as the home of *mariachi* music played by bands of trumpeters, guitarists and violinists. Its people, the *tapatíos*, have a reputation for being hospitable, friendly and artistic.

On the walls of the Hospicio Cabañas and the Palacio de Gobierno (Palace of Government), frescoes by José Clemente Orozco are a reminder that the three founders of the country's great mural tradition – Orozco, David Siquieros and Diego Rivera – came from northern and central Mexico. Guadalajara is the capital of Jalisco state, and Orozco was a Jaliscan, born in the town of Zapotlán in the west in 1883. He started his career as a cartoonist, and his work never lost its satirical edge, which is reflected in titles such as 'The rich banqueting while the workers quarrel' or 'The end of the old order'. Siquieros, whose paintings drew much of their inspiration from the plight and struggle of the workers, was born in Chihuahua state in the north-east. Some of his works are represented in Guadalajara's museums, as are many by Diego Rivera, born in Guanajuato in 1886.

Coming from a very different, though no less Mexican, tradition is the diminutive Virgin of Zapopán – known as the *zapopanita* – which is housed for most of the year in a basilica in the outskirts of Guadalajara. A Franciscan missionary and ardent champion of the Indians, Antonio de Segovia, originally dedicated her to the local people at the time of the conquest, and she has

Opposite: *Prickly pears and maguey plants line the road between Querétaro and San Miguel de Allende. They are the most characteristic plants of the arid central highlands. The prickly pear also figures in the Aztec device of an eagle battling with a serpent, which now forms part of the Mexican flag.*

Maguey hearts are pounded, and will later be distilled, to make the alcoholic spirit tequila. This is traditionally served with lime or tomato juice and salt. When drinking it, the trick is to swallow a mouthful of the tequila, then a few drops of lime or tomato juice, followed by a pinch of salt. In the south, the spirit mescal is extracted from maguey hearts – it is similar to tequila, only less refined.

remained one of Mexico's most widely venerated Virgins, rivalled only by her counterpart at Guadalupe. Between June and October each year, she is taken from her basilica and does a series of stints in churches in different parts of the city.

Farming, ancient and modern

North of the Bajío, a huge depression lies between the V-shaped arms of the Sierra Madre Oriental and the Sierra Madre Occidental. The land here was never as fertile as in the Bajío and for centuries it remained largely uncultivated. Then improved irrigation allowed a number of regions to develop as relatively prosperous arable or livestock-raising areas. Some, such as Aguascalientes, even developed important local wine industries. Here, though, as in much of the rest of rural Mexico, economic power remains very much in the hands of the large landowners, leaving smaller peasant farmers to eke out precarious existences. This naturally fuels continuing demands for agricultural reform.

Things were not always like this. Observers have long noted the potential of the more fertile regions of northern and central Mexico – among them Hernán Cortés, who wrote in 1521: 'An air of peace reigns in these lands and there is great fertility for anything sown in them.' In Aztec times, and even in the early centuries of Spanish rule, this was matched by a relatively equitable system of farming the land. Under the Aztecs, most cultivable lands belonged to rural communities known as *calpulli*, who farmed them jointly and benefited from what they produced. The system was continued in roughly the same form during most of the period of Spanish rule.

The change came in the late 18th century, when the colonial authorities issued a new set of commercial regulations. Paradoxically, these played a key part in the

The city of Guadalajara is one of the most gracious and elegant in the country. At its centre, four large squares form a kind of cross around the cathedral – this one is the Plaza de la Independencia. Guadalajara lies at the heart of charro *(cowboy) country; it also gave birth to* mariachi *music and houses one of Mexico's best-loved Virgins – the Virgin of Zapopán.*

later movement for independence. Creole landowners benefited most from the new code, and were the most influential supporters of the independence struggle. Later again, they also benefited from reforms set in place by President Benito Juárez in the 1860s. In dispossessing the Catholic church of its huge estates, Juárez also abolished collective ownership, and thus threw many peasants off farms they had worked for generations. It was the landowners who carved out for themselves the lion's share of the newly available land.

What followed was a 'golden age' – for the landowners – of huge haciendas and *ganaderías* (cattle ranches), with Indian workers, or *peones*, signed on for miserable wages. Farm workers lived in the bleakest of conditions and fell ever-more heavily into debt, due to a system of credit which obliged them to buy goods in *tiendas de rayas* (literally, 'wage shops') belonging to

*Flowers figure prominently
in the town of San Miguel
de Allende – either paper
flowers such as this, or
flowers made from a paste
of stale bread, which are
then painted in bright colours
and used to decorate
people's homes.*

*Most Mexicans have a
weakness for ices and ice
creams. Street sellers such
as this make a speciality of
water ices known as
nieve ('snow'). In this,
they follow in the footsteps
of their Aztec ancestors,
who enjoyed sorbets made
with real snow from Mount
Popocatépetl.*

Opposite: *Tomatoes, peas, avocados and assorted citrus fruit are among the foods on display in the market at Pátzcuaro. But the region is also noted for its ceramics, lacquer- and copperware, and for its masks and religious images made from a paste made with maize flour. Many of these craft traditions date from the times of the Tarascans, whose civilisation was a serious rival to that of the Aztecs before the Spanish conquest.*

Below right: *A Pátzcuaro market woman uses a basket as a hat against the midday sun. Her ancestors in pre-Columbian times were the Tarascans whose capital Tzintzuntzan lay not far away on the shores of Lake Pátzcuaro. Although they submitted more or less peacefully to the Spanish, they still suffered horrific massacres at the hands of the conquistador Nuño de Guzmán.*

the owners of the haciendas. About two-thirds of Mexico's cultivable land belonged to 9000 landowners.

Emiliano Zapata, the most popular leader during the revolutionary years at the start of the 20th century, sympathised with the peasants' anger, and proposed returning to something like the old order, making sure that this time the peasants really did benefit. This bore some fruit in 1915 when President Venustiano Carranza redistributed over 500,000 acres of land for collective farming (*ejidataria*). But it was only when President Lázaro Cárdenas came to power in the 1930s that more substantial areas – nearly 50 million acres – became *ejidos* or communal lands.

Under the new order, peasants had a life interest in communal lands, on the condition that they actually worked them themselves. If land remained uncultivated for three years, the farmer lost his right to it. Land on the *ejidos* was shared out according to its fertility and the quality of the soil. Generally, a farmer had a right to one part of *riego* (land that is well irrigated and fertile) or two parts of *temporal* (land that is more at the mercy of the elements). After an initial period of euphoria, however, the communal system led to complications. Children, for example, could inherit the right to communal land, but usually it was divided equally between them, thus creating plots that were too small to maintain a family. Once more, many peasants were forced to work as *peones* on the remaining large estates. In more recent years, the government has often been less than generous in providing credit and grants for the *ejidos*. Many are now barely scraping a living.

Among the landowners, dispossessed of their former haciendas, many have simply bought up large numbers

acquire larger, more viable holdings. But the poorest workers scarcely benefit and live off minimal wages.

These difficulties are particularly evident in the north. Here, huge tracts of land are given over to cash crops such as wheat or cotton. It is in the towns and countryside of these vast irrigated plains, worked by a new breed of college-educated farmers and managers, that the phenomenon of the *nueva burguesia* has emerged. They include cattle ranchers from the state of Chihuahua; arable farmers around Guadalajara; industrialists in the city of Monterrey – all of them with living standards further and further removed from those of the more traditional south.

In the lands of Pancho Villa

At the heart of the huge plain between the two branches of the Sierras Madre lies Chihuahua, capital of Mexico's largest and most productive state of the same name. This was the domain of the revolutionary hero Pancho Villa, whose home Quinta Luz in Chihuahua city is now a museum.

To this day, the whole epic story of Villa and his army, the 'Division of the North', remains a vivid memory for the people who live here. Certainly, it is replete with romantic images, of men on horseback

A market seller sorts citrus fruit in Pátzcuaro. Despite yearly inundations of tourists, the town remains thoroughly Mexican in feel – with sumptuously ornamented colonial churches and palaces, and rich Indian traditions of arts and crafts.

of small farms and then employed *peones*, just as they did in the old days, to work them. These farms – and others belonging to banks or large companies and run on an industrial scale as 'agri-businesses' – have increasingly received the bulk of government investment. In 1992, the law was changed to allow communal land to be sold or leased – thus permitting farmers to

riding into battle, carving their way across the country, financed – rather less romantically – by a US bank. Like some latter-day Robin Hood, Villa is remembered, in the romantic version of events, as robbing from the rich to mete out social justice for the poor. In fact, the truth – as usual – was less romantic. Coming from authentically peasant stock, Pancho Villa seems to have been motivated at least as much by the desire for power as for righting the wrongs of his people. He was a talented self-publicist who revelled in being a legend in his own lifetime. The story goes that when Hollywood came to Mexico to make a movie of his great deeds, he insisted on being filmed in most advantageous poses even as he led his troops into real battles. His death when it came was suitably dramatic: he was assassinated in 1923 while riding in a limousine, now on display in the Quinta Luz.

Bandit or hero, Villa lived to the full the life of the traditional Mexican *macho* (male). This swaggering mythical figure – always armed, shouldering his way manfully into *bodegas* (bars), ever ready for a fight – is also represented by the avenging 'hero', Hipólito, of the popular ballad of 'Rosita Alvirez':

Hipolito arrived at the ball
And went towards Rosa;
As she was the prettiest
Rosita was scornful of him.

'Rosita, don't insult me,
People will notice.'
'I don't care about people,
I don't want to dance with you.'

He put his hand to his waist
And drew his pistol.
Into the poor Rosita
Three bullets, no fewer, he shot.

The rebozo *shawl is often the only part of their traditional costume that Indian women still wear every day. This is largely because it is so useful. They can use it to keep them warm, to protect their heads from the sun, or simply to drape elegantly around their shoulders. They sit on it and use it to carry children or goods.*

Festivals in the north usually mean *charreadas*, the Mexican form of rodeo. Until relatively recently, the traditional outfit of the *charro* (cowboy) ranked as a kind of national costume: waistcoat-like jacket, buckskin trousers, overcoat with silver buttons and a broad-brimmed felt hat embroidered with gold thread. Nowadays, however, most men bring it out only for special occasions such as festivals and weddings.

At the *charreada* itself the men display prodigious skill with the lasso, launching themselves into full gallop as they hurl the lasso out in huge, perfectly executed circles, closing in on the cow they have to

trap. These are skills learnt in early childhood, and throughout the north you still see small boys in the streets of towns and villages practising with miniature lassoes. They perfect the art of making circles and then, at just the right moment, with a scarcely perceptible flick of the wrist, drop the loop around some substitute for the cow in a real *charreada*.

The *charro*, like the cowboy for Americans, has a key place in the mythology of Mexican patriotism, his values enshrined in traditional songs and ballads, known as *rancheras*, which have become a standard part of the repertoire of *mariachi* bands. The players accompany themselves on violins, huge bass guitars and trumpets, as they sing in the streets and squares of cities, and at family festivities, notably marriages – from which the bands get their name. Ballads or *corridos* are another staple part of *mariachi* fare; their rhyming couplets tell tales of tragedy and bloodletting, often mingled with characteristically black humour. These recount events from Mexico's history or cautionary tales of ancient crimes – such as the death of Rosita Alvirez.

It is hard to escape music and song in Mexico. During festivals, Indian villages still resound to the sound of pre-Columbian drums such as the *huehuetl* and

It is festival time in the Tarascan Indian village of Jerónimo Purenciecuaro. A group of women – wearing their traditional costumes for this special occasion – lead a procession, with a brass band following behind.

Satire plays an important part in the dance of the viejitos *('little old ones'). These two masked men represent the senile decrepitude which afflicted even the conquering Europeans in their old age.*

The Tarahumara Indians of Chihuahua state in the north-east are among the groups that have clung most steadfastly to their ancient way of life. They are still partly nomadic, living off mountain game such as goats, wolves and coyote.

the *teponaztli*. Throughout the country ingenious children and teenagers will turn just about any suitable object into a musical instrument: wooden whistles bored out of dry branches; flutes with just two or three stops, made out of anything from bone to bamboo or clay; pieces of wood which they bang or rub together; jam jars; boxes of nails; and even dried fruits with their seeds rattling inside them.

Home on the range

Spreading over the northern plains are huge *ganaderías* or cattle ranches, covering thousands of acres where the *charro* is still very much king and his skills a vital part of everyday life.

Meat and milk are essential parts of the local diet. The milk goes into enormous cups of *cafe con leche*

(white coffee), which are sold in the markets in the shade of large white-canvas stalls stretched between wobbly posts. The meat appears in dishes of *cabrito* (goat) or *machacado*-style (dried) beef. Boiled beef – or sometimes scrambled eggs – is also used to stuff the distinctive wheat tortillas of the north, known as *burritos*. For a refreshing contrast, you can sample one of the brightly coloured ices sold by children in the streets. At their best, these are delicious, made from crushed ice and various fruit juices, and evoke the sorbets enjoyed by the Aztecs, who had large earthenware jars of snow brought down from the heights of Mount Popocatépetl to make them.

Among the local Indian groups are the Tarahumaras, who live at the heart of one of the most spectacularly wild parts of the *sierras* of western Chihuahua state. The region is gouged with the deepest canyons in Mexico, including the astonishing Barranca del Cobre (Copper Canyon) whose craggy, many-hued heights rise from a carpet of dense tropical forest. The Tarahumaras once lived on the rich plains that spread out from the feet of the ranges named after them, the Serranía de Tarahumara, but were chased off the plains in the 16th century during a campaign led by the *conquistador* Francisco Vázquez de Coronado, whose explorations also led him into modern New Mexico and Kansas.

Today, the Tarahumaras live in modest dwellings of baked clay or even in mountain caves. Their principal livelihood comes from felling forest trees – from which they earn just enough to go to the local towns and buy any essential goods they cannot grow or make themselves. It is an austere life, relieved, however, by a succession of festivals, with both Christian and pagan origins: harvest festivals, and festivals when they sow their crops; festivals when they propitiate the gods with animal sacrifices and perform the dance of the owl (*tecolote*) to quell, for example, outbreaks of disease. These are occasions for drinking *tesguino*, a maize

The tiny chihuahua, with pointed ears and smooth fur, is one of the few well-known breeds of dog to originate in Latin America. As its name suggests, it came first from the state of Chihuahua.

The Sierra Tarahumara's huge canyons and towering limestone outcrops create some of the most awesome scenery in northern Mexico. Here the Tarahumara Indians found refuge from the conquering Spaniards, and here most of them remain, still making their homes in remote caves.

Of all Mexico's Indian peoples, the Huichols are most finely attuned to the supernatural world. Their principal gods are the Sun (whom they call the Great Father) and Fire (the Great Spirit). Other deities, such as the gods of water and fertility, govern practically every detail of everyday life.

Each Huichol village has its own special costume, but most consist of long shirts and baggy trousers, all finely embroidered with geometric patterns or stylised representations of animals.

alcohol, and for consuming *peyotl*, a sacred (and hallucinogenic) cactus. The ritual dance of the *peyotl*, with which the Tarahumaras usually celebrate a healing, is a kind of hymn of thanks performed at sunrise.

The sacred hunt for peyotl

A little farther south, in the Sierra Huichol, the cult of *peyotl* – or *jikuri*, as the range's Huichol Indians call it – assumes even more elaborate, and arduous, dimensions. The Tarahumaras gather the precious cactus on their own lands, but tradition demands that the Huichols seek the plant out some 250 miles away, across the peaks of the Sierra Madre Occidental, in the deserts of the central Mexican state of San Luis Potosí.

This extraordinary test of endurance, first through rugged mountain terrain with icy cold nights and then through baking deserts, lasts 40 days there and back again. But, for the Huichols, *jikuri* is a food for both soul and body, for gods and men: their maize harvests and success in hunting the great stags of their forests all depend on it. The journey itself is a key part of the ritual – from which women are strictly excluded. Sacred rites are performed at various holy places, shrines and grottos along the way. During one of these stops, on the Hill of the Star, these include confession, with individual pilgrims first examining their consciences alone, then in public; the gravest sin is adultery. No one would dream of opting out of these rituals, even if it means that later, on their return home, others will talk about them.

The pilgrims are not allowed to eat, drink or sleep, except in two places marked out by tradition. This means that they have to keep going, whatever the weather or their state of exhaustion, until they reach one or other of the sanctioned stops. Finally, at the end of the long march, the land of *peyotl*, known as Wirikota, appears before them. This brings the magic moment when they consume the first *jikuri*, and give themselves over to wonderful visions of stags and maize.

The return journey is more cheerful. Everyone carries his bundle of sacred cactus, which he can dip into at each stop. The pilgrims are further buoyed by the prospect of a warm welcome on their arrival from family and friends who have stayed behind. The return itself gives rise to another festival – lasting a month or more, in all – when they offer their *jikuri* first to the gods, and then share it out among the men.

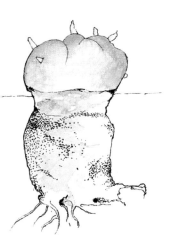

The peyotl plant (Lephophophora williamsii) *is known by the Huichols as* jikuri. *It is a small, rounded cactus containing the drug mescaline, which produces hallucinations.*

Tarascan charm

To the south again, the landscape becomes softer and more gently beautiful, leading eventually to one of the loveliest regions in the whole of Mexico: the Tarascan highlands, home of the Tarascan (or Purépecha) Indians, in the state of Michoacán. Here is Lake Pátzcuaro, one of the most beautiful – and photographed – lakes in the world. Its position is spectacular, in a mountain cradle, whose waters contain one of the richest fish populations of any freshwater lake in the world. Tarascan villages line its shores, though the bulk of the Tarascans live on the high plateaus of the surrounding volcanic *sierras*.

In the larger, mixed-race lakeside towns, the Tarascans' craft traditions are big business, due to the thousands of tourists who flock here each year. Among the chief attractions of the lake itself are the narrow dugout canoes of the local fishermen, and more

A Huichol healer in full festival attire wears the traditional ropopero, *a hat made from palm leaves and decorated with feathers and tassels.*

particularly their distinctive *mariposa* (butterfly) fishing nets. In the village of Janitzio, built on the largest of the islands, the dazzling whiteness of the nets forms a picturesque contrast with the brightly coloured clothes of the fishermen's children. Clambering up or down the village's *subidas*, or, narrow streets, they seem to stand out like brilliant tropical flowers or exotic fish.

Tzintzuntzan – the 'place of humming birds' (though you are unlikely to see a humming bird there now) – clings to a lakeside promontory. On its summit, you can still see the remains of an ancient ceremonial site, dating from the pre-Columbian Tarascan kingdom which, at the time of the Spanish conquest, included all of Michoacán and parts of modern Jalisco and Colima states. Dominating the village below is an impressive baroque church, which once belonged to a now-ruined Franciscan monastery, founded around 1530 by the Spanish bishop Vasco de Quiroga. Unusually for his time, Quiroga had a true appreciation of the Tarascans'

way of life – earning him the affectionate nickname, '*Tata Vasco*' (Daddy Vasco) – and he did much to encourage their crafts.

Today, maize and vegetables are the staple crops of the Tarascans of the *sierras*, while their fellows by the lake traditionally live by fishing its exquisite white fish, known as *blancos* (whites). As a result, the region is known almost as much for its gastronomy as for its beauty. On Sundays, these two worlds come together in

A Tarascan woman uses a bundle of twigs to comb her daughter's hair. Behind them spreads an inlet of Lake Pátzcuaro, one of inland Mexico's most famous beauty spots.

the barter market at Erongaricuaro on the lake's southern shore. This is a highly colourful occasion, with the mountain Tarascans often arriving by donkey, and the lakeside ones by canoe. They then set to, bartering fish for earthenware pots, wood for maize.

In the mountains, homes are simple affairs of logs built on a base of flat stones. Many have verandahs of carved wood, sheltering under roofs of palm leaves or wooden shingles held up by wooden posts. Inside, the walls are decorated with the beautiful ceramics that are produced throughout the district: large platters and jars, with a brilliant green glaze, coming from the village of Patamban; brown earthenware plates and bowls, with simple line designs showing lake fishermen carrying their catches, from Tzintzuntzan. Nor are the local potters content with simply reproducing traditional forms. Perhaps their finest creations are the utensils they make for the festivities around the Day of the Dead,

The 'butterfly' nets traditionally used by Lake Pátzcuaro's fishermen are now as often displayed for tourist cameras as for actual fishing. No amount of tourism, however, has been able to destroy the sheer beauty of the lake, cradled in a basin between volcanic mountains.

The cemetery bell on the island of Janitzio in Lake Pátzcuaro hangs ready to summon the faithful to the island's annual Day of the Dead vigil – one of the most colourful in Mexico. These women are laden with offerings which they will lay on the tombs of their dead relatives. Later will come a night of prayers and chants – interrupted only by the flashes of tourist cameras.

From the north of Mexico to the south, one of the first things a mother traditionally teaches her daughter is the art of tortear – that is, making tortillas. The process begins by grinding the maize on a low stone block or metate. The dough is mixed with a good pinch of powdered lime and moulded into shape by slapping hunks of it from one hand to the other. Finally, it is cooked.

which is celebrated by the Tarascans with particular gusto. Candlesticks, bowls for presenting offerings, incense burners are all adorned with fantastical arrays of leaves, flowers, prickly fruit, snakes and the fins, tails and scales of fishes.

It was here, in the state of Michoacán, not far from the town of Uruapan, that the earth opened one day in 1943 under the astonished eyes of an Indian farmer, Dionisio Pulido. He had been peacefully working on his *milpa* (maize field), when suddenly smoke began to emerge from it, followed by volcanic lava. He raised the alarm, and within hours the inhabitants of neighbouring San Juan Paracutín had evacuated their village. Now, only the belltower of its church pokes out from the ocean of lava spewed by the volcano during the course of a year or more. Its successive – and extremely spectacular – eruptions drew crowds of visitors to the region, which is still a favourite tourist spot.

There is, indeed, much to draw visitors to the Tarascan highlands: the *mariposa* nets of the Pátzcuaro fishermen, the glories of the volcanic landscape, and the splendours of the Tarascans' Day of the Dead celebra-tions (particularly at Janitzio, where the crowds of curious onlookers can often drown the devotions of the local Indians). There is also the Tarascans' dance of the *viejitos* (literally, 'little old ones') – among the most engaging of all Mexico's many traditional dances. This has as its central characters a group of performers dressed as old men. Their long white wigs and pallid masks painted with rosy cheeks and blue eyes are almost certainly a satirical dig at white-skinned Europeans, deformed by age and sickness. The dance consists essentially of a series of prancing leaps, which at times bear an uncanny resemblance to American tap dancing. The impression of impotent fury is reinforced as the dancers stab the ground with sticks and by the senile grins on the faces of the masks.

West of the sierras

Stretching up Mexico's far north-western flank are the ancient deserts of Sinaloa and Sonora states, now irrigated and given over to cereal crops in the north and

Lake and mountain provide a spectacular setting as a Tarascan woman on Janitzio island spins the cotton which she will later weave into long sheets of fabric. According to the archaeologists, cotton has been used in Mexico since at least 2400 BC, but it was the Spanish who introduced the varieties from which most of today's cotton plants are descended.

sugar cane in the south. Dotting the coast are a number of strangely isolated ports and tourist resorts: Guaymas, Los Mochis and Mazatlán. Mazatlán, in particular, is famous for its pre-Lenten carnival.

'It is significant that a land as sad as ours has so many *fiestas*, and such joyful *fiestas*,' wrote Mexico's great man of letters, Octavio Paz. 'Their frequency and brilliance, and the enthusiasm with which we throw ourselves into them, all suggest that, without them, we would fall apart. They set us free – even if only momentarily – from all the fruitless impulses and all the inflammable material we carry around inside ourselves.' Standing in stark contrast to the festivals described by Paz are the artificial ones, fabricated for the benefit of foreigners, eager for easy pleasures and little bothered about authenticity. One of the most characteristic instances of this consumer-led Mexican 'bazaar' is Tijuana, on the frontier with the United States. In this paradise of gambling and dance halls and 'typical' restaurants, everything is for sale.

The true Mexican *fiesta* – a state of mind and spirit as much as a particular occasion – survives despite all the pressures, as does the proudly different character of the people. In the central part of the fertile Yaqui river valley, in southern Sonora state, live the Yaqui Indians. Famous to this day for their warlike skills, they are the supreme embodiment of the independent spirit of Mexico's many native peoples. From the time of the Spanish conquest onwards, they have fought like lions – and with remarkable success – to preserve their autonomy and way of life. They rebelled against the Spanish authorities in 1710, and against the republican authorities in 1825. Under the dictator Porfirio Díaz, they suffered mass deportations, only to rise up again under the rule of President Alvaro Obregón – a Sonoran – in 1928. At the same period, they saw the waters of their sacred river diverted to irrigate the lands around the settlement of Ciudad Obregón, one of the President's pet projects. Thanks in part to proposals put forward by Obregón – who was, in fact, reasonably sympathetic towards their aspirations – they now enjoy a large measure of self-rule, with eight local governors for each of their principal towns.

Whales in spring

Remoter still, the long tongue of land known as Baja (Lower) California consists almost entirely of a wilderness, covered with strangely twisting *mezquite* plants and thorn bushes, relieved here and there by oases of relative fertility such as those given over to wine-growing. Over the centuries, the locals have fished for pearls, and also for fish in some of the richest waters off Mexico – marlin, skate and exotic flying fishes.

On the peninsula's western side, facing an immense spread of ocean, the Bay of Sebastian Vizcaíno plays host in early spring each year to a spectacle of haunting beauty. This is the place where California grey whales arrive in their hundreds from the icy waters of the Arctic to spawn and raise their young. Happily ignorant of the strife of the human world, and relatively safe from the attentions of whale-hunters, they frolic in the warm blue waters of the Pacific.

One child carries a basket of maize, the other a basket of orchids. Food and ornament ... the scene sums up two of the most insistent themes of Mexican life – the need to survive and the need for beauty.

Guatemala

Nature is turbulent as well as beautiful in Guatemala.
The country has glorious mountains, forests and highland lakes,
but it also lies on a geographical fault line which means that it is
regularly rocked by earthquakes. It has, too, a record of political
turmoil. For all that, it is one of the most fascinating countries in
Central America, rich in colourful Indian festivals and traditions
and hiding the secrets of the ancient Mayan civilisation that
flourished in the jungles of the Petén lowlands of the north long
before the Spanish arrived in the 16th century.

A crowd of Indian pilgrims watches a re-enactment of Christ's Passion during Holy Week. The vivid colours and lack of mourning are reminders that in Guatemala the days from Maundy Thursday to Easter Sunday are known as semana alegre, 'happy week'.

Men prepare for a religious procession outside the church of Saint Thomas in Chichicastenango. The church was built on top of a former Indian temple, and to this day Christianity and local Indian beliefs are inextricably mixed.

Previous page: The Quiché people's 'dance of the conquest' combines extravagance with a sense of irony. Spanish conquistadores and whites in general are depicted in a way that both exalts and ridicules them. This was how Guatemala's Indians sought to protect themselves from the influence of an invading culture.

THE MYSTERIOUS LAND OF THE MAYA   79

The Mysterious Land of the Maya

Nowhere in Latin America is Holy Week celebrated with a more extravagant mix of exuberance and sadness, revelry and religious fervour than in Guatemala's former capital, Antigua. Lying in a fertile mountain valley, dominated by the three great volcanoes of El Agua (Water), El Fuego (Fire) and Acatenango, to the west of the modern capital Guatemala City, Antigua provides a suitably dramatic setting. Imposing Spanish colonial palaces line cobbled streets, their entrances offering teasing glimpses of deliciously shady inner patios, where old noble families live out a sheltered existence waited on by Indian servants. Carved fountains play in old squares, while ornate baroque churches, many never restored after a catastrophic earthquake wrecked the city in 1773, seem to rise at just about every street corner.

For most of the year, Antigua has the attractively dilapidated air of a beautiful city that has lost its former importance. But during Holy Week all this vanishes. From throughout Guatemala and well beyond, thousands of visitors converge on the city for seven hectic days and nights of torchlit processions, music, dancing, fireworks and high religious drama.

The major festivities start on Palm Sunday afternoon with a re-enactment of Jesus's entry into Jerusalem. Crowds gather outside the church of La Merced in the north of the city and wait for a huge effigy of Jesus, borne on a large float or *anda* to emerge. Then they set off towards the Parque Central (Central Park). This is a lengthy business. The streets are packed, and every district of the city must have the honour of welcoming the massive effigy, which needs constant relays of men to carry it because of its sheer weight. By the time they reach the Plaza Mayor and are ready for the return journey to the church of La Merced, it is well after dark. Fireworks explode in the skies above; the air is thick with the smell of incense, coming from large burners swung by robed figures representing the Jews of ancient Jerusalem. Among the crowd, people's faces flicker in and out of the yellow light of flaming torches.

Monday, Tuesday and Wednesday are relatively quiet. This is the time for people to go to parties and concerts and wander through squares decorated with bright displays of flowers. There are few major processions, but the streets are never empty. The sounds of revelry emerge from bars, courtyards and homes, while by night the barrage of fireworks and crackers seems never ending. Then comes Maundy Thursday and the Procession of the Roman Soldiers. Men charge through the city, on foot or horseback, shouting out the tragic news of the *sentencia,* Jesus's death sentence. When night falls, the streets are carpeted with flowers, dyed sawdust, seeds and pine needles. The festivities last until dawn on Good Friday, and then merge into another procession from the church of La Merced. At midday, the Crucifixion is re-enacted, followed by a 'song of pardon' chanted outside the City Hall – after that, a prisoner from the city jail is traditionally set free. In the evening of Easter Saturday, women in black carry figures of the Virgin Mary, also clad in black and decked with blood-red roses, through the streets. By Easter Sunday, everyone is exhausted, and the visitors begin to leave.

Where nature excels in beauty

Guatemala can justly claim to be one of the most beautiful countries in Central America. Lying between Mexico to the north and Honduras, Belize and El Salvador to the east and south, it covers 42,000 square

Effigies of saints mingle with displays of plants and flowers in an Easter procession. Triumphal arches decorated with birds' nests and even iguanas' nests line the route. Nature almost invariably influences acts of worship in Guatemala.

miles (roughly the size of Ireland) and faces both the Caribbean and the Pacific. In the west, volcanic highlands rise sharply from narrow plains along the Pacific coast, their peaks looming majestically above fertile valleys. In the east, the dry valley of the Motagua river links the western highlands with the Caribbean coastline. To the north, the Verapaz highlands descend towards the Petén plain, whose dense and steaming jungles merge with those of Mexico's Yucatán peninsula. Monkeys clamber through the treetops and occasional flashes of bright colour mark the flight of a scarlet macaw or toucan.

There are at least 900 varieties of bird in Guatemala. The national bird (which also gives its name to the local currency) is the rare *quetzal*, with magnificent red breast, yellow beak and a brilliant emerald-green tail measuring up to 3 feet long. It has the distinction of building nests with two doors, so that it does not have to turn round inside and ruffle its feathers. The *cunzontl*, which looks rather like a maroon-coloured sparrow, is sometimes known as the 'bird with 400 voices' because of its wide repertoire of different songs; some people claim that these were the inspiration for the musical traditions of Guatemala's Mayan Indians. There is also a minute 'bird fly', smaller even than most humming birds, and a tiny, brightly coloured nightingale. Strange birds called *cucuchitos* bark like dogs and are said to warn of coming earthquakes.

Beauty mingles with violence. The volcanic highlands of the west run along a geographical fault line that has been responsible for devastating all three of the country's successive capitals: Antigua's predecessor Santiago de los Caballeros in an earthquake in 1542, Antigua itself in 1773 and Guatemala City in 1917, 1918 and 1976. Politics are no less unstable. Since Guatemala won its freedom from Spain in 1821, its governments have often been established by armed coups and the resulting regimes have frequently been unjust and cruel. A left-wing guerrilla insurgency in the 1970s and 80s led to savage reprisals and massacres of rural Indians by the military. Civilian rule (under the still watchful eye of the military) was established in 1985, but even that has been disturbed by attempted coups, one as recently as May 1993.

Some 55 per cent of Guatemalans are Indians, descended from the Maya whose ruined cities, built 2000 years ago, still stand in the remote jungles of the Petén lowlands. Most of the rest are *mestizos* (of mixed Indian and Spanish blood).

Despite centuries of oppression, the Maya Indians have clung fast to their traditions and culture, and in few places more so than in Chichicastenango in the western highlands. It was here, in the 17th century, that the Spanish priest Francisco Jiménez discovered the *Popol Vuh*, a Mayan account of the creation of the world, transcribed into Latin script by an unknown Indian of the local Quiché tribe. It reveals a down-to-earth humour with episodes such as a rebellion of household implements against their human masters and tyrants.

Catholic Christianity and ancient Mayan beliefs blend until they are nearly indistinguishable. In 1540, Spanish missionaries built Chichicastenango's church of St Thomas on top of a Mayan temple. Nowadays, the church is neatly divided down its centre: to the left are figures of various Mayan divinities; to the right are Christian saints. The long flight of steps leading up to it are black with the soot of candles left by worshipping Indians. The men cluster there in black woollen cloaks embroidered with flowers and butterflies; the women wear white embroidered blouses and long striped skirts, with their hair plaited with wool and rolled up on top of their heads. They light their candles and small sticks of a resin extracted from the *palo jijote* tree, using matches made from banana leaves. The resulting clouds of incense are believed to draw the attention of the gods.

In December each year, Chichicastenango gives itself over to another famous festival: the *fiesta de Santo Tomás*. Locals and visitors dance for eight hours on end,

Children grin, while a figure of Judas Iscariot dangles from an improvised gallows during Holy Week celebrations. Drama is never lacking when Guatemalans commemorate the events of Easter.

while the skies above echo to the thunder of fireworks. For some dances, the performers dress, Mayan-style, in jaguar skins; others have their roots in far-away Spain, and are ritual re-enactments of ancient battles between Christian Spaniards and Muslim Moors.

Land of festivals

Even by Latin American standards, Guatemala is a land of festivals. From January right through to December, scarcely a week seems to pass without some colourful celebration taking place in different towns and villages.

At Santiago Atitlán, lying on a sheltered inlet of Lake Atitlán in the western highlands, the Indians honour a strange personage named Maximón, part saint, part demon, whom they dress in yellow shoes and a tall European-style hat, often with a fat cigar hanging from his mouth. He is kept happy with offerings of rum and cigarettes, and on Good Friday is paraded through the village alongside an effigy of Christ.

The festival of *Ocho Monos* ('Eight Monkeys') at Momostenango, farther west, comes straight out of the Mayan calendar. This was somewhat complicated, since it involved, in fact, two calendars running concurrently, one based on a year of 260 days, the other on a solar year of 365 days – the two came together every 52 solar years, which equalled 73 260-day years. Ceremonials tended to follow the 260-day cycle and thousands of Indians still gather at the mountain of Chuitmesabal, near Momostenango, for New Year's festivities every 260 days. They pray before altars covered with broken pots – the remains of cooking pots families have accidentally broken during the previous 'year'. Worshippers also bring money, alcoholic spirits – and their troubles which they tell to the assembled priests and priestesses. These duly pass the tidings on to the gods, and the crowds spent the rest of the night in prayer around huge fires.

In a few places, Indian worship owes much to the vision of enlightened Catholic priests. At Esquipulas, near the Honduran border, the effigy of Christ is black – its 16th-century carver is said to have deliberately used dark wood so as not to offend the Indians. Esquipulas also houses the black god El Akau, deity of violent death; the Indians still perform the dance of *Los Negros* to honour simultaneously both Christ and El Akau.

No festival is complete without its special dance, which usually originated as part of a Mayan religious ritual. Some dances are also based on historical events, such as foreign invasions. One of these, the 'dance of the conquest', is performed by the Quiché and Cakchiquel Indians living on the shores of Lake Atitlán

Copal, a resin extracted from the palo jijote *tree, was orginally burned on the steps of Mayan temples. Today, Quiché descendants of the Maya of old burn it on the steps of Catholic churches.*

and re-creates the coming of the Spanish invaders in the 16th century. The dancers dress up in gold wigs, blonde moustaches, star-covered cloaks, and even carry parasols, which they open and close as they dance. They also, rather grimly, reproduce the brutal sound of Spanish laughter as they place gold collars around the necks of dancers representing the conquered Indians.

Hieroglyphics and men made from maize

When the Spanish arrived in Guatemala from Mexico in 1523, there were two main Indian groups living there. On the Pacific south-east coast were the Pipile, speaking a language closely related to the Mexican Aztec's Nahuatl. Living in the highlands, meanwhile, were the Quiché and Cakchiquel, together with less numerous

Colour is never far away among the Quiché people of Santiago Atitlán, a village on the shores of Lake Atitlán in Guatemala's western highlands. In recent years, girls such as these have had to share their village with growing numbers of artists drawn by the clear light and beautiful scenery of the region.

Catholic priests have effectively abandoned many of the churches around Lake Atitlán. The buildings have been taken over instead by the local Indians who worship surprising figures such as Maximón: usually depicted in a tall hat and yellow shoes and smoking a cigar.

groups such as the Tzutzuhil, Mam, Kekchi, Pokomchi, Pocomam, Itza, Lacandon and Chorti. All these spoke languages related to the Mayan tongue and were descended from the Maya or closely connected to them.

The Maya themselves had long since abandoned the great cities whose remains can be seen in the jungles of the north at places such as Uaxactún, Tikal, Piedras Negras and Quirigua. For 2000 years, they had developed a unique civilisation in the Petén. As well as their two calendars, they had created an advanced system of mathematics, and were skilled astronomers. They also developed a written language, surviving in hieroglyphic characters drawn on the bark of trees, which no one has yet managed to decipher fully. The rise and fall of the Mayan civilisation of the Petén remains one of the great mysteries of archaeology. All that is known for sure is that it went into rapid decline from the 10th century AD onwards, though the Maya's kinsmen in the Mexican Yucatán to the north survived a few centuries longer.

Among the Guatemalan descendants of the Maya, the Quiché recorded some of their stories and legends in the *Popol Vuh*. According to this, the human race was created by the 'forefather' gods Tepeu and Gucumatz. First of all, they formed the earth and clothed it with plants and animals. Then they set about fashioning mankind. This took four attempts. First, they used mud, but the resulting creatures disintegrated. Next, they tried wood, but these creatures had no minds and had to be scrapped on account of their stupidity. On their third attempt, they used flesh, but these creatures were prone to wickedness and also had to be destroyed – in a great flood, as in the Bible. For their fourth and successful experiment, the gods used maize dough. These men

This Biblical-looking scene could come from a Mediterranean village – but the site is the shore of Lake Atitlán. Conveniences such as running water are rare in these remote mountain valleys.

were the ancestors of the Quiché and proved a good deal more satisfactory, paying due honour and worship to their creators.

According to legend, the Quiché's greatest leader was E-Gag-Quicab, who succeeded in uniting the Indian tribes. In reality, the tribes were all too prone to feuding and this led to disaster. When the Spanish *conquistador* Pedro de Alvarado arrived in 1523 on the orders of Mexico's conqueror Hernán Cortés, they were unable to present a united front. They also failed to heed a message sent by the Aztec emperor Moctezuma warning them of Alvarado's hostile intentions.

Alvarado was accompanied by 300 Spaniards and a large number of Mexican Indian allies. Two Quiché kings, Oxib-Queh and Beleheb-Tzy, tried to trick the *conquistador* into 'peacefully' visiting their stronghold

Wood carriers with ingenious backpacks rest for a few moments on church steps. Indian pilgrims often burn candles and incense on the steps outside churches as offerings to the various saints and divinities, Christian and otherwise.

Gumarcaj, but Alvarado was taking no chances. He took Gumarcaj by surprise and had the two kings burned at the stake, before going on to take the towns of Zapotitlan and Telaju. The Indian prince Azumanche died in the course of a battle beside the river Xequigel, and, according to Quiché legend, Alvarado himself killed the Indian leader Tecún Umán in hand-to-hand combat on the plains of Quezaltenango.

Cruelty and more cruelty

The Spanish conquest continued with the rout of the Cakchiquel. Alvarado swiftly dispatched the Cakchiquel kings Beleheb-Cat and Cahi-Inoux, helped in his task by an epidemic of smallpox (hitherto unknown in the Americas) which preceded his advance and further weakened the Indian resistance. The Spaniards herded the survivors together in encampments known as *reducciones* for forced conversion to Christianity. Mayan places of worship were replaced with Catholic churches. Successive Indian rebellions over the next few decades were suppressed with similar brutality.

A year after his arrival, Alvarado founded a new capital, Santiago de los Caballeros, on the site of modern Antigua. He equipped this in grandiose style, and within ten years had built beautiful churches and convents with exquisite gardens. His own palace was decorated with purple and gold, and his wife, the arrogant and acquisitive Doña Beatriz de la Cueva, installed herself there with her daughter Leonora and 20 Spanish ladies-in-waiting. The austere Philip II dispatched sculptors and painters from Spain to beautify the new city, along with an effigy of the Virgin of Socorro sent from Mexico.

The Virgin of Socorro was one of the most sumptuous of all the Virgins of the Hispanic world, with a veil made of gold and so encrusted with jewels that they were said almost to blind onlookers. She also had a part to play in a romantic love intrigue. The story goes that Alvarado's daughter Leonora was in love with Pedro de Portocarro, an army captain serving under her father. Alvarado, however, was determined that she should

Two-storey estate homes like this are a common sight in the hot Alta Verapaz region of eastern Guatemala. The covered verandah gives protection from the sun,

while letting in a breeze during siesta time. Sleepers are soothed by the gentle rocking of their hammocks and the varied song of the cunzontl *bird.*

marry his brother-in-law Don Francisco de la Cueva. Leonora invoked the aid of the Virgin of Socorro, but seems not to have got it.

In 1541, Cortés called Alvarado back to Mexico to help him to quell an Indian rebellion. Alvarado was killed in battle with the Indians, and his widow Doña Beatriz declared herself the ruler of Guatemala. That same night, however, a violent storm and earthquake completely destroyed Santiago de los Caballeros. Don Francisco de la Cueva, the scorned suitor and sole survivor of the catastrophe, then went to search out the beautiful Leonora in her remote convent. She, too, had survived. The *cucuchito* bird had barked out its warning of the earthquake, but the Spaniards had not heard it. Alvarado's city was destroyed, though Doña Leonora and Don Francisco did marry as he had wished.

At its height in the centuries that followed, Guatemala was the heart of a vast colonial realm ruled over by a Spanish Captain-General. It included the state of Chiapas (now in Mexico), El Salvador, Honduras, Nicaragua and Costa Rica. There was a plentiful supply of Indian labour and thus little need for imported black slaves from Africa. Throughout the 17th and 18th centuries, the Indians worked the land for Spanish

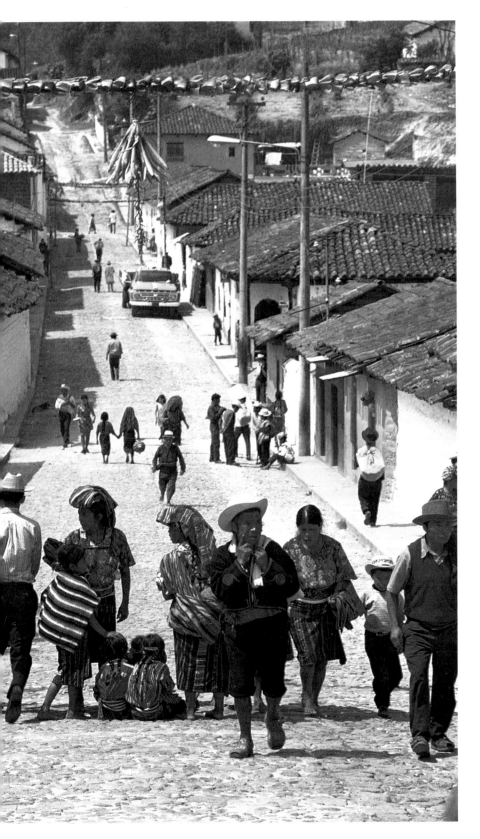

Quiché Indians bustle about their daily business in Chichicastenango. This was also where the Popol Vuh, *the so-called Quiché Bible containing an account of the creation of the world, was found in the 17th century.*

At Todos Santos, in the remote Cuchumatanes Cordillera near the frontier with Mexico, the local men wear long red and white striped trousers. People's costumes change from region to region in Guatemala. At Santiago de Sacatapéquez, near Guatemala City, the trousers are shorter with black stripes. Elsewhere in the mountain villages, men wear short woollen aprons with maroon and white squares.

Markets are festivals of colour and yet places of peace. Sellers like these do not yell out to potential customers, or thrust their wares at them. Their philosophy is simple: if people want onions, they will buy them, and if they do not want them, it is pointless to try to persuade them otherwise.

colonists and produced cocoa, cochineal and indigo (both used for dyeing cloth), tobacco, maize, beans, wheat and sugar cane.

Guatemala grew rich through Indian labour. Resentment among the colonists against Spanish bureaucracy grew, however, and when Napoleon invaded Spain in 1808 the Guatemalans started demanding independence. After the collapse of a Federal Republic of Central America established in 1821, El Salvador, Nicaragua, Honduras and Costa Rica each broke away from greater Guatemala. By 1839 Guatemala was on its own.

Yet more bloodshed

Guatemala's troubles did not end with independence. Slavery was abolished; the Indians were released from forced labour, and elections held, but instability continued. The fledgling democracy broke down and the call for a 'Strong Man' or *Caudillo* brought José Rafael Carrera to power in 1839 as Central America's first dictator. Carrera, a charismatic former drummer boy, abolished elections and entered Guatemala City on horseback at the head of a ragged army, whose rallying cry was 'Long live religion, and death to foreigners'.

Through the rest of the 19th century and into the 20th, Guatemala was ruled by a series of dictators. They included Justo Rufino Barrios, known as 'the Reformer', who confiscated Church property, attempted to re-

Most Quiché women have three huipil *shirts: one for childhood, one for marriage and one for burial. This woman sells* tamales *made of sugared maize, tortillas and tacos (fritters made of chicken or vegetable marrow).*

If pots like these get broken, the pieces will not be thrown away. Instead, they will be offered to the gods on the first day of the Mayan year at ceremonies held in the mountains of Chuitmesabal.

Oranges, tangerines and coconuts mingle with carved masks in this brilliant market scene. The masks include fair-bearded faces of Spanish *conquistadores,* suitable for the Quiché 'dance of the conquest'.

distribute wealth and was killed in 1885 while fighting to restore the Central American Republic. Manuel Estrada Cabrera's less liberal rule lasted 20 years until he was overthrown and declared insane in 1920. Between 1931 and 1944, General Jorge Ubico supported Hitler and awarded the monopoly of the nation's banana industry to the American United Fruit Company.

In 1952, a left-wing government under Jacobo Arbenz Guzmán tried to bring about agricultural reforms. It was toppled in a military coup backed by the banana barons and the CIA. After that, one military regime followed another, all demonstrating a common degree of cruelty towards the Indians, whom they had no scruples in using as scapegoats in revenge for guerrilla opposition to their rule. Soldiers would arrive in Indian villages, order men, women and children into the square and open fire. An estimated 100,000 people have been killed in this way since 1954.

The essential ingredient for a family meal: tortillas, which are usually accompanied by thick spicy stews or perhaps frijoles *(boiled black beans) and* chicharrones *(pork skin fried in oil), all seasoned with chilli.*

Indians and ladinos

During the colonial period, the Spanish tried to turn the Indians into Spanish-dominated peasants. The Indians, however, soon realised that life was not so attractive under the close eye of the white man, and took to the mountains instead.

There, they have gone on rearing their turkeys and black pigs, sowing maize and embroidering beautiful *huipil* shirts for the festivities of birth, marriage and death. They live in mud-walled *ranchos* with roofs made of straw and palm leaves, and sleep in hammocks or on *petates*, mats made of vegetable fibre. A single room houses the entire family, while the kitchen is a small room to one side, with a fire built on stones on the ground. Generally speaking, the higher the village, the poorer the houses. In the most mountainous regions, walls may be made of a mixture that includes cardboard

Maize is crushed in the traditional way using a pestle and mortar, and then flattened and shaped into a dough as here. Tortillas are a staple food, like bread in other parts of the world.

and branches, whereas in the valleys the walls are made of adobe blocks – bricks made from sun-dried clay.

Many Indians have to come down from their *ranchos* to work on the *fincas* (estates) of the whites, in order to harvest coffee, cotton and sugar cane, and for this reason they only live in the mountains for part of the year. In the bigger *fincas*, the white landowners build accommodation blocks for Indian *braceros* (workers) and their families. At best, this means a cement floor and a tin roof; at worst, an old wooden hut with a roof made of palm leaves.

Another group in the Guatemalan population is the *ladinos*, who are often largely Indian by blood but have become more Westernised than their fellows, speaking Spanish rather than one of the 30 or more Indian tongues and dialects. Falling a little uncomfortably between the minority of wealthy whites and the more traditional Indians, the *ladinos* have tended to be shunned by both: according to one saying, 'The *ladino* is someone who speaks badly, and whom you cannot trust'. They occupy the middle layers of Guatemalan society, though the poorest of them may work alongside Indians on the *fincas* of wealthy white landowners.

Indian families rarely visit the towns and cities, and when they do it is usually for the markets. In these, the women sit silent and apparently indifferent in front of their wares, which may include such exotic items as turtle eggs, crocodiles, skinned iguanas (delicious when served with tomatoes and red peppers) or chunks of wild boar. A smell of incense made from copal resin, vanilla, pepper and ginger floats in the air of the most colourful markets, such as the one at Chichicastenango. All around are piles of papayas, mangoes, guavas and bananas, along with beautiful cactus flowers, white orchids and, in the markets of the north of the country,

The Guatemalan method of weaving involves attaching the yarn to a tree and using the weaver's body weight to keep it taut. The very long yarn enables the weaving of the long narrow skirts favoured by Quiché women.

monjas blancas (white nuns), spectacular orchids that grow only in the jungles of the Petén.

Hilachas, a dish of boiled meat served with tortillas and a sauce (*recado*) that sears the tongue, bubbles in huge cooking pots in a corner of the market, and there are delicious cucumbers shaped like flowers. But the visitor should be careful. The food has been washed in marsh water, and can have disastrous effects on European digestive systems. *Tamales* made with sweetened maize or maize peppered with green chilli are safer for foreigners, as are tortillas made with maize flour (one woman grinds the maize with a pestle and mortar, while another flattens the dough). There are also *tacos* (chicken fritters with vegetable marrow) and *atoles*, sweetened maize shaped like Mayan pyramids and topped with cinnamon.

Elsewhere, beautiful Indian textiles are laid out for sale. You may also hear the strains of Indian flutes, pipes and drums, as well as the inevitable *marimba*, a xylophone-like instrument often played by two or more musicians at the same time. In Guatemala, it is impossible to imagine any special occasion without the subtle accompanying rhythm of the *marimba* and the melancholy sound of the Indian flute. The *marimba* originated, in fact, in Africa but found its way gradually through the whole of Central America after African slaves first introduced it to the continent. The flute is Indian through and through, and its soft, lilting whistle permeates all pre-Columbian dances: the 'dance of the stag', the 'dance of the snake' and others. The Quiché 'dance of the conquest' is accompanied by a special kind of flute called the *chirimía*.

A beautiful and terrible nature

From the great tropical plains of the north and the impenetrable jungle of the Petén, to the volcanic chain of the Pacific coast, the Guatemalan landscape is wild, dramatic, varied and beautiful. Guatemalan Indians enjoy no comfortable Western certainties in this unpredictable landscape, where volcanoes erupt and there is the sound of gunfire in the villages. Even the inhabitants of Guatemala City live a different life from their European counterparts. Badly damaged by an earthquake in 1917 and on several occasions since then, the city's low-rise buildings hide under the shadow of the volcanoes El Agua and El Fuego, which it shares with Antigua to the west.

The principal means of transport in Guatemala, as in much of Latin America, is the bus, where visitors may find themselves sitting next to a clutch of squawking chickens and a silent Indian. One such ramshackle vehicle, painted in every conceivable colour by its *ladino* driver, begins the long journey from Guatemala City 1000 feet up into the Sierra Grande to the west. It passes through the Tecpan pass at 2500 feet above sea level, where grass is scarce and the pine trees have a European look. It then skirts the shore of Lake Atitlán, with volcanoes including El Agua, El Fuego and Acatenango towering above it and still pouring their lava onto Antigua from time to time.

Quezaltenango, Guatemala's second city, lying north-west of Lake Atitlán, looks like a typically Spanish town, with wrought-iron grilles over the windows of its houses. But this was also once Xelahu,

Fishing on Lake Atitlán. The lake lies over 5000 feet above sea level and is surrounded by soaring, cloud-capped volcanic mountains. According to some local Indian beliefs, Atitlán is the navel of the world.

the Mayan 'Town of the Ten', governed by ten Quiché chiefs. Nearby is the tomb of Tecún Umán, the Indian leader killed in battle by Alvarado himself in 1523; the *conquistador* was so impressed by Tecún Umán's headdress of *quetzal* feathers that he named the neighbouring city 'Quetzal Citadel', or Quezaltenango. Another nearby spot is the sacred lake at Chicabel, inside the cone of an extinct volcano, where secret rites are carried out in May each year. These are designed to appease a variety of spirits and divinities – and outsiders are definitely not welcome.

The bus and others like it wheeze up and down the peaks and valleys of this extraordinary country. They cross chasms, arid plains and freezing plateaus and descend once more into warm and humid valleys such as that of Cobán in the Verapaz highlands to the east. Here are rich *fincas* with crops of coffee, vanilla, tea and cinnamon. Tropical flowers stud the valley sides, and you meet a few blonde-haired, blue-eyed Indians, the descendants of Germans who settled in the region in the 19th century and intermarried with the locals. They speak the Indian Kekchi tongue and the women attend festivals in *huipils* with big sleeves, long pleated skirts and silver necklaces.

The mysteries of the Petén

The land of the Maya is the cradle of this indigenous culture. The Maya did not live in the mountains of the south, nor in the balmy valleys of the west, but in the northern jungle of the Petén. This enormous territory of 20,000 square miles is now barely populated, but was home in Maya times to an estimated 15 million people.

Many theories have been put forward to try to explain why the Maya left the Petén, including the possibility that they were wiped out by yellow fever. But none of them is entirely satisfactory. What is certain is that the flight of the Maya was a turning point for the region, since no civilisation of comparable sophistication followed them.

Cortés was the first *conquistador* to cross the Petén: in 1524 on his way to subdue neighbouring Honduras. Near the modern town of Flores, set on an island in the jungle-encircled Lake Petén Itzá, his horse fell lame and he entrusted it to a group of friendly local Indians. They took the animal very much to heart but, since they had never seen one before, wondered what they should give this 'stag without horns' to eat. In the end, they gave it maize and alcohol and within a few days the unfortunate beast was dead. Worried that the white man would return, the Indians made a wooden statue of it, so that the gods – Cortés and company – would not be angry.

Cortés never came back, but at several points over

The quetzal *is the symbol of Guatemalan freedom. According to legend, when the Quiché leader Tecún Umán fell in battle against the Spaniards, a* quetzal *fell beside him. It is a bird of rare beauty, with red breast, yellow beak and long emerald-green tail. It cannot survive in captivity.*

The peccary – the wild pig of Central and South America – looks rather like a small wild boar. A gland secretes a powerful-smelling fluid that hunters have to remove immediately if the meat is to be eaten. The smell allows the peccary to recognise others of its own kind, since it has poor eyesight.

Bananas are among Guatemala's most important export crops. For many decades in the 20th century, the monopoly in the trade granted to the American-owned United Fruit Company gave it a potent influence over local politics. Coffee, sugar and cotton are other staple exports.

the next 200 years Spanish missionaries returned to the Petén, and at the top of a ruined temple they found the wooden statue of the horse being worshipped as the god of rain and storms. Eventually, in 1697, the Spanish attacked in force. Their priests wanted the Indians to stop worshipping the horse, but the Indians refused and escaped with it in a boat across Lake Petén Itzá. Unfortunately for them, the boat sank and with it the horse – although, according to a local legend, you can still sometimes see its outline in the waters of the lake.

Life abounds in this humid jungle. Mahogany, balsa and ebony all grow here, as does the *morro* tree with spectacular orchids clinging to its trunk and fruit that can be dried and used as cups. Beside long, winding rivers such as the Río de la Pasión and the Río Salinas are timber settlements – some active still, others abandoned – the active ones home to *chicleros*. Their job is to collect *chicle* resin, a basic ingredient in chewing gum, from sapodilla trees. The *chicleros* know the Petén like the backs of their hands.

The Petén is an animal-spotter's paradise, too. There are jaguar, puma, crocodiles, wild boar and tapir – slightly comical, short-legged beasts that look rather like a mix between a wild boar and a mini-elephant. The Indians hunt tapir with blowpipes that look like flutes.

Sleeping beauties in the forest

Flores is the gateway to the great Mayan sites. For many centuries, these lay undiscovered – a mystery, it seems, even to the local Indians – and many undoubtedly remain shrouded by jungle creepers as yet untouched by archaeologists or outside visitors. The first to be uncovered was at Tikal, found by accident in 1695 when a Spanish friar Andrés de Avendaño y Loyola got lost in the jungle. An army officer Colonel Modesto Mendes found others in 1848, and in 1960 a Frenchman Pierre Ivanoff made further discoveries.

In 1916, the American archaeologist Sylvanus Griswold Morley found an inscribed stone at Uaxactún, north of Tikal, bearing a date that he reckoned corresponded to AD 320. Morley advanced the theory that Mayan culture was born here in the Petén, and that the site including Tikal and Uaxactún spread over 10 square miles and included 3000 buildings. So far, only a handful of these have been found, including two temples of breathtaking beauty standing face to face. Their wooden sculptures have not survived, but the remaining stone ones are testimony to the skills of Mayan sculptors. The biggest of the temples to have been uncovered is the Temple of the Great Jaguar. It is a steep climb to the top of its pyramid, but once you get there your effort is rewarded with superb views over the jungle.

The Guatemalan writer, Miguel Angel Asturias (winner of the Nobel Prize for literature in 1967), tried to find words to convey the sensations he felt standing on top of the pyramid, seeking to penetrate at least some of the secrets of this mysterious civilisation: 'You must walk hard, listen hard, watch hard. You must eat roast quail, chew white copal [resin] and absorb, like wine taken to the point of drunkenness, the sound of the tiny birds which fly over the greenness. You will not truly become a party to this secret until then, the moment when you are alone with the sun on your head!'

The marimba *is a kind of xylophone descended from instruments introduced to Central America by African slaves. It has a more melancholy sound and a greater range than its classical counterpart. It is made of dried fruits, with a keyboard of hormigo wood.*

The West Indies

African, Carib and Arawak Indian, Spanish, British,
French, Dutch and Asian – the influences on the scattered
isles of the West Indies have been astonishingly diverse.
Equally diverse and spectacular are the landscapes.
From volcanic mountains to wide plains covered
with sugar cane, from sparkling palm-fringed beaches
to dense inland jungles, the islands encompass a glorious
range of scenery. History and politics have
often been difficult, but the islanders for the most part
retain an infectiously cheerful approach to life.

Each fishing boat drawn up at
Bellefontaine on Martinique
has its own name, drawn from
a variety of sources: from
ancient Greece (the Athenian
naval commander
Themistocles) to religion –
a misspelt slogan, meaning
'God protects'.

Open expressions are
matched by frank speaking.
The French patois of the
islands is littered with
pungent turns of phrase,
such as: an manman la
baleine (literally, 'a whale
lady', in other words 'a fat
lady'); an pété pié ('a cut
foot' – the last rum punch of
the evening, which often leads
to injuries).

Previous page:
An azure sea, stately palms
and the strangely shredded
leaves of banana trees: all are
essential ingredients of the
Caribbean 'idyll'.

Paradise Islands of the French West Indies

The landscape is like a broken puzzle that no one can put together again. Volcanoes – most, though not all, of them extinct – present jagged profiles against the skyline, their sides cracked with active fissures. Pools of boiling water and lava mud smoulder gently, giving off the rotten-egg smell of sulphur fumes. Pineapple plantations cover steep-sided, isolated hills or *mornes*, of similarly volcanic origin. They rise from plains that are clothed with swaying green expanses of sugar cane, neatly regimented rows of banana trees and areas of tropical forest, rooted in rich, humus-filled soil. Along stretches of the coast, the weirdly twisting roots of mangrove swamps create a near-impenetrable barrier between land and sea.

Elsewhere, wide sandy beaches are backed by dense stands of sea grape trees, whose leathery leaves (large enough and strong enough to serve as picnic plates) hide the burrows of land crabs. Overhead, the leaves of coconut palms flicker in the tug of the trade winds, filtering the sun's hot rays through a shimmering gauze of green; while higher still, huge frigate birds wheel through the azure skies, waiting for the return of the fishing boats. Cormorants are more impatient and dive in to plunge their black beaks into drowsy fish, idling in the still warm waters of coral reefs. There are turtles – though these have been over-hunted and are less common than they used to be – and, sheltering among the peeling thorn bushes, there are timid iguanas, which scamper off at speed, amidst a noisy crackling of dead leaves, at the first sound of human footsteps.

It all seems too beautiful to be true … and yet it isn't. Paradise exists, with its own problems, in the French Caribbean islands of Martinique and Guadeloupe and their smaller dependencies. They form two *Départements d'Outremer* (overseas departments) and are fully fledged members of the French republic, sending their elected members to the National Assembly in Paris.

Beyond the reach of time

The Iles des Saintes cluster 6 miles off Guadeloupe's southern tip, where the larger island's 4813-foot Soufrière mountain dominates the horizon with its cloud-enshrouded volcanic mass – the highest in the eastern Caribbean. The tiny archipelago consists of eight islands in all, but only two, Terre-de-Haut and Terre-de-Bas, are inhabited – and of them, Terre-de-Haut has the larger population.

Arriving from Pointe-à-Pitre on Guadeloupe, the pocket-sized plane stoops low over the high centre of Terre-de-Haut (the name means 'high ground', as opposed to Terre-de-Bas, 'low ground'), takes a wide swing and then plunges into a sort of trench carved into the side of the island. You descend, and are immediately greeted by a little cemetery bordering the runway on one side, shaded by an alley of angel-hair *filao* trees, where lizards dart among tombs ornamented with large pink shells.

The islands are definitely unusual. If every other Saintois seems to walk barefooted, it is not out of affectation, nor because he is poor, but simply because it is easier that way. The islanders' ancestors arrived here in the 17th century from Brittany, Normandy and the region around Poitiers in central France, and they have remained a tightly knit, still mostly white, community. Unlike their counterparts among most of the white settlers elsewhere in the Caribbean, they did not come to make quick fortunes – and in that, too, things have scarcely changed.

Indeed, there is little on Les Saintes to make the islanders rich. Rain is rare, and the cattle so scrawny that the sunbathing iguanas seem more likely to give milk. There has never been any sugar cane, coffee, cocoa or pineapples – and hence there has never been any need for slaves to work the barren soil. The first settlers became fishermen, and fishermen their descendants have remained.

Their chief settlement consists of a blue, yellow and red strip of tiny houses, overhung with coconut palms, that forms a rim around a single bay. Every day, their fishing boats appear on the horizon and converge on the bay, creating small white moustaches of spume in their eagerness to be home after ten hours at sea. Fishermen steer them onto the beach right in front of their homes

The marlin is the king of tropical sporting fish. It can be as much as 7 feet long and weigh well over 400 pounds. Hunting it has become a rich man's sport, involving powerful motor boats and specialised equipment. Once the beast has been hooked, the struggle to bring it in can last for hours, with the marlin making spectacular leaps out of the water. This, at least, is one battle where man does not necessarily emerge victorious.

Women sort and sell their husbands' catch. Generally, they keep the smaller fish for their own use, cooking them in delicious spicy stews or ragouts, while they sell the lobsters and crayfish to the tourist hotels.

and then offload blue nets and catches of red fish. A few of the older ones still wear the round straw *salako* hats that used also to be worn by Breton fishermen.

Others, too old perhaps to go out to sea, sit around in groups on benches or their doorsteps, taking advantage of the welcome shade. A few while away the time by bartering with visiting traders from Dominica; Dominica was once French and many of its people still speak a French patois, though France sold it to Britain in 1805 and it is now a member of the Commonwealth. The traders offer supplies from their more fertile island to the south: large green cooking bananas and plantains, sweet potatoes, yams and coconuts.

The Saintois have struck a happy balance between idleness and activity. They are not wealthy and have few creature comforts, but they do not lack for much, either. Above all, they enjoy the benefits of a beautiful setting and of a strong clan feeling, which ensures that few are allowed to go in need. That is why the rare Saintois who bother to emigrate in search of a 'better life' invariably come home again.

'There's no question of worrying our heads with huge influxes of tourists,' states one local mayor emphatically. 'Fishing is the livelihood for 90 per cent of the island; that leaves 10 per cent for hotels and picture postcards, which is enough not to upset the economy if people stop coming one day. There's no question, either, of developers taking over our beaches. We've made it just about impossible for them to build, and that's fine by us.'

Nature gave Les Saintes their glorious environment, and the locals are determined to preserve it. Equally, they are not going to let outsiders exploit any of their home's more man-made charms: such as the tiny quayside square where passengers disembark from the boat that plies daily between Terre-de-Haut and Guadeloupe. The square forms another wonderful introduction to the island. Ornamenting it are just three lamp-posts, a small square lighthouse and a cast-iron statue of Marianne (the symbolic maiden, also seen on French currency, who represents the republic). She gazes out beyond the pier, across the narrow strait, towards the forest-clothed slopes of Guadeloupe.

What the scene lacks in grandeur, it more than makes up for in pure tropical delight. The air is thick with the warm scent of conifers and the more acid tang of limes. Hummingbirds – jet black but with emerald-green metallic sheens – skim from flower to flower among the luxuriant creepers that clamber over fences and walls.

Out to sea, a large cutter with red sails, coming from Pointe-à-Pitre on Guadeloupe, curves round the smaller, uninhabited island of Cabrit and makes for the breakwater, disappearing momentarily behind a clump of coconut palms.

Dominating a nearby height is Fort Napoléon, from where there are superb views of the surrounding islands. Although the fort never witnessed a shot fired in anger, there are displays giving a French account of the battle of the Saints, fought off the islands' shores in 1782. This was one of the key naval engagements of the War of American Independence, in which the British Admiral George Rodney defeated a French fleet under the Comte de Grasse. The French, as allies of the American rebels, were intent on capturing Britain's most important West Indian colony, Jamaica, thereby dealing a blow to the British war effort on the American mainland. Their defeat put paid to that scheme.

'Yes,' says one Saintois, 'we're a friendly bunch. But you have to be careful, too. As we say, if you shout at a dog that barks, you'll end up quarrelling with his master. Here, if you don't share my opinion, you're my enemy … You should see what it's like during election times. What with all the *ti'punch* going round, things get pretty lively, if you see what I mean.'

Ti'punch (rum punch) promotes fun as well as bouts of bickering, however. It is hard to feel lonely anywhere in the West Indies, thanks to the endless rounds of parties that are such a vital part of everyday life. And where would they be without rum? The French islands alone produce 3.6 million gallons of it a year, of which 70 per cent goes for export. The rest, more than a million gallons, stays behind, mostly consumed by

Opposite: Like fishermen the world over, this man has to spend long hours keeping his nets in good order. His hat, however, is strictly Martiniquan. It is a bakoua; *its high crown and wide brim provide agreeably natural air conditioning.*

The fish caught in coastal waters are generally small. Fishermen have to venture into the deeper waters of the Dominica Passage, between the Iles des Saintes and Dominica to catch larger ones. This is the domain of the Saintois who use powerful outboard motors to take them out to sea.

Everyone lends a hand to draw in a large senne *net, usually dragged through the sea by two dugout fishing boats, or* gommiers. *These men are at work on the beach at Fond Lahaye, the spot where the first French colonists landed on Martinique in 1635.*

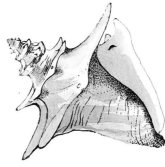

The delicate pink of conch shells makes them much-prized decorative objects. They are also valued for their firm flesh (known as lambis *in the French West Indies).* Lambis *is one of the ingredients in* blaff, *a stew which also includes red snapper or sea urchin, onions, lime juice and white wine.*

locals, with a generous helping hand from visitors. Even on Les Saintes, with their tiny population of fewer than 3000 people, rum shops are commonplace.

Freebooters and conquistadores

In 1492 Christopher Columbus made his first landfall in the New World when he stepped ashore on San Salvador (or Watling Island) in the Bahamas. At the time of his arrival, Indian groups, now loosely referred to as the Arawaks, lived in the larger islands of the western Caribbean. The smaller islands of the east were populated by the more warlike Caribs, who had already exterminated most of their previous Arawak inhabitants. The Caribs, after whom the sea was named, also had a fearsome reputation for eating prisoners captured in battle; the word 'cannibal' is derived from their Spanish name *Caribal*.

Neither Caribs nor Arawaks, however, were a match for the Spanish settlers and *conquistadores* who followed Columbus, and within ten years of his landfall an estimated population of 1.2 million native Indians had shrunk to little more than 12,000.

Not that the Spanish stayed long in most of the islands. Hypnotised by discoveries of gold and silver in Mexico and Peru, they turned their attention more to the mainland, allowing other Europeans – notably the British and French – to establish themselves in the West Indies, first as freebooting pirates, and later as colonists. Barren as they were of precious minerals, the islands nevertheless opened up many rich possibilities that the

conquistadores had not bothered to exploit. Spices, tobacco, indigo, coffee, cocoa and, later, sugar cane all would prove to be as valuable in their way as the gold and silver of the mainland.

By the mid-17th century, Spain retained islands such as Cuba and Hispaniola (now divided between Haiti and the Dominican Republic) and exercised fairly perfunctory control over many others. As the century went on the real powers among the islands came increasingly to be the British, the French and, to a lesser extent, the Dutch. For the British and the French the process of colonisation began almost simultaneously, and on the same small island: St Kitts, part of the group to the

Two women, laden with shopping bags, make their way home across Fort-de-France's central park, La Savane. In the background rises a white marble statue of Joséphine de Beauharnais, later Napoleon's Empress Joséphine.

A traditional wooden case on the island of Marie-Galante reveals all the delicate craftsmanship that once went into such homes: fine fretwork under the eaves, shutters on the doors to let the air in but keep the sun out, and a perfect sense of colour. On this house, as on many others, a corrugated iron roof has replaced the old wooden shingles.

north of Guadeloupe. Here, in January 1624, the Englishman Thomas Warner established his country's first official colony in the West Indies. A year later, the French freebooter Pierre Belain d'Esnambuc (a Norman by birth), weary of 20 years of little profit from preying on the Spanish treasure fleets, arrived on board his four-cannoned brigantine, the *Espérance*. He and Warner reached a remarkably amicable agreement by which the English were allowed the central parts of the island and the French the two tips. They agreed to join forces in the event of an attack from surviving Carib groups or the Spanish.

The agreement lasted long enough for the two groups to establish themselves and to prove the potential of such colonies – but not much longer. By the 1660s, the British and French were open rivals, each out to grab as much land as possible in the rich Caribbean seas.

Where wine beats beer

Things worked out rather better on St Martin, farther north of St Kitts. Here, it was the French and Dutch who arrived within days of each other in March 1648. The Dutch were, on the whole, more interested in trade than in establishing colonies of settlers on the islands, but

Green bananas, callaloo (a spinach-like vegetable), knobbly, pear-shaped christophines and banana-like plantains are on display in this corner of a Fort-de-France market. Boiled green bananas (more highly scented than when yellow) are excellent with fatty meats, such as pork. Christophines are generally grilled with grated cheese and breadcrumbs to make christophine au gratin.

Daytime traffic jams are normal on Pointe-à-Pitre's main shopping street, rue Frébault. After the shops shut at five o'clock, though, it is practically deserted. Guadeloupans tend to go to bed early and rise early.

Over three centuries later, the legal position remains exactly the same, making Marigot, capital of the French portion, one of the most remarkable administrative centres in the whole of the French republic. Taxes, duties, customs and other impediments to commerce are virtually unknown, and St Martin as a whole has become a kind of bounty land for jetloads of tourists in search of hi-fis, cameras, superb havana cigars and fashionable clothes.

In fact, there is a noticeable difference between the two sections. Philipsburg, capital of the Dutch part (officially, Sint Maarten), consists essentially of one long street, full of tempting shops that are kept alive by custom brought in by one of the busiest airports in the Caribbean. Marigot is more modestly served by the small, twin-engined aircraft of Air Guadeloupe. The trademarks of the great Parisian cosmetics and fashion houses are most in evidence in its shops.

St Martin is full of quirks. Until relatively recently, people on one side of the island had to go through telephone exchanges in Paris and Amsterdam if they wanted to make a call to friends just a mile or so away. For those in difficulties with the law, life is remarkably well organised. At the first sight of a flashing police light, all they have to do is nip across a frontier that exists only on paper. Add to all this a fine tradition of cooking, and it is hardly surprising that St Martin is so popular with tourists, who have no objection to escaping from the rigours of winter climates back at home.

Paris on the Caribbean

A natural amphitheatre of high hills tumbles into the sea around the 17th-century Fort St Louis. Turning its back to the crowd of sightseers gathered on a flight of concrete steps leading down towards the harbour is a

Pointe-à-Pitre's covered market sells every kind of local fruit, vegetable and spice. Also on sale are magic potions and spells, to mend broken hearts and physical ailments. It is a short walk to the Place de la Victoire, overlooking the old harbour.

nevertheless seized (and still retain) a few bases in the Caribbean, such as Sint Eustatius, Saba, Aruba, Curaçao and Bonaire.

The two groups on St Martin decided to share the island. The French positioned themselves at one end of the island, the Dutch at the other. Both groups then set out towards the centre: they would draw the frontier line at the point where they met. They kept to the agreement, and a commemorative pyramid still marks the spot. In fact, the French did rather better out of the deal, ending up with roughly two-thirds of the island, against the Dutch third. As the (French) guide who shows visitors round likes to point out, the story reveals the superior virtues of wine over beer.

statue of Pierre Belain d'Esnambuc – who, after his adventures on St Kitts, went on to establish the first French settlement on Martinique in 1635. Perched on his stone plinth, the 'founder of France's colonial destiny' (in the words of the inscription beneath) faces out into the harbour of what is now Martinique's capital, Fort-de-France. He stands with a bronze finger pointing to the vessels anchored there: in particular, three large white cruise ships, disgorging their tourists in groups of 25 on motor launches. There are few among them who would not agree that the bay of Fort-de-France is one of the most beautiful in the world.

Life has certainly moved on since the time of Belain d'Esnambuc, when Cardinal Richelieu ruled France in the name of King Louis XIII and when the newly formed Company of the Isles of America press-ganged assorted vagabonds from port taverns and sent them out to settle new territories for the glory of their country and the profit of the company's shareholders. Not far away, the walls of Fort St Louis – still a French military base – are a reminder, too, that the settlers had to be constantly on their guard against attacks from the island's Caribs or, later, from the marauding British. During the Seven Years' War (1756–62), for instance, the British seized both Martinique and Guadeloupe, though at the end of the war they returned them to France in exchange for Canada and various smaller West Indian islands – so keen was the French King Louis XV to retain his most important sugar-rich domains.

The fortifications are also a reminder that the wealth of the islands relied on the labour of African slaves, frequently ready to rebel and inflict what vengeance they could on their often brutal owners. Indeed, Martinique was re-occupied by the British between 1793 and 1802, at the specific request of the local plantation-owners, who were terrified of the effects of the French Revolution. They feared that slaves, spurred on by the revolution, would rise up and slaughter them, as they had done on many other islands.

The scene today is more peaceful. Market women and souvenir sellers ply their wares at the foot of Belain d'Esnambuc's statue. Behind the statue, the park of La Savane is a delicious sanctuary of palms, tamarind trees and exotic shrubs. In the neighbouring grid of arrow-straight streets, with names such as rue Victor-Hugo, rue Lamartine and rue de la République (the same street names you will find in Guadeloupe's Pointe-à-Pitre or, for that matter, in Paris), shops offer the full range of modern consumer goods.

Only the tropical luxuriance and beauty of the surroundings reminds you that you are in the Caribbean. It was this which inspired the first volunteer settlers, who arrived before the introduction of slavery and worked the land without wages in return for a smallholding at the end of three years. The beauty has not faded with the centuries, nor have the coconut palms, lush green forests, tree ferns and (since the Spanish introduced them into the Caribbean from the Canary Islands) banana trees. The soil is rich and fruits flourish: guavas, sweetsops, star apples, sapodillas, pineapples, avocados, coconuts, mangoes and pawpaws.

Cry freedom

Europe's great year of revolutions, 1848, left its mark on the French West Indies as well. One of the first acts of the republic briefly established in France was to bring to fruition a lifetime's campaigning by the Alsatian politician Victor Schoelcher. An edict was passed banning the French slave trade – which until then had carried off thousands of slaves from Africa each year – and definitively freeing all slaves in France's overseas dominions; similar legislation during the Revolution of

Some of the older women on St Barthélémy still wear the traditional quichenotte *bonnet, which their ancestors brought from Brittany over 300 years ago. It is a practical piece of headware providing shade from the sun. The name is believed to be a corruption of the English 'kiss me not' – which indicates another reason for its shape.*

1789 had been only patchily applied. 'The Republic does not know how to make distinctions in the human family,' announced Schoelcher – still revered as a hero in the French islands. 'It excludes no one from its immortal motto: Liberty, Equality, Fraternity.'

Created overseas departments after the Second World War in 1946, Martinique and Guadeloupe and their people have sought to apply the motto as best they can – and the islands' development in the years since the war has been impressive. Roads that were once the domain of ox-carts and horse-drawn buggies are now tarmac in two or even four lanes, while islanders enjoy the full benefits of the French welfare state, from free healthcare to family allowances.

For all that, the islands are dogged by problems. In the first place, slavery still evokes bitterness. These painful memories were most eloquently expressed in the mid-20th century by the leaders of the *négritude* movement, such as the black Martiniquan writers Aimé Césaire (a former mayor of Fort-de-France) and Frantz Fanon. Then there are economic problems. Imports greatly exceed exports, so that the French islands have little hope of providing anything like full employment – leading to a constant drain of young people emigrating to mainland France. To make matters worse, the high costs of the welfare system (although heavily subsidised by Paris) get transmitted to their staple export crops, such as bananas, pineapples and cane, which are thus less able to compete in world markets.

Adieu foulard, adieu madras,
Adieu grain d'or, adieu collier-chou.
Doudou à moi i ka pati
Hélas, hélas, cé pou toujou! ...

Farewell silk scarf, farewell madras,
Farewell gold bead, farewell necklace.
Woman of mine, I have to leave
Alas, alas, it's for ever! ...

This patois rhyme evokes the lost delights of colourful madras headdresses and the gold-bead necklaces traditionally worn by French West Indian women (*doudous*). It was composed by the Marquis de Bouillé, an 18th-century governor of Guadeloupe and cousin of the aristocratic revolutionary, the Marquis de la Fayette. The nostalgic sentiments would be echoed by many of today's surviving members of the old 'planter' class, as more and more of their beautiful homes, with wide shady verandahs, get swallowed up in an all-engulfing wave of concrete and air-conditioning.

Few such homes are left today in and around Fort-de-France or in Guadeloupe's chief towns, Pointe-à-Pitre and Basse-Terre. The rare survivors are mostly in the country areas where the old ways – both good and bad – survive in many places. These are often grand affairs, using a mixture of stone and wood, built at the heart of estates by *hommes libres* (freemen), as the planters used to refer to themselves. Frequently, they have just one storey, surrounded on all sides by a wide verandah, to keep out the sun's glare, with french windows opening onto spacious rooms inside, thus ensuring the free circulation of air. Traditionally, they

This old wooden mansion – once the town house of a wealthy planter or merchant – is a fine example of creole architecture. Though costly to maintain, a few such homes survive in the Didier district of Fort-de-France, overlooking the city centre.

are painted a sparkling white, which gives them their cool, aristocratic beauty. They are an endangered species, however, even in the countryside, since wood is now a good deal more expensive than cement.

The traditional *cases* (smaller homes) of the poorer people have survived much better, probably because of their sheer convenience: they can easily be added to, or reduced in size, as circumstances demand. Essentially, they consist of large, single-storey wooden boxes, with a door and two windows at the front. They are usually roofed with corrugated iron, instead of the old wooden

The broad leaves of a breadfruit tree provide generous shade for four young boys. They illustrate that the mingling of the races is well-advanced in the West Indies.

Nowadays, in the French West Indies, cattle such as these are raised on a small scale for beef and household milk. Much of the beef eaten on the islands, however, is imported.

Cutting cane takes two strokes of the machete – to cut the stalk near the base, then to remove the grass-like foliage on top. The islands' relatively hilly terrain makes mechanical cutting difficult. Seasonal cane-cutters are a powerful force and are represented by well-organised unions.

A machine crushes the cane to extract the juice which is allowed to ferment for a few days in large vats, before distillation begins. Competition from the more highly mechanised sugar industries of countries such as Australia has forced many French West Indian factories to concentrate on rum production.

shingles that used to protect them from the fury of tropical storms and hurricanes. They are painted in brilliant shades of yellow, red, blue and green and, if there is enough room, often have a small verandah at the front. The kitchen is usually a smaller shack set apart from the home, to keep away the heat and smells.

Faire sa case – to build one's home – is still a great event in many of the more old-fashioned country areas. It marks the moment when a young man founds his own family. Often, the whole neighbourhood turns out to help him in his task.

The quest for identity

Recent decades have witnessed a huge migration from the rural areas of the islands, with inevitable consequences for city landscapes. When a population such as that of Fort-de-France – 100,000 people, or just under a third of Martinique's total population – doubles in less than 20 years, what housing exists suffers immense strain. Shantytowns spread along the shoreline by the day, and the coastal strip, 50 paces wide, that used to be reserved for maritime defences has long since disappeared – despite sporadic attempts by the authorities to dislodge the shanty-dwellers.

Even so, the island towns and cities retain some grace. Nothing can deprive Fort-de-France, for example, of the beauty of its bay, or the spacious grandeur of La Savane, where Belain d'Esnambuc shares the place of honour with a marble statue of Napoleon's Martiniquan-born empress, Joséphine. The modern concrete blocks that have almost taken over Pointe-à-Pitre have spared its wonderful Place de la Victoire, while La Darse, the old harbour in front of it, still bobs with inter-island schooners and pleasure yachts, set against a spectacular backdrop of volcanic mountains.

Martinique and Guadeloupe have clambered aboard the train of progress … and have undoubtedly benefited as a result. The contrast with the neighbouring islands of the former British West Indies – each of them going

The raton laveur *(racoon) is the emblem of Guadeloupe's large Natural Park, which occupies much of the area around La Soufrière on the island's western half. It is heavily protected, and still very rare – though it is possible to see small families of racoons on some of the park's forest trails.*

Anthurium lilies have become valuable exports for the islands, especially Martinique. They need humidity and flourish on rich volcanic soil in the shade of larger trees. Crateloads of them are flown daily to mainland France, for sale in florists' shops.

it alone with, perhaps, just a few thousand inhabitants – is ample testimony to that. The average income on the French islands is six times that of most of their neighbours. But relative economic prosperity does not solve everything. Cut off from their African roots by the trauma of slavery – and more recently, by a French-oriented system of schooling – the people of the islands have yet to build a sense of true identity. The French authorities compound the problem – with the best of intentions – by pouring in more money.

A number of local black leaders demand autonomy or even full independence, but the price of that would be the loss of French subsidies and all the benefits of family allowances and free healthcare.

The delights of La Désirade

The island of La Désirade – covering just 8 1/2 square miles and with a population of around 1600 people – is one of the least-known delights of the French West Indies. A narrow slice of land, lying about a quarter-of-an-hour by steamer off Guadeloupe's eastern tip, it is not immediately inviting, but on better acquaintance reveals a rugged charm. Its interior consists of a high limestone plateau, where the locals go from time to time to shoot agoutis, burrowing rodents that look strangely like squirrels from the front, and like hares from behind. This plateau shelves away in steep cliffs on all sides, leaving a narrow strip of coastal plain in the south. It is

just wide enough to fit in a few fields, rows of small houses and a jetty, where the grey provision ship from Guadeloupe moors.

A single road runs parallel with the coast, skirting its various inlets, from the island's western tip as far as a lighthouse-cum-meteorological station in the middle of a patch of baking, desert-like terrain in the east. On the way, you pass the ruins of a former leper colony and a leper cemetery, now the more-or-less undisputed domain of a few sunbathing iguanas.

The leper colony was closed down in 1954, after more than 200 years, but the memories of it perhaps explain why La Désirade has never developed as a tourist destination. Another factor may be the manchineel (*mancenillier*) trees that form a dense barrier along parts of the coast; they are tall, handsome trees, whose wood is excellent for furniture-making, but a tiny drop of their latex on the skin can cause a painful inflammation (the Caribs used the latex to tip their poison arrows).

The dryness of the island is a third factor. One of the curious features of the eastern Caribbean is that places of almost Sahara-like aridity lie within a few miles of places with similar soil where more generous rains create lush profusion. The explanation lies in the north-east trade winds, laden with the humidity of the Atlantic. They release their loads only when they reach cooler highlands, such as those around Soufrière on Guadeloupe or around Martinique's 4583-foot Mount Pelée. Les Saintes, La Désirade and the larger neigh-

Pineapples on Martinique, especially in the Morne-Rouge district in the north, near Mont Pelée, are picked by hand when still green, and loaded by conveyor belt onto a waiting truck. It is labour-intensive work, providing an important source of employment and export earnings.

bouring island of Marie-Galante are left to swelter in the rain shadow.

For all that, La Désirade and its people have huge charm. A friendly '*Comment ça va?*' ('How are you?') greets visitors in the street; locals have not grown resentful of tourists. They readily invite you into their homes, where all is usually a picture of orderliness. Nor are these the island's only pleasures. A stiff hour's walk across the island from the main settlement Grande-Anse leads to Pointe du Nord, with spectacular views of the

Ox-carts, known in the French islands as cabrouets, *are still used to carry cut cane to the sugar factories and rum distilleries because they are cheaper than trucks.*

rugged north coast and the huge natural arch of Porte d'Enfer (Gate of Hell). On the south coast, around the hamlet of Souffleur, there are wonderful deserted beaches, while the even tinier settlement of Baie-Mahault, farther east, offers the rare delight of Chez Céce, a bar and restaurant serving delicious seafood and many varieties of rum punch.

These tiny islands of the eastern Caribbean are amazingly diverse. The people of Les Saintes come from almost exactly the same stock in Normandy, Brittany and around Poitiers as the people of St Barthélémy, farther to the north; both have kept themselves to themselves over the centuries, mingling very little with the other races of the neighbouring islands. And yet both have evolved in quite different ways. The Saintois are mostly fishermen, while the Saint-Barts (as they are known) have developed a more commercial sense. Traditionally, they were the region's rum smugglers, though more recently they have taken to selling imported perfumes and liqueurs to millionaire tourists. They do at least have one thing in common with the Saintois: they keep alive many of the old ways. They still speak an ancient Norman dialect (as well, mostly, as English), and some of the older women still wear the traditional starched white *quichenotte* bonnet.

Marie-Galante is different again. Comparatively large at 60 square miles, it has glorious sandy beaches sheltered by offshore coral reefs, and the spectacular Trou à Diable, a huge cavern reached along forest trails. It also has two former plantation homes, Château Murat and Brîlle, that are open to the public. Like La Désirade it is relatively undeveloped as a tourist destination.

Back on La Désirade, tradition continues in the all-enveloping calm. A motor scooter sputters along the coastal road, but only momentarily drowns the gentle plash of waves lapping on long sandy beaches. Inside a village house, a voice on the radio croons a song from between the wars. And the housewife stands on her doorstep, using a coconut broom to brush off intrusive specks of sand.

A crowd of spectators waits eagerly for the results of a gommier *– fishing-boat – race. These races are one of the key features of village festivals. Enthusiasts lay heavy bets, and consume large quantities of* ti'punch *– rum punch.*

The islands may be French, but this competitor in a gommier – fishing-boat – race has an English name: 'Let Me Pass'. The entries come from rival villages, and each boat bears the brilliant colours of its village. The lush green of coastal vegetation and the blue of sea and sky combine to offer an outstanding spectacle.

Madras skirt and top, lace petticoat, necklaces and earrings of gold beads: the traditional finery of the island costume is part of the entertainment at a tourist hotel. These events undoubtedly have some charm, but the real spirit of the French West Indies lies in the music, blared out from local radio stations or played live at village festivals.

Men gather for a cockfight, a bloody pursuit which arouses the same enthusiasm among some French West Indians as horseracing does in Europe. The fights are battled out in small pits – there are around 80 of them on Guadeloupe alone, and almost as many on Martinique – with a round floor of beaten earth.

The ancestors of the French islands' fighting cocks came from Spain. They are specifically bred for their aggression, and rigorously trained. Many poor breeders and trainers deprive themselves of red meat which they feed to their champions.

elaborate earrings and, above all, their checked madras headdresses, which are tied with a cockade at one side or the other to indicate whether the wearer is married or free. They then process through the streets, carrying baskets overflowing with all the wealth of the islands' produce: fish, *lambis* (conch), crayfish and lobsters, kid, crabs, avocados and mangoes. Following in their train is a crowd of men, drawn on by the scent of cinnamon, *colombo* (the distinctive curry of the islands), guava jam and coconut.

The islands have inspired poets, such as the modernist Saint-John Perse (pen-name of the distinguished French diplomat Alexis Saint-Léger Léger, who was born in Guadeloupe in 1887). And they continue to inspire craftsmen, such as Martinique's skilled furniture-makers, who use the local mahogany to create huge four-poster beds and elegant rocking chairs. The islands' power to enchant is still evident in the weekly fashion parade of Sunday Mass, and equally in the magic potions and remedies – love balms, holy water for breaking spells and devices to ward off the evil eye – which are sold among the fruit and vegetables of the markets. It is there too in a medley of beliefs, which

mean that many of the islands' good Catholics – even the most educated of them – will resort as readily to the *quimboiseur* (wise man and healer) as to the pharmacist, with the explanation: 'If it doesn't do any good, it doesn't do any harm, either.'

History and slavery may have cut the black islanders off from many of their roots. But their ancient, African traditions of story-telling survive. The islanders retain a rich repertoire of tales, directly related to the tales of West African ancestors. These stories are peopled with figures such as the ingenious Brer Rabbit (as he is known on the former British islands), who is always plagued with troubles, but always manages to turn events to his own advantage. The people also retain a more sinister belief in zombies, the living dead, who are supremely useful in bringing fractious children to order.

Large sums of money change hands at cockfights, where betting and ti'punch *are key elements in the fun. Bets are laid when the cocks are presented to one another in the pit or ring, but before they are let loose to fight.*

Culinary splendours

Not surprisingly, the French West Indies are famous for the talents of their cooks, especially those of Guadeloupe. These are organised under the banner of their own association, the Cuistot Mutuel, and have their own annual festival in mid-August, the Fête des Cuisinières. This is an orgy of parades, music, dancing – and, of course, good food. The women dress up in their traditional finery – long embroidered skirts, blouses decorated with flowers, gold-bead necklaces,

An authentic culture

The culture of the West Indies is rooted in the celebrations of everyday life, and – as in most parts of the world – has little to do with the exotic extravaganzas put on for the benefit of tourists in their hotels. The French islands, for example, are famous for the grace of the *biguine*, their best-known dance. This has a variety of influences – African, European and Latin American. But the true *biguine*, in all its raw sensuality, has no more place in the dinner-time entertainments of the hotels, than would the cock or mongoose-versus-snake fights that entertain crowds of gamblers throughout the islands. For the real street flavour of the *biguine*, you have to go to one of the local dance contests where, to the blare of violins, electric guitars and synthesizers, couples from neighbouring towns and villages compete fiercely for the honour – and profit – of cash prizes.

The islanders do, indeed, have an ample sense of celebration, although the locals conform only very superficially to the carefree stereotypes often used to describe them. Their pre-Lenten carnivals, for instance, often last weeks rather than days, and reach a dramatic climax on Ash Wednesday when – in an interesting jumble of Christian and African traditions – crowds dressed in black and white process through the streets for the funeral of the carnival king Vaval. They also have a number of other dances, as well as the *biguine*, many of them rooted very directly in their African past: such as the *bel-air, calinda, haut-taille* and *laghia*. For the islanders, these dances and celebrations are a release – temporary, at least – from the various worries that beset them: unemployment, hardship, racial tensions and the sense of being dependents, rather than masters of their own destiny.

For all their tropical abundance, life on the islands has never been wholly easy. Nature, as well as man, has seen to that. One of the most dramatic exhibitions of nature's power came on Martinique in May 1902, when Mont Pelée erupted at the northern end of the island, engulfing the city of St Pierre, then the capital. Despite ample warning that an eruption was on the way, the French colonial authorities had insisted that nothing was amiss, the governor himself deliberately staying in the city as an example to others. He paid for his folly with his life. St Pierre's 30,000 inhabitants were killed in just three minutes as an explosive, burning cloud of ash and gas rushed down the side of the volcano to the sea. Only one person survived: a stevedore who had been jailed for brawling. He was protected by the thick stone walls of his prison – and was almost immediately afterwards granted a pardon.

The islands have since been spared a repetition of devastation on that scale but lesser disasters are a fairly constant menace. Soufrière on Guadeloupe threatened a dangerous eruption in 1976, causing widespread panic to evacuate the area, though it turned out to be a relatively modest smouldering. Much more real has been the havoc – in lost lives, ruined houses and wrecked banana and sugar crops – left by hurricanes, such as Hurricane David in 1979 and Hurricane Hugo in 1989. Nature has endowed the islands with a scarcely believable tropical beauty, but when it wants to be, it can be as destructive as it is often bountiful.

Waves lap the beach beneath a dwarf coconut palm. In the distance, sails stud a bright blue horizon. The magic of the Caribbean is inspiring – for all the islands' problems, natural or man-made.

Hispaniola – The Divided Island

Columbus had a particular fondness for Hispaniola. He first spotted it on December 5, 1492, and named it *Isla Española*, 'Spanish Island'. Today, Hispaniola is divided between two countries, the Dominican Republic to the east and Haiti to the west. The Spanish-speaking Dominican Republic, despite a turbulent past and a good deal of poverty, now enjoys a greater measure of political stability and makes reasonable profits from tourism, sugar and gold and silver mining. By contrast, Haiti, once a French colony, is synonymous with political repression, acute poverty, Voodoo, dances, drums, spirit possessions, spells and zombies.

Hispaniola covers nearly 30,000 square miles and is the most mountainous island of the Greater Antilles, which also include Cuba, Jamaica and Puerto Rico. In the Dominican Republic, Pico Duarte in the central Cordillera reaches over 10,000 feet above sea level and is the highest point in the West Indies. The highest mountains in Haiti reach nearly 9000 feet. Haitians like to say that their country is shaped like a crocodile about

to bite Cuba's tail; but what really makes Hispaniola different is its variations of climate and landscape.

In the Haitian capital, Port-au-Prince, for example, the atmosphere in the lower part of the town – which includes the port, the commercial and administrative centre and the most densely populated areas – is torrid at the best of times. But the narrow coastal strip soon gives way to mountain flanks with residential suburbs like Pétionville. The road twists and turns through woods and past crumbling mansions, modern villas and peasant huts. At 2000 feet above sea level, the climate is cooler and the capital's centre is left sweltering below.

Beyond Pétionville the road climbs another 4000 feet to Kenscoff. Here is the Chalet des Fleurs, where acres of flowers are grown for shipment by air to the United States. Farmers grow cabbages, carrots, potatoes, strawberries and other fruits and vegetables. The climate is mild and the nights are cool all the year round. At the end of the road is the Furcy television-relay station, at 7000 feet above sea level an impressive

A basket-maker uses her head to carry her wares to market in Haiti's capital, Port-au-Prince. She needs the help of a friendly passer-by to get them on her head and to take them off again at the end of the journey. She has to walk for several hours from her village in the mountains. Using any kind of public transport would wipe out her meagre profits.

look-out point, so long as the weather is clear and the wind has blown away the ocean mists. From Furcy, too, there is a good view of La Selle (The Saddle), Haiti's highest mountain – 8793 feet. The steep slopes of La Selle are covered with pine forest in which escaping slaves once took refuge from French plantation owners.

In the north, on the Atlantic coast, north-east trade winds blow from April to June, followed by north-westerlies from September to November. The south coast, facing the Caribbean, is fanned by east winds from August to October. All these winds, loaded with humidity, run headlong into the mountains. As they climb, temperatures drop rapidly, turning the humidity to rain. But although they water the summits, the winds soon heat up again on the way down and sweep across the dry plains of the interior. This is particularly true of northern Haiti, where the contrast is greatest between the fertile northern plain exposed to winds from the Atlantic, and the dry stretches on the other side of the mountains, near Gonaïves, and on the country's north-western peninsula.

The result is huge variety. Coral beaches lined with coconut palms look as if they came straight from Polynesia, plains of sugar-cane as if they came from neighbouring Cuba. There are deserts of cactus and thorn bushes, as in north-east Brazil; rice paddies, as in Indochina; terraced fields, as in the Andes; fertile plains, as in East Africa; and slopes covered with conifers, as in Switzerland.

A conspiracy of history

The Dominican Republic comprises nearly two-thirds of Hispaniola, but its population of just under 7.5 million people is only marginally larger than Haiti's – which is 6.7 million. Haiti's population is predominantly black, while most Dominicans are *mestizos*, that is, mixed race. There are still areas of jungle in the Dominican Republic, whereas in Haiti nearly every scrap of land is inhabited, though much of it is unsuitable for cultivation, thanks to the erosion resulting from years of more or less indiscriminate tree-felling. Haiti is more crowded, more rural, poorer and badly served with roads. The Dominican Republic has comparatively affluent towns, while its factories, museums, libraries, cinemas, newspapers and radio and television stations are mostly much better equipped than those of Haiti.

Such contrasts abound. The Spanish-speaking Dominican Republic has close links with the rest of

When making their fishing boats, the Haitians still use techniques developed on the coasts of France many centuries ago. The patchwork sail is hardly elegant, but from a distance the eye is fooled into missing the scars of poverty.

Latin America. Haiti, on the other hand, is the only independent country in the Americas with French as one of its official tongues. Like the Dominican Republic, it is a member of the Organisation of American States, but it has less contact with its predominantly Spanish- and English-speaking neighbours. Moreover, French as it is spoken in France is used by less than 10 per cent of the population; the rest speak a French-based Creole. French visitors can make themselves understood but will have trouble understanding two Haitians in conversation with each other. Haiti has relatively little contact even with the other French-speaking territories in the Caribbean. It has some links with Jamaica, none with Cuba, is openly suspicious of the Dominican Republic and is frightened of the United States.

Santo Domingo, the capital of the Dominican Republic, is proud of its historical heritage. It was founded in 1496 by Columbus's brother Bartolomé, and retained its links with the family when Christopher Columbus's son Diego came to the island as Spain's viceroy in 1509, with his wife María de Toledo. During their period of governorship, the city of Santo Domingo flourished as Spain's most important base in the New World. Later in the 16th century, in 1586, it was sacked by the English freebooter Sir Francis Drake, but much of it has survived. Drake stopped short his destruction of the city at Diego Columbus's old house, when the Spanish agreed to pay his ransom demands.

Today, the old city contains a remarkable collection of Spanish civil, military and ecclesiastical buildings from the 16th century. They include Diego Columbus's house and the Alcázar, the castle he built in 1514. These and many other buildings have been restored and in places reconstructed according to the original plans and with the same materials used by the 16th-century Spanish. In Mexico, Peru and other Latin American countries, Spanish art and architecture are essentially baroque, but in Santo Domingo things are different. There are no gildings, flourishes or overpowering details, and its buildings do not reflect an obsession with gold and conquest. Instead, they mirror the earlier, more formal style of Spain after its reconquest from the Moors. There are gothic vaults, romanesque arches and a hint of Moorish in its architecture – all of them majestic and austere expressions of strength and power. Santo Domingo also has a lively modern city which has grown up around the old colonial quarter.

Port-au-Prince presents a very different picture, though it too has plenty of colour and a vibrancy of its own. It has no colonial jewel at its heart and is a maze of tantalising streets interspersed with haphazard modern developments. The stench of animals and scent of spices fill the teeming markets. Beggars line the streets outside the more expensive hotels, while in front of them cars and lorries compete with horses and donkey carts. Hordes of people emerge from *tap-taps*, primitive buses painted with crude pictures, prayers and proverbs, and stream into the narrow streets. Its few museums and galleries include among their exhibits the anchor from Columbus's flagship and paintings by Haiti's talented 'naive' artists – such as André Pierre and Wilson Bugaud, both with worldwide reputations – many of whom are also leading practitioners of Voodoo.

Unlike Santo Domingo, which is set on the edge of a plain, Port-au-Prince has only been able to expand up the flanks of the surrounding mountains. The roads to the high part of the city climb past deep ravines which are dry for most of the year, but when the rains come turn into menacing torrents. When that happens, and in spite of efforts to improve the drainage system, the ravines overflow and the roads become deathtraps. Pedestrians and drivers are occasionally washed down to the sea in terrifying flash floods. The following morning, in the modern quarter at the foot of the mountains with most of the ministries and embassies, men toil with wheelbarrows to clear away the mud.

Fortunately, good humour is a common quality in Port-au-Prince – and it is needed. There are virtually no pavements except in the few wealthy areas, and even there they are often full of holes and neglected by the residents. The centre of Port-au-Prince is crisscrossed with covered arcades, but there are not always links between the different sections and they are peppered with open drains. When the road climbs uphill, as it often does, the different levels cause further problems and involve leaps and jumps of up to a yard.

The great cattle ranch

Hispaniola was the Spaniards' first base in their conquest of the Americas. Its capital Santo Domingo – originally given the name of La Nueva Isabela, after Queen Isabela of Castile – was the first city they founded in the New World, their first port, first administrative centre, first bishopric and home to their first colonial university. At the same time, the Taino Indians who

Coconut palms originated in Asia, and it was the Spanish who introduced them to the West Indies, where until then they had been unknown. The warm sea breezes blowing over islands such as Hispaniola are perfect for coconuts, and the palms were soon flourishing all around their coasts.

A rocky shoreline along parts of the Dominican Republic's coast means that swimming pools have to be built beside tourist bungalows. The development of tourism and the hotel trade is one factor giving the country a decisive advantage over its poorer neighbour.

already inhabited the island were among their first victims. Ravaged by European diseases to which they had no immunity, demoralised by the invaders' firepower and degraded by forced labour, they rapidly saw the destruction of their way of life. Within a few decades of the Spaniards' arrival, the native Indians had almost entirely died out.

At first, the Spanish tried planting vines and cereals, but neither proved a success. Livestock did better and herds soon multiplied in the savannahs and glades of the island. The Spanish also found some gold and other precious and semi-precious minerals (the Dominican Republic still has extensive deposits of amber and the largest operating gold mine in the Caribbean). By the late 16th century, however, the Spanish had mostly shifted their search for gold to Mexico and Peru, and accordingly lost much of their interest in the West Indian islands. Santo Domingo was downgraded as a colonial capital, and the pretty town built by Bartolomé and Diego Columbus was no longer a prestigious posting for colonial officials. The rural areas of the island became a gigantic cattle ranch.

Other European powers, however, were interested. Excluded from a share of the conquest of much of the rest of the Americas, British and French pirates and freebooters haunted the north coast of Hispaniola,

A Texan-style broad-brimmed hat marks out a Dominican rancher. The Spanish introduced cattle to Hispaniola, and cattle have remained one of the fundamentals of Dominican agriculture ever since. Today, hides and skins are exported as well as meat. Improvements have been made by crossbreeding local livestock with Indian Brahman cattle.

buying large quantities of leather and skins from Spanish farmers in return for goods from Paris, London and Amsterdam. At the beginning of the 17th century the Spanish authorities, opposed to this trade between their colonies and countries other than Spain, took steps to suppress it. The settlements on the north and west coasts of Hispaniola were evacuated and the Spanish population was concentrated around Santo Domingo.

Unfortunately for the Spanish, the decision backfired. French and other European freebooters first set up on the small island of La Tortue (or Turtle Island) off the north coast of modern Haiti, and then on

Hispaniola itself. They formed themselves into groups with names such as the Brethren of the Coast and had elaborate initiation rites for new members. According to one version of events, some Taino Indians surviving on Tortue taught them how to cure meat on a barbecue or *boucan* – from which came the word 'buccaneer'. These ragged pirates gradually turned themselves into accomplished hunters of the herds that by now ran wild. Having secured a supply of food, some of the new colonists built settlements and created the first plantations, thanks to the efforts of white convict gangs sent by the boatload from France.

The western part of Hispaniola officially came under the control of France with the Treaty of Ryswick in 1697. The aim of the French in what they called Saint Domingue was to secure a cheap and plentiful supply of sugar. The era of the Haitian slave trade had begun.

The slave garden of France

In the Atlantic triangle bounded by Europe, Africa and the Americas, slave labour was a currency bought and sold in exchange for arms and goods made in Europe. The near-extinction of the native Indians in the West

It is common to see Haitian women smoking pipes known as cachimbos. *The men, on the other hand, only use* cachimbos *very occasionally. It is also rare to see men carrying big loads on their heads, whereas the women will carry baskets, as here, or even just a purse and a tin of food.*

In Santo Domingo, the edges of the market are one big outdoor café where a few pesos can buy all kinds of fruit, cooked dishes and drinks. Fruit-juice sellers with mobile stalls like this are just waiting to turn their oranges into a refreshing juice.

Furniture – including the chairs used by the children in this photograph – is so scarce in Haiti that it is often passed from home to home for special occasions. The letters 'EM' on the central pillar indicate that the anti-malaria agency has passed this building as safe in its efforts to free the country from the disease.

Indies led to the importation of African slaves. These were brought in slave ships to places like Saint Domingue, and the sugar and coffee they laboured to produce was then exported to western Europe.

The territory in the west of Hispaniola – the name Haiti comes from *Hay-Ti*, 'mountainous country' in the Taino Indian language – was cultivated and many forests destroyed to create sugar-cane plantations. Settlements were built and more land cleared for sugar refineries. The slave-driven economy reached as far as the lower slopes of the mountains, where in the cooler climate coffee plantations were established. The Haitian countryside still bears the traces of that era in an unbalanced economy. There was no attempt to develop diversified commercial enterprises; the sole aim was to

produce as much sugar and coffee as possible. Now, although most of the plantations have long since been broken up, agriculture remains the chief occupation in Haiti. The problem today is the smallness of the holdings, which on average cover just under 4 acres. Many farmers are able at best to grow enough only to feed their own families.

In the Spanish part of the island conditions were always different. The Spanish never established big plantations, but left vast stretches of land where herds of cattle roamed at will. The population was scattered and contained a lower proportion of African slaves; looking after the livestock required only a small labour force.

There was an informal relationship between the two territories. In French Saint Domingue, the slave-

Catholicism is the official religion of Haiti, though Protestant churches have also been established in the country since the 19th century. Voodoo, however, is Haiti's most famous religion, based on African beliefs but mingled with some Christian rites and symbols. Its rituals are not always as sinister and bloody as many popular films and novels would have one believe.

powered agricultural economy was a net exporter of food crops, and yet had problems in providing enough food for its own population. Meat had to be imported, legally or otherwise, across the border from the Spanish part of the island.

During the 18th century, the contrasts intensified. Slaves were imported to the French part in ever greater numbers. The production of sugar cane and coffee rose, but living conditions deteriorated. This applied not only to the slaves, but also to parts of the poorer white and mixed-race (mulatto) population who nursed a growing resentment against the richer French colonists.

White insecurity was aggravated by the statistics. In 1681, French Saint Domingue had a total population of 6648 people, made up of 4336 whites, 2102 slaves and 210 freed slaves. A century later the slave trade had reached new heights: in the nine years between 1780 and 1789 an estimated 150,000 slaves were imported into the colony. By 1789 there were 30,000 whites, compared with the 465,000 black slaves. Some 28,000 emancipated slaves and their descendants were becoming richer, and now owned a third of the land and a quarter of the slaves, but were still discontented because they did not have full citizenship.

At the same time, the Spanish part of the island, which was twice as big, had less than a quarter of the population of the French part. There were 30,000 whites, as many as in the French part, but only 15,000 slaves and 80,000 freed men and women – a pattern which continues to this day, with a densely populated black republic in Haiti adjoining a relatively sparsely populated *mestizo* Dominican Republic.

Blood and fury

The French Revolution of 1789 had an explosive effect on the French part of Hispaniola. In 1791, the black slaves rose against the planters with a ferocity reminiscent of France's Reign of Terror. Leadership of the revolution then passed into the hands of the remarkable black Haitian Toussaint L'Ouverture, a former slave who had helped his French master to escape during the 1791 uprising and would later do much to try to reconcile blacks, whites and mulattos on the island. By 1801, Toussaint was undisputed master not only of Haiti but of the whole of Hispaniola, having invaded the

Haiti's 'naive' art is now world famous. In works like this, the soft green and yellow of the vegetation and the fresh blue of streams, are a far cry from the barrenness which afflicts so much of Haiti today.

Spanish half earlier that year. In May, he made himself the island's governor-general for life, though he never cut official ties with France and, indeed, went out of his way to convince the new French leader Napoleon Bonaparte of his loyalty.

This, however, was not good enough for Napoleon, who sent 70 warships and 45,000 men under his brother-in-law, General Charles Leclerc, to take back firm control of the troublesome island. Leclerc arrived in January 1802. There was some fierce fighting which saw most of the island's white and mulattos and even some of the black leaders defect to the French side. In June, Toussaint accepted an invitation to the French headquarters to discuss an armistice. Despite a promise of safe-conduct, he was seized, thrown into the hold of a ship and sent to France, where he was imprisoned in a fortress in the Jura Mountains along the Swiss border. His appeals to Napoleon for mercy were eloquent: 'I will not conceal my faults from you. I have committed some. What man is exempt? But I have too high an idea of the justice of the First Magistrate of the French people, to doubt a moment of his clemency.'

The French leader, however, had no intention of yielding. Toussaint, bedridden with pneumonia in the unaccustomed cold of France, was denied proper medical treatment and, on the morning of April 7, 1803, his jailers found him dead, sitting in a chair beside an empty fireplace.

The remaining Haitian generals resumed hostilities with a vengeance. In 1803, any surviving French people who had not already succumbed to an outbreak of yellow fever were massacred, and on January 1, 1804, the country officially declared its independence from France, with the name of Haiti. After the United States, it was the second country in the Americas to throw off the European colonial yoke. It was also the only country in the Americas to win independence through an armed slave revolt.

The Haitians paid a high price for their independence. The immediate effect was financial: when France finally agreed to recognise the nation of Haiti in 1825, it was in exchange for huge compensation payments to the former French settlers. Paying off this debt seriously destabilised the Haitian economy. The country was

Opposite: *Haitian farmers' wives carry most things on their heads, including, as here, a live turkey. The owner barely seems to have noticed the photographer who caught her here in a lane of the market at Jacmel, a small port on the south coast.*

The tap-tap is a national institution in Haiti. These small lorries converted into buses are the most common means of getting around the island. At the rear of the wooden superstructure there is usually a saying, prayer or proverb – in this case 'Give me faith'.

politically and economically punished by the rest of the world and ignored for the rest of the 19th century – an isolation whose effects continue to this day.

Independence moreover had been won by arms, and in the century that followed internal disagreements were mostly fought out and settled in the same bloody way. As early as 1806, Toussaint L'Ouverture's former lieutenant Jean-Jacques Dessalines (who had taken a leaf from Napoleon's book by having himself crowned Emperor Jacques I) was killed while trying to suppress a mulatto rebellion. Civil war then broke out between the black general Henri Christophe based in the north and the liberal mulatto Alexandre Sabès Pétion based in the south. Haiti remained divided between a northern kingdom headed by Christophe as King Henry I (as a great admirer of the British monarchy, he anglicised his name to Henry) and a southern republic led until 1818 by Pétion. Only in 1820 was the western half of Hispaniola reunited under Pétion's successor Jean-Pierre Boyer.

Boyer ruled until overthrown in a rebellion in 1843. From then until 1915, Haiti had 20 different rulers, of whom all but four were either assassinated or overthrown by force. Interminable conflicts, calls to arms, revolutions and counter-revolutions became the norm, though they never dampened the Haitians' determination to preserve their independence and banish forever the tyranny of slavery. In the end, however, they did temporarily lose their independence when the United States – mindful, among other things, of Haiti's strategic position on the sea routes to the newly completed Panama Canal – sent in the marines, and went on to occupy the country from 1915 to 1934.

Domestic politics among the urban elite in Haiti has long been dominated by the complexities of the racial mix. On the one side are the mulatto descendants of freed slaves, for whom independence brought Haitian nationality and recognition of their property. On the other side are the descendants of the generals and officers of the independence struggle, usually but by no means always black, who won their freedom with the bullet and bayonet. In politics, the mulattos tend on the whole to be more liberal, with a wider international perspective. The others are more inclined to rule in the name of the masses, and tend more towards dictatorship.

The poor people of the cities will sell anything in order to survive, from a shoe shine to a clean windscreen, lottery tickets to sugar-cane stems and coconuts. This man with his tricycle is selling his wares in the streets of the Dominican capital Santo Domingo.

For many peasants in remote rural areas, the market is the big social event of the week. They can choose from a wide variety of produce, like these farmers at the fish market at Lully in Haiti. They can also meet friends and catch up on the latest gossip.

Playing on the frustrations of the growing black bourgeoisie, President François Duvalier after he was elected in 1957 took away much of the political power of the mulatto faction, though they kept most of their economic dominance. 'Papa Doc' – so called because he had been a physician before his rise to political prominence – established a dictatorship based on repression and extortion and enforced by the infamous *tontons macoutes*. This ruthless presidential militia – named after *Tonton Macoute,* an ogre-like figure in Haitian folklore who kidnaps naughty children – savagely persecuted those of the old elite who had not already fled, as well as undermining the influence of the army.

most strongly into play. The Haitians not only have a language of their own – Creole, essentially a French dialect, though mingled with many African words and grammatical forms – but also a religion: Voodoo. This has its roots in African religious beliefs – 'Voodoo' comes from a West African word meaning 'spirit, deity' – though it also incorporates Catholic elements, which were originally introduced to disguise Voodoo rites from disapproving French plantation owners. Although not always as luridly sensational as depicted in many films and novels, rituals in Voodoo temples or *péristyles* are undoubtedly colourful, usually involving generous libations of rum and the sacrifice of cocks. A *houngan*

The Haitian factor

The rural poor have played little part in the political conflict between the mulattos and blacks, liberals and nationalists. Exploiting the uncertainty and disharmony of the post-independence order, the former slaves settled the land wherever they were, set up their communities and smallholdings and created the small-scale peasantry that exists to this day.

It is in the countryside, on the other hand, that the so-called 'Haitian factor' – referring to all that is most distinctive about Haitian life and culture – has come

Itinerant Haitian tinker women travel the country on donkeys, often covering long distances. They are commonly known as Madame Sara – *after a migratory bird of that name. Their husbands, meanwhile, farm the family smallholding.*

Ragged clothes, but brilliant colours, are the mark of a typical Haitian market scene. Despite the fearsome reputation of their Voodoo ceremonies, most Haitians are also extremely good-natured.

The Dominican Republic is traditionally a land of stockbreeding, which in the old days secretly supplied its French neighbour with meat – thus getting around strict Spanish regulations concerning trade with other nations. Today, the importance of stockbreeding has diminished, but with 2.2 million head of cattle the Dominican Republic still supports nearly twice as much livestock as Haiti.

A Dominican smallholder tends his beehives. In the most fertile areas of the republic, the tobacco and sugar plantations are mostly owned by a few large farmers or multi-national corporations. Smallholders proliferate in the less productive areas.

(priest) presides and the gods, or *loas*, are invoked to the pulsating beat of drums. Believers writhe on the ground in the phenomenon of 'spirit possession'.

Voodoo and Catholicism now often exist in a strange interdependence, with people frequently going to Mass one day and a Voodoo ceremony the next – despite the strictures of the more orthodox Catholic clergy. Certain Voodoo deities have even taken on the characteristics of Christian saints. The goddess Erzulie Freda, for example, originated in Dahomey in West Africa, but in Haiti is closely identified with the Virgin Mary. The tombs in officially Catholic cemeteries often have little strips of red and black cloth attached to them – red and black are the colours of Baron Samedi, the Voodoo god of the dead.

The benefits of tourism

Haiti's turbulent history and the fearsome reputation of Voodoo have helped to prevent tourism from developing on a large scale in the country. In this, as in so much else, it stands in marked contrast with the Dominican Republic. Haiti has areas of rugged beauty unmatched by its neighbour, but it also suffers the disadvantage of having fewer good beaches and lacks the facilities for scuba-diving and fishing; much of its coast is rocky, and its beaches are often muddy and surrounded by mangrove swamps. It also lacks the equivalent of the Dominican Republic's Cordillera, with attractions for walkers, riders and hunters.

These imbalances between the two countries increase the problems of underdevelopment. The Dominican Republic has much more space, fewer people per square mile and bigger towns. Haiti has a large rural underclass and a problem of violence. The disappearance of virtually all its wildlife means there is little prospect of

creating national parks; the Dominican Republic has five of them. Even if the Haitians were able to promote their tourist industry more successfully, they would still have to solve the problem of installing luxury hotels and other facilities amidst a largely impoverished – and potentially resentful – population.

Once again, there is a huge contrast with the Dominican Republic, whose tourist attractions include the astonishing country club built by the American multinational corporation Gulf and Western near La Romana sugar processing plants. This has a private airstrip, a tennis village, two golf courses, a shooting range, a bareback-riding stadium and a polo ground which opens onto thousands of acres of grass and woods. There are marvellous beaches and a lagoon for sailing. Sailing, swimming and fishing are popular and each year the club is the venue for international sea-fishing and watersports competitions.

Ten minutes away, on a hill overlooking the sea, Gulf and Western have also built Altos de Chavón in the style of a 16th-century Spanish village. As well as that, there is an American-style recreational centre with a museum, art galleries, shops, restaurants and artists' and sculptors' studios. The tourist developments on the north coast of the Dominican Republic are still more sophisticated, with Florida-style resort complexes,

The instrument may be made out of a tin can left over from an international aid campaign, but it is clearly descended from the zither played by this boy's ancestors in Africa. Success as a popular musician offers one of the few escape routes from poverty.

Bottom: *During the Lent and Easter celebrations each year,* Rara *musicians wander through Haiti's towns and countryside with drums and bamboo flutes, which they both blow and strike with a stick to keep time. Rara music and dances have their roots in Voodoo ceremonies and ultimately in the religious rituals of Africa.*

enjoying the added attraction of a better climate than the southern United States. Of course, few local people get the chance to enjoy all these expensive pleasures, but at least they provide a certain amount of employment (in a country where, in spite of a relative prosperity compared with Haiti, 29 per cent of the workforce are unemployed) and some benefit for the national treasury.

In large measure these benefits are the result of history. The Dominican Republic shares the same island as Haiti but not the same past. Its road to independence was less bloody and ultimately less costly, though still fraught with setbacks. It started in 1795 when the Treaty

of Basle gave the Spanish part of the island to France. Beaten by their former slaves in Haiti, French forces regrouped in Santo Domingo with a view to mounting a counter-attack; this in turn led to the counter-strike by Toussaint L'Ouverture onto Dominican soil.

After Toussaint's fall the Dominican territory broke free, only to be annexed once more by Haiti in 1822. But the Dominicans took a dim view of the occupation and of being liable for part of the huge debt imposed by France in return for Haiti's independence. Dominican forces under the writer Juan Pablo Duarte eventually ejected the Haitians and the two countries separated again in 1844. Haitian aggression continued, however, and at one point even pushed the Dominicans into an alliance with Isabella II of Spain. In an event unique in the history of the Americas, the Dominican Republic actually reverted to being a Spanish colony in 1861. Further insurrections soon led to independence once more in 1865.

In 1868 a failed attempt at independence in nearby Cuba led to an influx of rich Cuban sugar planters into the Dominican Republic, where they re-established their businesses. A year later, the Dominican president, still fearing invasion from Haiti, offered his country for annexation to the United States – an offer which the US Senate eventually refused. The power of the sugar barons grew, meanwhile, as did American investment in the country, and in due course this led to American occupation. In 1916, US marines disembarked at Santo Domingo, on the pretext of restoring order, a year after they had occupied Haiti. They left Santo Domingo sooner than they did Port-au-Prince (in 1924 rather than 1934) but Dominican customs and excise administration would remain under American control until 1940. When Fidel Castro came to power in Cuba in 1959, there was a further influx of Cuban sugar planters and hoteliers.

Over the years, the Dominican Republic suffered under a series of brutal dictators – 'men on horseback' as they were known in the 19th century – and 1930 saw the rise to power of one of the most ruthless, and grotesque, of them all. He was the self-styled 'His Excellency Generalisimo Doctor Rafael Léonidas Trujillo Molina, Honourable President of the Republic, Benefactor of the Homeland and Restorer of Financial Independence'. This megalomaniac had 2000 statues of himself erected around the country. He renamed the

The central pillar of a Voodoo temple or péristyle *symbolises the channel through which the* loas *(gods) make their presence felt. Initiates sacrifice white birds, while a priest* (houngan) *presides with a glittering banner in honour of Dambala, the god of knowledge, usually depicted in the form of a snake. Spirit possession of various members of the assembly then follows. Foreign visitors are not always welcome in Voodoo ceremonies.*

capital Ciudad Trujillo (Trujillo City) and used his initials (RLTM) as the basis for a motto blazoned throughout the country: *Rectitud-Libertad-Trabajo-Moralidad* ('Rectitude-Liberty-Work-Morality').

Between 1937 and 1941, Trujillo and his armed forces used the threat of increased Haitian influence to carry out a policy of 'Dominicanisation' along the border between the two countries. The massacres that followed reputedly left between 10,000 and 20,000 Creole-speaking people of Haitian extraction dead. Even the Dominican authorities admitted to 17,000 people massacred, and this eventually led to reparations being paid by the Dominican Republic to Haiti.

The republic became a kind of private fiefdom for Trujillo and his family. Eventually a group of rebels determined to free the country from his grip. He was assassinated in 1961 and the 2000 statues were pulled down shortly afterwards. Since then the country's most resilient political figure has been Joaquín Balaguer, who started out as one of Trujillo's protégés: he narrowly won his sixth term as president in 1990, aged 83. Today, the Dominican Republic has reasonably fair elections, a growing tourist industry and a comparatively prosperous sugar-cane and cattle sector. It also has ambitions to play a greater role in the politics of the Caribbean, though it is hampered in these by a large foreign debt.

Haiti by contrast has suffered yet another setback. As recently as 1986 it looked as though the republic could achieve a significant step towards greater freedom and prosperity. That year, President Jean-Claude 'Baby Doc' Duvalier – who had succeeded his father 'Papa Doc' at the age of 19 in 1971 – was deposed and fled into exile on the French Riviera. A joint civilian and military government set up in his place foiled a coup attempt by associates of Duvalier, and made strenuous efforts to recover the hundreds of millions of dollars

thought to have been looted from the country's treasury by members of the Duvalier family and their hangers-on. Economically, it seemed that Haiti was making long overdue progress. The 620,000 small farms were producing cash crops such as coffee, sisal, sugar and cocoa – albeit on an insufficient and inefficient scale – as well as subsistence crops such as maize, rice, millet and beans. Assembly plants supplied sports goods, toys, clothes and pharmaceuticals for the American market. Foreign investors, mainly from the USA and France, were attracted by significant tax concessions and low labour costs. Tourism was slowly increasing, although Haitian expatriates returning home from the USA made up many of the visitors.

At the same time, the institutions of democracy – among them, a constitution and chamber of deputies – were established or strengthened. Jean-Bertrand Aristide, an ordained Roman Catholic priest, became president of Haiti in 1991 after winning 67 per cent of the votes in an internationally monitored election a few months earlier.

Yet all these signs of progress were halted when, only seven months after he was installed as president, Jean-Bertrand Aristide was forced into exile and the army once again took power. The international community insisted on the restoration of Aristide and imposed a political and economic embargo which seriously weakened Haiti's fragile recovery. The bloodshed increased and there was controversy over the Vatican's apparent condonement of the latest military regime. The international embargo resulted in famine in the north of the country and a general worsening in the already precarious condition of the rural poor.

Haiti is still one of the poorest countries in the world and the poor relation to its next-door neighbour, which is still an importer of unskilled Haitian labour. This immigration causes problems of racial tension. The

A machete, a bottle of rum and 'magic' mud are key ingredients in the annual celebrations in honour of the Voodoo loa *(god) Ogoun. He is the blacksmith god, patron of fire and war. In the days of slavery, black Haitians often identified their gods with Christian saints – partly as a means of disguising their religious rituals from disapproving white plantation owners and Catholic priests. Ogoun was identified with St James the Great, so that July 25, on which the Catholic church commemorates St James, is also Ogoun's day.*

Dominican Republic barely conceals its distaste for a black Haitian migrant working class on its territory, whose most conspicuous characteristics, Creole and Voodoo, are anathema to the Dominican way of life. Over 500 years after Columbus landed in 1492, ancient contrasts still haunt Hispaniola. In spite of their attractions to visitors, Haiti and the Dominican Republic preserve their own cultures and mutual suspicions, as if reluctant to make the changes needed to redress the imbalances between them.

Hopes that failed

One place above all, perhaps, stands for the high aspirations of Haiti's founders – and of the failure to live up to most of them. Rising from a summit on the north coast, near the country's second city Cap Haïtien, are the astonishing remains of what many Haitians like to claim as the 'eighth wonder of the world': the Citadelle La Ferrière, completed in 1816 and the brainchild of King Henry Christophe. Fearful of a renewed French invasion, he designed it as a retreat where the newly independent Haitians could hold out against invading troops. He was ruthless in pursuing its construction. Some 20,000 workers were assigned to the task, many of them dying in the process. The finished fortress was capable of housing a garrison of 15,000 men and was stocked with enough food and ammunition to last a siege of 12 months. In places its walls were 30 feet thick; it included a hospital, kitchens, storerooms, a foundry, dormitories and treasure chambers.

A little farther down the mountain slopes are the ruins of Henry Christophe's own residence of Sans Souci, named after the more famous palace built by the 18th-century Prussian king, Frederick the Great. Like La Citadelle, it is now largely overgrown with jungle, but in its time it too was a startling measure of Christophe's ambitions as a black ruler claiming equality with the white monarchs of Europe. It had huge audience chambers, banqueting halls and private apartments for Christophe, his Queen and two daughters, all sumptuously paved with marble and furnished with tapestries and gilt mirrors imported from Europe. It even had an under-floor system of pipes with spring water flowing through them to help to keep the rooms cool. Here, Christophe maintained a truly royal pomp, surrounded by a court which included a newly created hereditary nobility. There were 4 princes, 8 dukes (including the picturesquely titled Duc de la Marmelade), 22 counts (including the Comte de Limonade) and 37 barons.

Christophe seems to have started out with the best of intentions, determined to give his new black realm a dignity that hostile foreign powers would have to acknowledge. Unfortunately, his rule became increasingly despotic and conditions for the poorer people ended up scarcely any better than they were under slavery. Rebellion broke out in 1820 and on October 8 the King, partially paralysed by a stroke and deserted even by his army, shot himself, using (the story goes) a silver bullet. He was buried in La Citadelle, where a tablet still bears the inscription: *'Je renais de mes cendres'*, 'I will rise again from my ashes'.

For all its terror and corruption, the Duvalier regime in Haiti managed to inspire a degree of loyalty, especially in the country areas. Jean-Claudisme – *support for Jean-Claude 'Baby Doc' Duvalier – had its adherents, such as this young man in brilliant red, though they were not able to save the younger Duvalier from luxurious exile on the French Riviera.*

Cuba – Land of the Green Crocodile

Misunderstandings about Cuba existed as long ago as October 27, 1492, when Christopher Columbus reached the island during his first voyage to the New World. Columbus's object was to find a sea route, west across the Atlantic, to Asia. Somewhat optimistically, he mistook Cuba for a piece of mainland, and thought he had stumbled on a province belonging to China. Only later did the Spanish *conquistadores* realise that another continent, America, with its attendant isles of the Caribbean (of which Cuba, at over 44,000 square miles, is the largest), stood between them and the riches of the Asiatic empires.

Nearly 500 years after Columbus's first voyage, in 1989, Cuba celebrated the 30th anniversary of the *triunfo de la Revolución*, the triumph of its Communist revolution. Nobody was under any illusions about its geographical position any longer, but misunderstandings did – and do – definitely persist about the long, narrow island, described by one of its poets, Nicolas Guillén, as:

... swimming on the map
Like a long green crocodile
With eyes of water and of stone.

Revolution!

The year was 1959, and all over the world left-wing intellectuals were singing the praises of a handful of 30-year-olds who had just overthrown the Cuban dictator Fulgencio Batista (a former army sergeant whose corrupt and repressive regime had ruled the country on and off since 1933). The young men, known as *los barbudos* ('the bearded ones'), because of their luxuriant side-whiskers, had been victorious at the end of a tough guerrilla campaign, led by the former law student Fidel Castro and his Argentinian-born lieutenant Ernesto ('Che') Guevara. Youth, idealistic intentions and heroism in the fight against Batista had a huge romantic appeal; and the young men's shaggy faces, touting large local cigars, adorned posters and pamphlets everywhere.

Their newly conquered capital, Havana, became a Mecca for intellectuals from all over Europe and the Americas. They came like pilgrims to soak up an atmosphere where youthful leaders, who never seemed to need any sleep, gave interviews at three o'clock in the morning before heading on to ministerial meetings a couple of hours later. The air was thick with idealistic

schemes, such as the challenge Castro threw down at the headquarters of the United Nations in New York: that his regime would eliminate illiteracy in Cuba in less than a year. This was no idle gesture, since at least 700,000 Cubans could neither read nor write – and Castro was as good as his word. He and his fellows mobilised an army of 264,000 volunteers who spread out into city slums and the countryside, equipped with books – and spectacles: 167,000 pairs were distributed to old people. In the end, they taught exactly 707,212 of their countrymen and women to read and write.

A youthful Fidel Castro is pictured with his trademark cigar. In 1989, a now greying leader celebrated the 30th anniversary of his revolution.

The crocodile – or more precisely, the cayman, a family of crocodiles unique to the tropical regions of the Americas – has long been a symbol of Cuba. As early as 1517, it figured on the coins of a special Cuban currency, issued by King Ferdinand 'the Catholic' of Spain.

But the tide of goodwill soon turned. Castro was also determined to take over the economy and run it along true socialist lines. Close ties were established with Moscow and, with the Cold War in full swing, a jittery United States – with the added worry of large pre-revolutionary investments in Cuba – broke off diplomatic relations. In April 1961, the administration of President John F. Kennedy gave open backing to a failed attempt at invasion by 1600 anti-Castro Cuban exiles landing on the south coast at the Bay of Pigs (Playa Girón). A year later in October 1962, the world tottered on the brink of nuclear war after US spy planes discovered nuclear missile bases on Cuba, only 90 miles off the Florida coast. The US Navy was mobilised to blockade the island and prevent Soviet ships carrying missiles from reaching it. Only at the last minute did the Soviet leader Nikita Khrushchev back down.

For many people, especially in the United States, Cuba became the 'bad boy' of international politics. In the wake of the revolution, there were mass arrests of anti-Communists and thousands of exiles poured into the United States. Havana welcomed hijackers – acting

Plant tendrils hang from ancient balconies in Havana's Old City. In the background rises the Capitolio, symbol of the United States' former domination of the island. It was built in 1929 to house the Cuban parliament, and was based on Washington's Capitol. It is now Havana's Museum of Natural Science.

The twin towers of the American-built Hotel Nacional rise above Havana's seafront Malecón in the Vedado district. In the middle distance looms the tower block of the ultra-modern Hermanos Ameijeiras Hospital, dominating much of the Old City.

in the name of various international terrorist organisations. Che Guevara, and others inspired by his example, announced their desire to export revolution to the other troubled spots of the world: Latin America, Africa and the Middle East. Guevara himself would in due course die for the cause, when captured and executed by the Bolivian army in 1967. From being a model of idealism, Cuba entered conservative demonology as the source of all kinds of evil: Moscow's offshore agent in the Caribbean, where 10.6 million Cubans lived in near-destitution and terror of the secret police.

More moustaches than beards

Eleven hours on board a Russian-built Ilyushin belonging to the airline Cubana de Aviación are drawing to an end, and a glimpse through the porthole reveals the lights of Havana sparkling in the distance. The flight has come from Paris – one of the places in western Europe, along with Stansted, Berlin, Brussels, Madrid and Lisbon, that offers a direct air link to Cuba. The plane lands, and a suffocating blanket of warm, humid air greets the passengers. Gradually, they become

Little love is now lost between the capitalist United States and Communist Cuba. For all that, baseball remains the island's most popular sport. Indeed, sports of all kinds are encouraged, and Cuba has an impressive Olympic record.

acclimatised to the surroundings. Almost immediately one 'myth' about Cuba is destroyed. Cuban men do not all have Castro-style beards. In fact, moustaches drooping down the sides of the mouth, in the style of Che Guevara, seem more popular.

The taxi and bus ride from the airport to the centre of Havana passes through a series of plywood triumphal arches which are regularly erected across the road to commemorate the anniversaries of key moments in the revolutionary struggle: such as the attack on July 26, 1953 on the Moncada, an army barracks in the south-eastern seaport of Santiago de Cuba. Castro led the attack and was captured. Later, however, he managed to leave the island, returning in 1955 to launch a new, and finally victorious, uprising.

Also lining the route are billboards and large model rockets. The rockets – less warlike than they may appear – commemorate the remarkable feats of Arnaldo Tamayo, the first Cuban in space, who went up as part of a Soviet space mission. The billboards are a mix. Some are purely commercial, proclaiming the merits of Havana Club, the most popular local brand of rum, or of various makes of cigar. Others consist of revolutionary slogans, such as: *'Ayer, hoy y siempre: estudio, trabajo y fusil'* ('Yesterday, today and for ever: study, work

and gun') – a reminder of the regime's constant pre-occupation with possible invasion. Others again preach the virtues of saving money, economising on energy or taking care of precious tools and equipment. Another reflects the government's concern at the growing numbers of Cubans longing to escape a rapidly deteriorating economic situation (due, above all, to the collapse of Cuba's former backer, the Soviet Union) by fleeing to the United States: *'Aquí me quedo'*, 'I'm staying here'.

The delights of Havana

To discover the real heart of Cuba, the best place to start is Havana. It is hard not to be seduced by one of the oldest, and most beautiful, capitals in the New World, whose Old City was recently officially designated by UNESCO as a World Heritage Site.

The seafront Malecón is Havana's only main thoroughfare without an accompanying avenue of trees. Here, the attraction is the sea itself, whose waves in stormy weather come crashing over the breakwater and parapet. They lick across the highway and tumble at the feet of buildings which crowd the approaches to the port

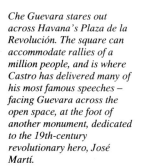

Che Guevara stares out across Havana's Plaza de la Revolución. The square can accommodate rallies of a million people, and is where Castro has delivered many of his most famous speeches – facing Guevara across the open space, at the foot of another monument, dedicated to the 19th-century revolutionary hero, José Martí.

area, their fronts all painted in a cheerful medley of pastel shades.

East along the seafront is the Castillo de la Fuerza, Havana's most ancient fortress, started in 1538. In front of this stretches the small wood-paved Plaza de Armas, which is dominated by a statue of the 19th-century fighter for independence and the freedom of Cuba's slaves, Carlos Manuel Céspedes. Immediately to the left is a small shady chapel, the Templete, built in 1828 beside a column marking the site where the first Mass was supposed to have been celebrated on Cuban soil in 1519 under a large cotton (ceiba) tree. Inside, a series of frescoes by the French painter Jean-Baptiste Vermay fills three walls, giving a wonderfully detailed depiction of the people who took part in the first Mass, and of their costumes.

Opposite the Templete, on the other side of the square, rises the former Palacio de los Capitanes Generales, where the Spanish governors and later the Cuban presidents lived until 1917. It is a masterpiece of

A Cuban teenager peers over the top of a suitably red drape. The Castro regime sees the island's youth a precious resource, and spares no effort to educate youngsters in revolutionary values.

Military bands form an inevitable part of state occasions and parades. But Cuba's real musical genius lies in the dancing rhythms of the conga, rumba, guajira and others, creating a hypnotic blend of Spanish and African influences.

local baroque architecture, dating from 1780; the principal reception rooms have been restored and furnished with fine specimens of colonial furniture, paintings and other ornaments.

Inland from the Plaza de Armas, two narrow streets – Calle Obispo and Calle O'Reilly – lead to the city's Parque Central (Central Park). Both are lined with shops that have a positively Victorian atmosphere: polished mahogany counters, old-fashioned glass display cases and pottery jars containing medicines and perfumes. A short walk north leads to the Plaza de la Catedral, which has some more fine specimens of colonial baroque, including the cathedral's own impressive façade. This in turn leads to Calle Empedrado, with Havana's most famous watering spot: the Bodeguita del Medio, whose regular clients included the American writer Ernest Hemingway.

To sample some of its excellent creole cooking, diners sometimes have to book in advance. But Hemingway's favourite cocktail, *mojito*, is served at the bar. The bartender puts a few leaves of *hierba buena*, a kind of mint, at the bottom of a glass and covers them with a spoonful of caster sugar, which he then grinds into the leaves. He adds the juice of a lime, some ice cubes, fizzy mineral water and mixes the whole concoction. Finally, he adds some white rum, and mixes it all again, before handing it over.

Farther west in the newer Vedado district, which was developed in the late 19th and early 20th centuries, is Avenida Cinco (Fifth Avenue): the streets and avenues in this part of Havana are given numbers and letters, as in New York, and are divided into 'blocks'. Avenida Cinco is particularly elegant, divided down its centre by rows of flowerbeds and a line of delicately shaped pines, lime trees, poincianas and royal palms. Rising on either side are the wonderful former homes of Havana's wealthy elite. No extravagance of style was too much for them: Greek-style capitals top colonnaded entrances; and caryatids (pillars shaped like human figures) support finely wrought balconies. Other mansions were evidently modelled on Scottish baronial fortresses, Bavarian castles and Venetian palaces.

Museums abound in Havana. Among the most interesting is the Museum of the Revolution, which is housed in the former Presidential Palace. In pride of place in front of it is the small yacht *Granma*, which smuggled Castro and a group of companions back to Cuba in 1956, at the start of their last, victorious campaign. There is also the National Museum of Fine Arts, with some impressive examples of modern Cuban painting, and – back on the Plaza de la Catedral – the Museo de Alfabetización, dedicated to the literacy campaign of the early Castro years. Another interesting memorial is Room 511 at the Hotel Ambos Mundos, kept as a showpiece for visitors. This was where Ernest Hemingway lived for several years in the 1930s – it also offers some of the best views of old Havana.

Finally, there is one of Havana's most distinctive sights: the huge and dilapidated American limousines that have somehow survived the decades since the Revolution – Plymouths, Chevrolets, Cadillacs, Dodges, Mercurys and Studebakers, dating from the 1950s or even 40s. Lovingly repainted in bright colours, they jolt, wobble and rumble along the potholed streets, though petrol shortages now mean that more and more of them spend most of their time parked (or abandoned) at the street sides. Moving or stationary, they form a living motor museum, held together by improvised spare parts,

Motorbikes, sidecars and ancient American Chevrolets, Oldsmobiles and Cadillacs are among the delights of Cuban cities, such as Havana. The cars mostly date from the pre-Revolutionary 1950s, and are miraculously held together by the mechanical improvisations of the locals.

The United States' economic blockade of Cuba has meant there are no spare parts for a decaying reserve of mostly American-made trucks. This truck is offloading a precious cargo of bananas in Havana's Old City. But generally it is difficult to get farm produce from the countryside into the cities – hence the frequent absence of fresh foods from city shops and markets.

and overshadow the upstart Ladas and Mz motor bikes (with sidecar), imported from the former Soviet Union. In fact, car ownership is still rare in Cuba. The squads of smartly dressed traffic police, in light-blue uniforms and spurred boots, seem almost redundant.

A taste of Africa

When Columbus first arrived Cuba was inhabited by up to 350,000 Arawak Indians – divided into three large 'clans', the Ciboney, the Guanahatabey and the Taino.

But they have left few traces. Apart from a few rock carvings and drawings, they are remembered chiefly for their heroic resistance to the *conquistador* Diego de Velázquez, who landed on the island in 1511 with 300 followers and over the next few years established most of the first colonial settlements, including Havana. The Indians were almost entirely wiped out within four years of his arrival.

It was in the 17th century that Cuba began to show the first signs of local patriotic feeling, as its creole population (almost all of Spanish extraction) reacted against colonial domination from Madrid. This was

Dominoes are a passion with many Cubans. They often play the game in the street outside their homes, where the air is cooler. No money changes hands – openly, at least – since gambling was banned after the Revolution.

encouraged by an influx of creole settlers and their slaves from the neighbouring island of Jamaica, which had been seized from the Spanish by British forces in 1655. In 1762, at the end of the Seven Years' War, Britain briefly seized Cuba, too, but after a year returned it to Spain in exchange for Florida.

The real struggle for independence began in the 19th century. An abortive uprising against Spain in 1809 was followed in 1868 by a much more serious rebellion, led by the liberal landowner Carlos Manuel Céspedes. This rumbled on for ten years before the rebels signed an armistice with the Spanish authorities. It did yield one important result, however. Although slavery had been officially abolished in the Spanish empire in 1847, emancipation had never been properly carried out in Cuba. Céspedes set the example by freeing his own slaves, and shortly after the rebellion, in 1880, slavery, too, came to an end.

A talented poet and orator, José Martí, was the inspiration behind Cuba's final, victorious bid for independence. He led another rebellion in 1895, and was almost immediately killed, on May 19. Thanks largely to his earlier efforts as a propagandist, however, the Cuban cause now had backing from the United

States. In 1898, following an incident in February during which the US battleship *Maine* was blown up in Havana harbour, Washington declared war on Madrid. American troops landed on Cuba and, later in the year, an American squadron defeated a Spanish fleet off Santiago. By December peace had been signed and American forces controlled the whole island. Spain had lost its last foothold in the Americas.

The island of Cuba was not yet wholly free, however. The Americans maintained a military government on the island until 1902, when they handed over to the first Cuban president, Tomás Estrada Palma. Even then,

the island's freedom was limited. According to the so-called Platt Amendment, which became part of a treaty between the two countries, the United States reserved the right to intervene in the island's domestic affairs, in order to safeguard American interests. The United States also kept control of two naval bases on Cuba – one of which, Guantánamo Bay in the south-east, it has retained to this day. In return, Washington offered the island import preferences for Cuban sugar. Cuba had, in effect, become an American 'neo-colony'.

The long years of struggle have left their mark, and all are now duly recorded in the island's museums. But there is, of course, another strand of influence, from Africa. Most museums have sections dwelling on the horrors of slavery; a few, such as the one at Guanabacoa, just outside Havana, delve more fully into African culture and religion, and their influence on Cuba. 'The Cuban represents a mingling of European and African cultures,' Castro has stated. In fact, the African influence is far less strong in Cuba than in most other West Indian countries. Only 12 per cent of the population define themselves as black; 66 per cent register themselves as white, though many have African blood as well. For all that, a black African influence is real enough, particularly in the island's rich musical traditions: in the percussive rhythms and drumming of *rumba*, a form of singing and dancing; and in the shows and cabarets that were one of the most popular entertainments of pre-Revolutionary Havana and have continued even in the more puritan era since then.

Treasure cities and fields of cane

Santiago de Cuba – the island's second-largest city – has streets shelving steeply to its port area. These are lined with fine old wooden houses and stone palaces (many of them recently restored). There is a small

Inland Cuba's most attractive scenery lies on the edges of the island's mountain ranges or sierras. Here, a hamlet nestles beneath the mountain slopes, a lone royal palm prodding skyward. Cars are virtually unknown in these country districts, and the horse is still the most useful means of getting around.

The marshes of the Zapata Peninsula on the south coast are home to some 40,000 fearsome crocodiles. The peninsula even boasts the world's second-largest crocodile farm, at Guamá. It forms part of the local 'tourist institute'.

central square where young people like to meet at dusk. The people here are famous for a more relaxed approach to life than their counterparts in Havana. Their speech is different, too: more lilting and musical. In the evenings, they meet at one of various *casas de la trova* – uniquely Cuban institutions, where people listen to traditional music (often songs of love and revolution). In late July, Santiago's midsummer carnival, lasting a week or more, climaxes in the celebrations of National Rebellion Day, commemorating Castro's attack on the city's Moncada barracks on July 26, 1953. Santiago also has José Martí's tomb in its Santa Efigenia cemetery; and a huge cotton tree, in whose ample shade the representatives of Spain and the United States signed the peace that ended the war of 1898.

Farther west along the south coast, Trinidad is even more steeped in the past. Wealthy merchants' houses topped with tiled roofs line the cobbled streets of a city centre that seems unchanged since the 17th century. These bear witness to the wealth and treasure that once flowed through its port, when Trinidad was Cuba's richest city. It was founded in 1514, as a base for Spanish exploration of the New World; and it was from here that Hernán Cortés set sail in 1518, on his way to conquer the Aztec empire and Mexico.

In contrast to the cities with their history and colonial architecture, the Cuban countryside can often appear somewhat dull, with little of the naturally baroque luxuriance of other West Indian islands. From the moment Columbus repaid the local Indians for introducing him to tobacco with a few sugar-cane seedlings brought from the Canary Islands, nature in Cuba has had to bow to man. As more and more Spanish settlers arrived, the island's lowland forests were gradually felled to make way for cane. Forests do survive in the mountain areas, notably in the region around Soroa in the west, where ranks of palms and cedars mingle in strangely contrasting patterns. But the plains around them have long since been domesticated.

Here, cane is king. Driving across the plains on long, straight roads, cane fields spread out on all sides. There are a few breaks in the monotony, however – around Cienfuegos, west of Trinidad in the south, for example, where the landscape is covered with orange, grapefruit and lime trees, and the occasional mango orchard. On the north coast, east of Havana, Matanzas province also stands out: in rolling dairy country, which bears a surprising resemblance in places to parts of the English West Country, except that royal palms stud the skyline rather than oaks and apple trees.

The province of Pinar del Río, in the island's far

A headscarf hides the curlers that many Cuban women wear even at work during the day. This girl is one of the island's 12 per cent black minority – though most Cubans have some African blood.

west is different, too. Here, it is tobacco, not cane, that rules – and (making the region exceptional in another sense, too) 80 per cent of the land is still owned privately, rather than by the state. There is an undeniable beauty in the contrast between the bright green of the large tobacco leaves and the rich red of the soil.

Inland Cuba may be lacking in tropical exuberance, but the island possesses over 4000 miles of coastline, much of it extremely beautiful. Beaches at famous resorts such as Varadero (on the north coast, some 90 miles east of Havana) enjoy the additional beauty of sea sheltered by long coral reefs, creating huge, pond-still expanses of dazzling emerald green. Sadly, though, the beaches are often littered.

The nanny state

The Cubans are among the friendliest, best-natured people imaginable. It is not hard to get to know them, since they are also extremely curious. Usually, they approach strangers, and only rarely do they do it out of any kind of self-interest – though a few 'hasslers', particularly in Havana's Parque Central, do propose black-market deals to tourists, hoping to exchange their own pesos for precious US dollars. Or they ask visiting foreigners to buy them goods that are on sale only in the island's special tourist shops.

But there is still room for misunderstanding even with the friendliest, least demanding locals. The peso itself is a source of huge confusion, even though foreigners rarely use it. An almost entirely artificial, official exchange rate means that US$1 buys only 0.76 pesos. Consequently, when Cubans tell foreign friends the cost of various goods on the island, they can seem exorbitantly expensive. On top of that, there is the complicated business of ration cards. These come in two kinds, both of which local people can buy fairly cheaply: the first (known as *libretas*) ensure that everyone is able to get enough food; with the second, people can acquire various basic manufactured goods, essentially clothes, shoes and household items. The situation has been made worse in recent years as Cuba's economic situation has deteriorated. It is now almost impossible to buy even the most basic manufactured goods, except in the 'dollar' tourist shops.

The Cuban welfare state, meanwhile, is as complicated as it is comprehensive. There is no income tax – except on a few peasant smallholders, who have kept the private ownership of their land, and on some craftsmen, who are officially 'free' or self-employed. On the other hand, people living in state-owned accommodation (the majority of the population) do have to pay 10 per cent of what they earn as rent – no matter how large or small their home is. This is remarkably little, though the cost of gas, electricity and telephones to some extent make up for it. The cost of food, of course, is kept low by the *libreta* ration-card system.

Charges are made for medicines, but all other health expenses are borne by the state. In 1987, there was one doctor for every 377 people, though the health system has contracted with Cuba's economic crisis. The picture is similar in the education system. Basics such as books and exercise books are free, and – as in healthcare – the system is growing. More than 23 per cent of Cubans are students, at school, university or in other forms of fulltime education. It is hardly surprising then that the provisional budget for health and education in 1989 ate up almost a quarter of the state's total revenue.

The expenses of the school system are particularly high. At the beginning of every term, each child is given – free – three shirts, three pairs of shorts, a belt and a pair of shoes. Schoolchildren also receive two free snacks every day during term, one in the morning and

Cuba's coat of arms was designed in the 19th century by the poet Miguel Teurba Tolon: the diagonal stripes echo the national flag; the royal palm set against a mountainous background evokes the countryside; and the key represents Cuba's strategic position in the northern Caribbean.

Large families are no problem in Cuba. Free clothes, free schooling and at least two state-run holidays a year at 'pioneer camps' are among the provisions.

A group of Cuban men relax at the end of the day in a casa de la trova *(literally, 'house of the minstrel'), where they can listen to traditional Cuban music and enjoy a* mojito *cocktail or a rum punch. On the wall above them are paintings of well-known local musicians and singers.*

According to the poet Cirilo Villaverde, the slender elegance of the royal palm 'embodies the liberty and independence of the young republic'. It grows everywhere, in towns and cities, along beaches and in the countryside. The new constitution of 1976 raised it to the status of a 'symbol of the republic'.

one in the afternoon – workers are similarly offered two free snacks and a free lunch at work. A child – 'that most precious of goods', as José Martí stated in the 19th century – is thus almost entirely looked after by the state. This, of course, has its advantages, but does not please everyone. Many parents feel that their children are virtually kidnapped by the state. Even during the holidays, children are sent away, at least twice a year, to take part in 15-day 'pioneer camps' in the country.

Since 1982, all Cubans have been allowed to buy their own homes, or to build new ones – before then, the privilege had been confined to a relative few. The new freedom to build is especially popular. The only problem is finding the materials. As so often in Cuba, money is not the difficulty (in any case, credit is virtually free). But land has to be acquired, and there is an almost permanent shortage of cement. Homebuilders have to learn the virtues of patience, or prove to the authorities that they deserve special priority. Often, they pool their skills and what materials they have with friends, and thus manage to construct a new home.

Cars are another problem. Cubans cannot go to a garage and buy a car. Unless they already possess, or manage to acquire, an ancient American Chevrolet or the like, they are entirely dependent on their bosses. Once again, it is not how much money they have that counts, but how well they get on with the powers that be, and whether sufficient revolutionary 'merit' has been earned.

It is a system with obvious flaws, and yet for a long time most Cubans seemed to get by. People had a lively sense of the pleasures of life. Their clothes were usually homemade, but almost always smart. Restaurants were invariably packed on Friday and Saturday nights, with long queues forming outside even the most expensive of

them, such as Havana's Floridita (another of Ernest Hemingway's favourite haunts). The best cabarets and musical shows were equally difficult to get into. But factors such as the demise of the former Soviet Union have changed all this. The Cuban government has great difficulty in feeding its population, let along keeping it provided with comparative luxuries. There is tightly controlled food rationing and a serious problem of malnutrition, leading in recent years to epidemics of illnesses almost certainly related to an inadequate diet.

The pleasures now available to Cubans are more limited: plenty of dancing and, from time to time, a romantic weekend *à deux* in a *posada* (an old lodging house) in the country. For these outings, accommodation is admittedly somewhat limited. Increasingly, the big tourist hotels – often dating from the years before the Revolution – are kept exclusively for foreign visitors with hard currency.

Cuba boasts nearly 5 million head of cattle, most of them dairy cows. This means no shortage of milk and milk products, including some fine cheeses. The provinces of Matanzas, Camagüey and Cienfuegos in the centre of the island are the principal dairy areas. Also important is the Isle of Youth (formerly Isle of Pines), lying off the south-west coast.

Divorce – Cuban-style

Flats are hard to come by, and often tiny – with several generations of one family crammed into a few rooms. As a result, privacy is at a premium, and divorce increasingly common. In the early days of the Revolution, this was considered something of a luxury – a revolutionary conquest – and divorces could be obtained free. Now it costs 100 pesos, and does not necessarily solve the problems. Many divorced couples have to go on living together, because they cannot find alternative accommodation.

Finding any privacy is even more of a problem for courting couples. In the old days, they used to make for the beaches, but bad relations with the United States and the constant fear of invasion have largely put a stop to that – beaches are now patrolled at night. That leaves the *posadas*, where a room can be hired – anonymously – by the hour. Even married couples avail themselves of that privilege.

For ordinary people, economic fluctuations are reflected in the shops: shelves that are full or empty (more often empty than full nowadays), according to world sugar prices. For the government, a cent off the world price of a pound of sugar means some US$40 million less in the state coffers.

In an attempt to reduce its dependence on sugar, Cuba has attempted to diversify its economy. But how to find the necessary amounts of hard currency? The government has launched various schemes designed to bring in dollars: notably the development of tourism – more than 500,000 Western tourists visited the island in 1991. This, in turn, brings further ironies. There, in the big hotels' special tourist shops (off limits for locals) are rows and rows of the very goods that many Cubans most desire: radios, jeans, French perfumes, televisions

Most Cubans live in the towns and cities, though the island's principal wealth is agricultural products. This often leads to a shortage of labour at croptime, so that volunteers such as these are encouraged to leave their offices and factories for a week or two to help out in the country. They may be rewarded with watches, motorcycles, or even a foreign holiday.

Once picked, tobacco leaves are strung up to dry in huge hangars. The lower racks are the ones that have been most recently picked. They are then gradually shifted higher as spaces become available.

Entire fields are covered with enormous awnings of cheese-cloth as the tobacco plants reach maturity. The awnings allow the leaves to ripen evenly, and protect the upper leaves from being scorched by the sun.

In one of the final stages of packing, a factory worker arranges groups of cigars according to the colour of their outer leaves. This means that when the boxes are opened, the cigars inside will present a uniform appearance.

and cassette recorders. These create a permanent focus for dissatisfaction, which in 1980 expressed itself in one of the most telling outbursts of discontent the Castro regime has suffered.

Two years earlier, in 1978, the government had set up a Panama-based company called Cimex, to channel hard currency into Cuba. The situation at the time was dire. For the last two years, world sugar prices had stood at an all-time low: 9 cents a pound – compared with an average price of 30 cents a pound in 1974, and 21 cents in 1975. Despite the fact that the Cubans were selling to the Soviet Union at a slightly higher price than the world average, prices were extremely low, and would continue that way – in July 1990 the world price still stood at only 12 cents per pound.

The government was losing huge amounts of revenue, and to limit its losses decided on desperate remedies. One was to exploit the million or more exiled Cubans who had fled in the early days of the Castro regime and were mostly living in nearby Florida. They decided to lure them back to the island for holidays to visit relatives who had stayed behind, bringing their dollars with them. The idea was probably encouraged by negotiations then under way with the administration of President Jimmy Carter, which aimed at normalising relations between Washington and Havana. Cimex was put in charge of the operation but it had some unforeseen consequences.

The exiled Cubans returned in their thousands, bearing not only dollars, but also gifts of televisions, radios, jeans and other commodities for their relatives. It was enough to turn the heads of all but the regime's most hardened supporters.

To aggravate matters, the economy took yet another turn for the worse. By the end of November 1979, a blue mildew had destroyed 85 per cent of the tobacco crop in less than three months. Then Cuban cane fell victim to a 'rust' blight – with the loss over the next two years of 1.5 million tons of raw sugar. The crisis was growing, and the government had to act to defuse it. In Washington, meanwhile, the Carter administration

Two vegueros, *or tobacco-growers, inspect the drying leaves with all the care and pride of wine-makers examining a choice vintage.*

The earthy smell of tobacco combined with the highly perfumed scent of cedarwood boxes are part of the attraction of cigar smoking. Even the labels are often minor works of art.

With smart straw hat, neck scarf and earrings, this woman is not on the poverty line. Yet, along with many other Cubans, she may well hanker after the consumer delights that her island cannot offer her.

Cubans boast that, 'Sugar is our oil.' The island's 400-year-old sugar industry has been substantially modernised since the Revolution. Today, these mechanical cane-cutters (below) gather in more than half the national crop. They are slowly replacing the macheteros, *or cane-cutters (opposite).*

was insisting that no further progress could be made in negotiations, unless Cubans who wanted to leave the island were given the right to do so freely. Finally, Castro decided to let them go: he invited 'those who wish to leave the island to do so'. In a highly unpleasant shock, both for Castro and for the American authorities with the task of receiving them, an estimated 800,000 Cubans immediately volunteered. It was hardly a vote of confidence in 20 years of Castro-style Communism.

In the end, some 125,000 people (including many criminals released from the island's prisons and patients from its mental asylums) left from the little port of Mariel, west of Havana. The rest were condemned to stay behind – less because of the Cuban government's reluctance to let them go, than because of the limited number of visas issued by the United States and other Western governments.

Stay or leave?

A number of question marks hang over the future of the Castro regime. There is the constant threat of another Mariel, of more recruits joining the ranks of the 800,000 who wanted to leave. Above all, there is the fear that the government will be rejected by the very sector of the population it has done most to woo: the young. The security of free healthcare, education and, until recently, full employment, all rank among the regime's undeniable achievements – especially when Cuba is compared with most of its neighbour in the Caribbean. At the same time, Cubans born since the Revolution tend to take these things for granted. Assured of the basics, many of them long for luxuries: a car, holidays abroad or fashionable clothes.

A civil servant at the Ministry of the Interior remains hopeful. 'It's true', he concedes, 'that the facilities of the West tempt our young people. They are undoubtedly ready to engage in a bit of illegal trafficking in order to acquire a pair of jeans or a cassette recorder, but that doesn't go very far. We only have to announce that Nicaragua needs more teachers, and they're queueing up to volunteer.' He adds: 'There are still between 750,000 and a million Cubans who do not accept our conception of society and who want to leave ... But the countries they want to go to shut the door on them.'

Human rights abuses undoubtedly exist, but the situation is almost certainly less black than it was painted in the early 1980s. In September 1988, the human rights watchdog Amnesty International, for instance, acknowledged a certain improvement in Cuba's human rights record. And in September the following year, the United Nations' Commission for Human Rights rejected a proposed US resolution condemning the Castro regime.

There are different ways of looking at accounts of repression in Cuba. The Jehovah's Witnesses are persecuted (but then they are strongly opposed to the regime). Catholic churches are often almost empty on Sundays – equally, in the words of one priest, a professor at a large Catholic seminary in Havana: 'They were hardly full before the Revolution.' In any case,

there has been some dialogue between Castro and the local leaders of the Catholic church since 1984. At the start of 1989, there was even the possibility of a visit from the Pope.

Critics speak of the activities of the secret police. On the other hand, Cuba never did have the traditions of a Western democracy. Moreover, it considers itself a country at war with a hostile outside world – a view shared by many ordinary Cubans, who readily sign up for organisations such as the Committees for the Defence of the Revolution (CDR). These were originally established, as their name suggests, to defend the Revolution's achievements and to prevent possible attempts to destabilise the regime. Every district has its CDR, and every night it nominates one of its members to patrol the streets and watch out for illicit activities; as a result, the streets and squares of Cuban cities at night are among the safest in the world. The committees also engage in other, unquestionably wholesome activities: organising home helps for hard-pressed families, arranging blood donations, rubbish clearance and so on. Nor do they lack for volunteers. Their membership is estimated at up to 5 million (out of a total Cuban population of over 10 million).

A troop of horsemen riding through the streets of Trinidad on Cuba's south coast give it the air of the Wild West. Despite the present dilapidation of parts of Trinidad, it was once the richest city in the West Indies: much of the gold and treasure of the Spanish Main passed through its port.

One Cuban explained his feelings to a visiting French journalist: 'You experienced exactly the same situation in France. After your revolution, the whole of Europe ganged up on you to try to dam a flow of ideas that terrified them. Today, to try to isolate us, the United States has instituted a blockade – a very efficient one, so that goods, if they arrive, do so only by extremely circuitous means, which makes imports much more expensive for us. But we have no more intention of submitting than you did in 1789. We will not give up our principles; we understand that we have no choice. In effect, it's *"Patria o muerte"* ["Homeland or death"] …'

Profit with honour

There is, of course, one important difference between the French and Cuban revolutions. Twenty-six years after the fall of the Bastille in 1789 came the defeat of Napoleon's France at Waterloo. Over 30 years after Cuba's Revolution, Castro is still in command.

Even so, things are changing. 'When we came to power,' says the Cuban ambassador to UNESCO, Alfredo Guevara (no relation to Che), 'we lacked everything. Most professional people – doctors and engineers – had chosen to emigrate. All our efforts were directed towards technology. Many other things we were obliged to neglect … Today, we are starting to stand back a bit, in order to analyse things better, to focus on the human aspect …'

The last decade or so has seen astonishing changes. First of all, in the early 1980s, there was a tentative loosening of state controls on the economy. Among

Cuba has an overwhelmingly youthful population: more than 40 per cent are under 20 years old. The survival of the Castro regime thus depends on the support of people such as this young girl.

other things, this envisaged companies run, almost along Western lines, by directors, who were responsible for managing their businesses effectively, rather than simply obeying the diktats of revolutionary bureaucrats. 'Profit' was no longer a dirty word. On top of that, Cubans were allowed to set up their own businesses – though the conditions for doing so varied somewhat. In some areas, the privilege was confined to individual craftsmen and artisans, who were not allowed to 'exploit' labour by having underlings working for them. Elsewhere, the budding entrepreneur was allowed to employ up to three or sometimes five workers.

In 1986, however, Castro changed tack. There were

complaints that private farmers, truckers and food-sellers, in particular, were making undue profits at the expense of their fellow citizens and undermining the co-operative achievements of the Revolution. In May 1986, the authorities decided to close the new 'free' crafts' and farmers' markets and a programme of 'rectification' (of previous errors) was imposed instead. Strict controls and state planning were once more the keys to the economy, although earlier reforms which allowed foreigners to invest in Cuba – especially in tourism – remained in place. Foreigners can still set up limited companies, with or without state involvement or part-ownership, as they wish.

Castro is determined to carry through his policy of economic diversification, and in his hunt for the necessary hard currency seems willing to take many risks. Over the years, Cubans have become accustomed to demands for sacrifice, as they export more and more lobsters, cigars, citrus fruit and so on, to bring in dollars. Now it is the turn of tourism, and the call for sacrifice is even more acute. People longing for new homes see more and more new hotels sprouting along the coastline. Queueing patiently outside restaurants on Saturday evenings, they see dollar-bearing tourists jumping the queue.

Many remain proud of their achievements – that no Cuban baby lacks for milk, that their medical care is among the most advanced in the developing world (Cuban doctors had carried out their 37th successful heart-transplant operation by 1987) – but for many, their patience is beginning to wear thin. 'Everything for the Revolution, nothing but the Revolution,' runs the slogan, to which a few disgruntled Cubans reply: 'Everything for tourists, nothing for Cubans.'

Recent events have not been altogether kind to Castro. The collapse of the former Soviet Union, in particular, meant the loss of a lifeline. In the old days, Soviet aid to Havana included more than 13 million tons of oil and petroleum products every year at prices well below the world average. This was far more than Cuba needed, and it was able to sell the excess on world markets at a handsome profit, bringing in some US$500 million each year between 1983 and 1985. Then, as the Soviet bloc crumbled in Eastern Europe in 1989, Cuba experienced its own upheavals; some of its highest-ranking officials were tried and executed for drugs trafficking, corruption and other abuses of power – at one point, it seemed that even Castro's brother and faithful lieutenant, Raúl, might be implicated.

Castro has fought on, none the less, making certain changes, but insisting on stern loyalty to Communist ideals. Constitutional adjustments in 1990 extended democratic accountability in local assemblies and the National Assembly in Havana. Rationing has been tightened during a continuing 'special period' – a kind of economic state of emergency – and the fight against corruption has been stepped up, leading to hundreds of arrests. Ironic talk of 'Castroika' and a gradual breaking up of the Cuban Communist state, along the lines of the break-up of Soviet power, seems only to have stung the *Líder Máximo* ('Supreme Leader') into renewed zeal. For the time being at least, he continues to duck and weave as the world changes around him, but he remains defiant in his pursuit of a Communist Utopia.

Cabaret shows, such as this one at Havana's Tropicana night club, survived the Revolution almost intact. The chief change was in the clientele. Before the Revolution, audiences consisted of American tourists – for whom Havana was a favourite hot spot. After the Revolution, the Americans fled and the clubs were thrown open to all comers.

Isles Under the Sun

The scattering of small islands that arcs around the Caribbean's eastern rim reveals the sheer diversity of the region. Divided into the Windward Islands to the south and the Leeward Islands to the north (because of their relative positions to the prevailing north-east trade winds blowing in from the Atlantic), some islands are little more than sandbanks. Others rise to volcanic cones with boiling lava pools, hot springs and unexplored tropical jungle. Others again are more domesticated: Barbados, lying farther out into the Atlantic, is still sometimes called Bimshire or Little England, in part because of its green and rolling terraces.

The diversity of the islands' peoples and cultures is also remarkable. In their colonial heyday, in the 18th century, when sugar was still king, the British and French fought fiercely over these smaller islands. St Lucia changed hands more than ten times between Britain and France in the 200 years before 1803. After that, it remained British and is now a member of the Commonwealth, but the local people still speak a French patois as well as English. This was the heritage that gave birth to the island's Nobel Prize-winning poet Derek Walcott. Elsewhere, on Barbados, for example, there are 'poor white' communities – the Redshanks – as well as the still-powerful descendants of the island's white 'plantocracy'. The last 2000 or so Carib Indians – who populated the whole of the eastern Caribbean before the arrival of European colonists, and gave the sea its name – live in a reservation in eastern Dominica.

Trinidad (geographically, more a detached part of the neighbouring South American mainland, than part of the island group) presents a rich cultural brew. African, British, French and Spanish influences blend with a large Asian minority (around 40 per cent of the population), descended from indentured labourers brought from India as plantation workers after Britain abolished slavery in its empire in 1834. This was the mixed culture that produced the island's famous pre-Lenten Carnival, its distinctive calypso music and a string of notable writers, including the Naipaul brothers, V.S. and Shiva.

Eel island and Nelson's Dockyard

The islands in the Lesser Antilles' north-east corner include Anguilla, a barren coral strip covering barely 35 square miles. It was discovered by Christopher Columbus in 1493 and probably owes its name to the Spanish *anguilla*, 'eel', because of its long, narrow shape. Its 7000 inhabitants, mostly of African descent,

Rafting on the Rio Grande is one of the great tourist attractions of eastern Jamaica. Bamboo rafts in the river's upper reaches are gently poled downstream through some of the island's most spectacular scenery, with the Blue Mountains rising behind. The rafts were originally used for transporting bananas; it was the filmstar Errol Flynn, with a home nearby, who spotted the tourist potential.

live largely by lobster fishing, tourism (thanks to excellent beaches) and salt extraction from seawater. They may be small in number, but in 1969 Britain was obliged to send troops to the island, to restore order after the Anguillans broke from domination by the larger island of St Kitts to the south. Anguilla is now a self-governing dependency of the United Kingdom.

St Kitts (or St Christopher) was the birthplace of both British and French colonialism in the West Indies, when colonists led on the one side by the Englishman Thomas Warner, and on the other by the Frenchman Pierre Belain d'Esnambuc, settled there in the 1620s. They shared the island (just 68 square miles) amicably at first, until the British ousted the French in 1783. Dominating the north-west coast are the impressive British fortifications of Brimstone Hill – one of various so-called 'Gibraltars of the Caribbean' – started in 1690.

Since 1983, the tiny volcanic island of Nevis, 2 miles south-east of St Kitts, has formed part of the state of St Kitts-Nevis, independent within the Commonwealth. In the old days, Nevis's thermal pools made it a spa resort for health-seekers from neighbouring islands. Nowadays, its beaches are its chief allure for visitors.

Farther east, Antigua and Barbuda form another joint state. In the 18th century, Antigua was one of Britain's most important naval bases in the West Indies. At English Harbour, in a perfectly sheltered inlet at its south-eastern corner, it has the remains of a naval dockyard – where Horatio Nelson was once based. Since the Second World War, Nelson's Dockyard, as it is now known, has been restored, and is among the island's tourist attractions.

Barbuda is very different. A flat, scrubby saucer of an island, it was the personal fiefdom of the Codrington family from Barbados between 1685 and 1860 – they leased it from the British crown for the rent of 'one fat pig' a year. In the early days, they used it for experiments in slave breeding; they also introduced game for hunting, including wild pigs and English fallow deer, which continue to thrive.

South of Antigua and the neighbouring small island

of Montserrat (still a British colony) lies the French island Guadeloupe, and beyond that Dominica, which Columbus discovered on a Sunday – *domingo* in Spanish – in 1493. It is one of the wildest and loveliest of the islands of the Lesser Antilles, rising to the 4747-foot volcanic peak, Morne Diablotin. Three-quarters of the island – including the Carib Indian reservation – is still covered in forest. Because farming was difficult on its mountainous slopes, it never attracted as many settlers as the other islands. Even so, the French and British fought fiercely over it until 1805, when France finally ceded it to Britain; most Dominicans still speak French patois among themselves.

Under the volcano

St Lucia is another island of volcanoes, with Mount Gimie, its highest peak, rising to 3117 feet. Its best-known landmarks are the twin Pitons – Gros Piton and Petit Piton – on the west coast, which rise directly from the sea to more than 2460 feet. Nearby are the remains of a collapsed volcanic crater, once 8 miles in diameter. Vents, or *soufrières*, in its sides still exude sulphurous gases (giving off a distinctive rotten-egg smell), and there are boiling mud and water pools. St Lucia's tropical exuberance has also made it a popular film location, whose credits include *Dr Doolittle* and *Superman Two*.

St Vincent was another Carib stronghold, and a base for the Caribs' expeditions against European settlers on the neighbouring islands. They were more welcoming to black slaves. When a Dutch ship was wrecked off St Vincent in 1675, a group of slaves on board made it safely to dry land, where they mingled with the Caribs to create a new race of 'Black Caribs'. Their descendants still live in parts of the north-west. Only in the early 18th century did the French and British seriously attempt to settle the island, and even then the Caribs and Black Caribs resisted until finally defeated in 1797. During the same period, St Vincent had ping-ponged back and forth between Britain and France, until finally ceded to Britain in 1783.

The tiny isles of Bequia, Mustique, Canouan, Mayreau and Union Island, south of St Vincent, form part of the same state of St Vincent and the Grenadines, which won independence from Britain in 1979. They are exclusive paradises, peopled largely by long-established locals, millionaires and a few visiting yachtsmen. On Bequia (pronounced 'Bek-wee'), sperm whale hunting was the traditional livelihood, though most of the hunters are now old men and catch only a few whales each year. The season lasts from February to May, and they go after their prey in 26-foot cedarwood canoes, armed with harpoons. The 'flensing' (cutting up the whale) is done on a neighbouring islet.

A Portuguese captain first sighted Barbados, and named it *Os Barbados* ('the bearded one'), after the bearded fig trees growing along its beaches. English settlers arrived in 1627, and it remained British until independence in 1966, giving it one of the most stable histories of any Caribbean island. The British influence is unmistakeable: neat homes and gardens; fine planta-

Pink clouds of flamingos feeding in salt marshes are a spectacular sight. With their long necks bent almost double, they use their beaks to rake the mud in their search for food. They are particularly common on the Dutch island of Bonaire.

West Indians have no fear of colour. The bright hues of flowering plants and trees are reflected in the brilliant shades of small homes such as this. Palms and banana trees lend some welcome shade.

tion 'great houses'; uniformed policemen; bewigged and gowned magistrates; a central Trafalgar Square (duly presided over by a statue of Nelson) in the capital Bridgetown, and, above all, perhaps, cricket – one of the most lasting, and unifying legacies left by Britain in its former West Indian colonies.

Despite its small size (166 square miles), Barbados is one of the most prosperous of the West Indian islands, thanks more to good management than to natural resources. The Barbadians – or Bajans – are on the whole hard-working, and have been spared the political turbulence that has afflicted many of the other islands; the House of Assembly, founded in 1630, is one of the oldest parliamentary assemblies in the Western Hemisphere. Sugar is still the main export, though tourism is a bigger money-spinner. Barbados is also one of the most densely populated places on earth, with an average of 1550 people per square mile (compared with 596 per square mile in the United Kingdom).

Grenada, the southernmost main island of the Lesser Antilles, is very different. Its mountainous volcanic scenery contrasts with Barbados's gentle contours, as does its recent history. It hit world headlines in 1979 when a bloodless coup installed a new government with strongly Marxist leanings. Links with Cuba and the former Soviet Union created alarm among Grenada's pro-Western neighbours, and this culminated in 1983 with an invasion by troops from the United States and the other Commonwealth islands. Since then, Grenada has settled down again to a more peaceable existence. Indeed, wandering through the streets of the capital St George's, backed by green hills and facing onto a brilliant blue sea, it is hard to believe that it could ever have been the object of such political intrigue. Of much more immediate interest are the wonderful products sold in its markets (earning it the nickname, 'the Isle of Spices'): nutmegs, mace, cloves, cocoa and bananas.

Trinidad's capital, Port of Spain, leaves you in no doubt about its mixed influences. The spacious, well-clipped lawns and botanical gardens of its central Queen's Park Savannah are unmistakeably British (Britain captured the island from Spain in 1797, though there has also been a strong French influence over the centuries). Elsewhere are Hindu temples, the pointed minarets of mosques, synagogues and churches of every conceivable Christian denomination. Trinidad is remarkable in other ways, too. It is one of the world's oldest oil-producing nations (the first well was drilled in 1867) and the astonishing 114-acre oozing mass of its Pitch Lake is the world's main source of natural asphalt. These have made Trinidad one of the West Indies' richest islands, though falling oil prices in recent years

The façade alone remains of Old King's House, the former residence of Jamaica's British governors, which was gutted by fire in 1925. But it is still grand enough to testify to the importance of what was once Britain's richest sugar island. It stands in Spanish Town, the capital until 1870 when the seat of government was moved to the more thriving city of Kingston in 1872.

Crafts and arts flourish in Jamaica. Markets and roadside stalls sell baskets, carved heads and polished shells to tourists. But Jamaica also boasts potters, sculptors, painters and a formidable dance theatre, with worldwide reputations.

Hibiscus flowers in bright shades of red, pink, purple and orange are among the chief glories of West Indian gardens and roadsides.

have resulted in tumbling living standards. Trinidad was also the birthplace of calypso (which started as songs of punchy political satire and comment) and steel bands, which developed during this century, using oil drums, tins, dustbins and cooking pans as ingeniously improvised musical instruments.

Lying 19 miles north-east of Trinidad is its smaller companion isle Tobago – together they form the Commonwealth state of Trinidad and Tobago. Tobago's chief resources are wonderful beaches, the glories of its Buccoo Reef and a luxuriant plant and birdlife inland. Not surprisingly, tourism is its mainstay.

early 18th century but, since the abolition of slavery in their realms in the mid-19th century, had found them more of a liability than a benefit. They were therefore happy to sell them to the United States, for whom their commanding position on the Anegada Passage – one of the key points of entry from the Atlantic into the Caribbean and its approaches to the Panama Canal – gave them a crucial strategic importance.

The British Virgin Islands (or BVI as they are often known) consist of more than 40 islands and islets, with a population of over 16,000, of whom more than 13,000 live on Tortola. They are, above all, a tourist and

Co-ownership in the Virgin Islands

Lying to the east of Puerto Rico, the Virgin Islands are officially part of the Lesser Antilles, although history as well as the deep waters of the Anegada Passage to their west have kept them slightly apart from their neighbours. Nowadays, they are shared between the Americans and the British.

The USA never conquered its islands. It bought St Thomas, St Croix and St John, plus a scattering of tiny cays and islets, from Denmark in 1917 for the sum of US$25 million. The Danes had settled the islands in the

yachting haven, with wonderful beaches and bays, and strange formations such as The Baths on Virgin Gorda. These are huge boulders which form a kind of natural sea pool with underwater caverns.

Dutch fragments in Caribbean seas

Across the Anegada Passage to the east, the tiny island of St Martin (just over 34 square miles in all) lies immediately to the south of Anguilla and is neatly divided into two: the northern portion belonging to

France, the southern, slightly smaller portion (Sint Maarten) belonging to the Netherlands. The influence of the motherland is noticeable in the sparkling white churches and tidily gabled houses of Sint Maarten's capital, Philipsburg, but few of its inhabitants speak much Dutch any more, finding English more useful.

Sint Eustatius – or Statia – lies 35 miles south of Sint Maarten and is even tinier, at just 8 square miles. It consists essentially of two extinct volcanoes joined by a stretch of lowland. Even by the standards of the Lesser Antilles, its past was complicated, having changed hands no fewer than 22 times between 1632 when the Dutch established their first settlement there and 1816, when they regained it for good at the end of the Napoleonic wars. It was firmly under Dutch rule at the peak of its prosperity in the 18th century. At that point, it was one of the most important trading ports in the Caribbean (known as the Golden Rock), and its harbour played host to some 3500 ships each year.

It played a key role, too, in the American colonies' struggle for independence, and the islanders still celebrate November 16 every year. This commemorates the day in 1776 when, according to tradition, local officials were the first representatives of a foreign power to recognise a ship flying the colours of the new American republic by firing a gun salute. The Statians also kept the revolutionaries provided with essential supplies, but paid dearly for their support. Incensed at the islanders' presumption, the British invaded Statia in 1781 and sacked its warehouses and homes. Craftily, the Royal Navy continued flying the Dutch flag, and thus managed to capture a number of American and other enemy merchant vessels.

Saba to the west – the third of the Dutch West Indies' 'Three S's' – consists of one extinct volcano. The inhabitants of the flattest country in Europe made a colony of the steepest island in the Caribbean, rising sheer from the sea with neither beaches nor a natural harbour. In the old days, the locals (about half of them black, the other half white, descended from Scottish and English, as well as Dutch, settlers) would repel unwelcome outsiders by hurling rocks from the cliffs. To launch their boats, they lowered them by rope down the mountainside, with the crew scrambling after them as best they could.

The Netherlands' 'ABC' islands – from west to east, Aruba, Curaçao and Bonaire – though officially part of the Lesser Antilles, lie well over 500 miles away from the Three S's, off the north-western coast of Venezuela. For the most part flat and scrubby, they have low rainfall and in places are covered with twisted groves of cactuses. Oil-refining is a key industry on Aruba and Curaçao (much of the oil coming from the nearby Venezuelan fields), while Bonaire is a nature paradise whose reefs and nesting birds – among them, herons, pelicans and flamingos – draw large numbers of wildlife tourists. In 1986, Aruba broke away from the rest of the Netherlands Antilles (which form an autonomous region within the Kingdom of the Netherlands), with the aim of achieving full independence in 1996.

Although Dutch influence is unmistakeable, especially in the canals and brightly painted gabled houses of Curaçao's capital, Willemstad, the islands can also claim to be among the most cosmopolitan places on earth. For a start, the native Arawak Indians were less ruthlessly exterminated here than in the rest of the Caribbean, and their blood flows in the veins of much of the population of Aruba and Bonaire. Then there are layers of African, Dutch, Portuguese, French, British, Jewish, Asian and now Turkish (workers were brought in to help man the oil refineries). Symbolic of this mix is the most widely spoken local language, Papiamento. This started off as a dialect spoken by Jewish settlers from Portugal in the 17th century, but since then it has picked up a vocabulary and grammar from just about every tongue used in the Caribbean. It is still largely a spoken language, but local scholars are seeking to turn it into a written one too, with fixed rules of spelling.

Green, yellow and red are the colours of the Rastafarian movement, which has its roots in Jamaica. The figure in the plumed hat is Marcus Garvey, a Jamaican-born black rights' champion of the early 20th century.

A Carib girl from Dominica is among the few survivors of her race left in the West Indies. Dominica's rugged terrain helped the Caribs to hold out there longer than elsewhere. Since 1903, they have formed a kind of state within the state, in a 3700-acre 'reservation' in the north-east.

Coconuts are staples of the St Vincent economy. Oil extracted from the white flesh is used in soaps and cosmetics, and the fibrous husks can be made into matting and baskets.

Scattered Riches in the Bahamas

Seen from the skies, the Bahamas are like a scattering of green jewels fringed with gold against the turquoise setting of the sea. Some 700 islands – of which barely 100 are inhabited – fleck the Atlantic Ocean off the coasts of Florida and Cuba. Their highest point, no more than 207 feet above sea level, is Mount Alvernia on Cat Island in the east. Surrounding these islands is a sprinkling of about 2400 rocky islets, or 'cays', circled by coral reefs and inhabited by a few sea birds. Islands and islets add up to a total surface area of 5380 square miles, a little larger than Jamaica.

Although only the southern islands are technically within the tropics, all enjoy an enviable climate of perpetual summer, tempered by the trade winds during the hottest months, and kept warm in winter by the northern flow of the Gulf Stream, bringing with it rich shoals of migrating fish. Not surprisingly, the Bahamas include some of the world's most famous centres of sport fishing, including the Bimini Islands, lying closest to Florida, where the American writer Ernest Hemingway – himself a keen fisherman – lived and wrote *The Old Man and the Sea*. The prey here are blue and white marlin, swordfish, giant tuna fish, barracudas, dolphins and sharks.

With delicious weather and the convenience of hundreds of marinas, capable of hosting the most imposing and luxurious of ocean-going yachts, the Bahamas have much to offer the wealthy foreigner. They are an easy 20 minutes' flight from Miami, and only 2 1/2 hours from New York. They are not only a holidaymaker's paradise, but also an international tax haven and a business and banking centre.

There is an undeniable, frequently rather indolent charm about the islands, symbolised by the 'lazy trees' or 'lazing trees' – huge mango trees that preside over the centre of many of the older villages. This is where locals traditionally seek the midday shade, and laze away an hour or two with their neighbours. However, the Bahamians take their role as hosts to a booming international tourist trade seriously. Out of an overwhelmingly youthful population – almost half of the Bahamas' 264,000 inhabitants are under 20 years old – two in three work in the tourist industry. Most years, they expect to welcome more than 3 million visitors, mainly from the United States.

There are two chief centres of population and business: New Providence Island, with the capital Nassau; and Grand Bahama, to the north, with the islands' other principal city, Freeport. Freeport, with a huge tourist complex (the largest in the West Indies) and an International Bazaar, is probably the most Americanised. Elsewhere, the small towns and the countryside retain a colonial charm. Unmistakeably Victorian public buildings are painted in delicate shades of pink and white. Larger colonial homes, often built of wood and painted in pastel shades, are surrounded by wide, shady verandahs and set in beautifully kept gardens, with well-trimmed lawns and flower beds brimming with bright hibiscus blossoms. White churches rise at the centre of villages, and often there is even a green, for games of cricket or (revealing the growing American influence) baseball.

Natural wonders include the 'blue holes' found on

A small verandahed home on Dominica nestles within a scene of superabundant tropical profusion. Dominica is one of the wildest, least discovered islands of the Lesser Antilles chain.

Smartly uniformed schoolgirls in the St Lucian capital Castries peer curiously into the local bar. Although St Lucia was British from 1803 until independence in 1979, many residents still speak a French patois – a heritage of earlier French rule.

Beautifully carpentered wooden homes are a feature of Antigua's capital, St John's. The island, with well-sheltered natural harbours and a strategic position in the Caribbean's north-eastern corner, was an important British naval base in the 18th century.

making full use of thousands of secret, well-sheltered anchorages. Later, they were joined by Loyalists escaping America after the Revolution (1775–83) and then by Southerners fleeing the American Civil War of 1861–65. African slaves, meanwhile, provided the bulk of the work force, and today their descendants account for some 80 per cent of the population.

Fun for the Bahamians lies in festivals of calypso, reggae music, or limbo dancing, where the dancers shuffle under low-slung horizontal poles in extraordinary, acrobatic contortions. Then there are the celebrations known as 'jumpings', which are outings, often including a picnic feast, organised by the local church – congregations remain large in the Bahamas. Other highlights include the Junkanoo festivities at Christmas, which involve noisy, costumed parades

Cricket is a passion on Montserrat as on the other British and Commonwealth islands. A common sight during test matches is people walking along with tiny transistor radios glued to their ears.

some islands, but particularly on the largest, Andros. These are large, steep-sided inland tunnels where the ocean rises through the islands' coral foundations. Even more impressive is the Andros Barrier Reef. It is about 125 miles long, second only in size to Australia's Great Barrier Reef.

The truth behind the idyll

As in the rest of the West Indies, the population is mixed. The original Arawak Indian inhabitants were enslaved by the Spanish to work on other islands, though the Spanish themselves never settled in the Bahamas. The first European settlers arrived in the 17th century and were an unlikely mix of English Puritans, escaping religious persecution at home, and pirates, through town and city streets, often accompanied by the ringing of cowbells. These have their roots in African customs, and according to legend are named after a popular rebel slave leader, John Canoe.

For foreign visitors, the islands have idyllic charm. For the locals, inevitably, things are a little different. Thanks to the revenues of tourism and international business, the Commonwealth of the Bahamas – as it officially became after independence from Britain in 1973 – is still one of the richest countries in the Caribbean. But unemployment is high among the young people, many of whom seek seasonal work in the United States. The situation is made worse by immigration – much of it illegal – from neighbouring, less fortunate islands, notably Haiti.

Jamaica – fairest isle that eyes have beheld

For Christopher Columbus, who first reached Jamaica on May 5, 1494, it was quite simply 'the fairest isle that eyes have beheld'. With soaring mountains, broad and fertile river valleys and sparkling beaches, it has never lacked for admirers since then. In the 20th century alone, the filmstar Errol Flynn, the playwright and wit Noël Coward and James Bond's creator, Ian Fleming, chose to make their homes there.

Indeed, Jamaica – its name comes from the Arawak Indian Xaymaca, meaning 'land of wood and water' – is living proof that fame bears little direct relation to size. For a small Caribbean island, it is extraordinarily

renowned. Few foreign visitors will not already be familiar, for example, with at least some Jamaican folk and 'calypso' songs or with the distinctive rhythms of Jamaican reggae and rap. Most will have tasted Jamaican rum. And yet, of course, there is another, very different Jamaica. A tropical paradise it undoubtedly is, but one that reveals another face to its own people; for them, there are occasional violent outbursts, exploding – with tragic irony – against a background of superabundant natural beauty.

Arriving by sea or air, the visitor's first impression is of rugged terrain, red earth and thick, disorderly vegetation, surrounded by waters of the deepest blue. Although the third largest of the Caribbean islands – and the largest of the former British islands – Jamaica is still comparatively small: just under 140 miles long and 50 miles wide. Even so, it encompasses an astonishing range of landscapes. When volcanoes first sprouted from the Caribbean depths, Jamaica emerged with a thick limestone coating, formed by an accumulation of marine sediment – thousands of shells and plankton debris. Then, about 100 million years ago, it sank once more beneath the waves, to re-emerge around 20 million years ago with a still thicker limestone covering. Today, the results of that process can be seen in the rich chaos of the interior highlands.

Mountains cover much of the island, of which the most beautiful are the Blue Mountains, reaching their highest point in Blue Mountain Peak at 7402 feet. Lying at the eastern end of Jamaica, they are covered with thick forests and gouged by the paths of rivers, where thermal springs alternate with tumbling cascades. At

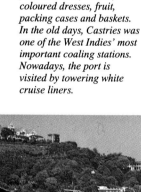

A harbourside scene in St Lucia's capital Castries presents a confusion of coloured dresses, fruit, packing cases and baskets. In the old days, Castries was one of the West Indies' most important coaling stations. Nowadays, the port is visited by towering white cruise liners.

Bananas are big business throughout the Caribbean, although Britain's membership of the European Community has posed a few problems for the former British islands' most important market. These St Lucian workers are processing and packing bananas ready for export.

their feet, the forests give way to fields of sugar cane and plantations of bananas and oranges.

The north coast is particularly beautiful. From the small banana port of Port Antonio in the north-east, with a somewhat dusty air of British colonialism, to the tourist town of Montego Bay in the north-west, the shoreline is studded with a succession of long sandy beaches and narrow rocky creeks. Following the coast road, the sea shimmers in a hundred different shades of blue, turquoise and green under skies of dazzling blue, and all the time the hot, dry smell of vegetation seizes visitors by the throat. Dunn's River Falls, between the towns of Ocho Rios and St Ann's Bay, tumble down a huge natural stairway of rock. Discovery Bay offers

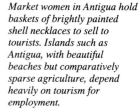

Market women in Antigua hold baskets of brightly painted shell necklaces to sell to tourists. Islands such as Antigua, with beautiful beaches but comparatively sparse agriculture, depend heavily on tourism for employment.

The mongoose was introduced into the West Indies from India to control rats that played havoc with sugar cane plants. It was hugely successful, and at the same time wiped out all the snakes on some islands. Jamaica, for example, no longer has any snakes.

Opposite: *Small-scale fishermen with long dugout canoes and nets trawl the Caribbean waters for fish to sell to tourist hotels and local people.*

finely filtered golden sands and a profusion of palm trees. Other beaches are shaded by stands of coconut palms and rambling bougainvillea.

Montego Bay – or Mo Bay, as the locals call it – is the smartest and most famous of the island's resorts. Between November and April, the height of the tourist season, rows of bronzing bathers line the sands of the Doctor's Cave beach. Luxury hotels and villas – the winter homes of assorted American millionaires, show-business stars, European dukes and press barons – have a Hollywood-style flamboyance. People top up their tans, lying glass in hand beside their swimming pools, and in the cool of the evenings haunt restaurants and each other's parties. Beautifully kept golf courses, well-sprinkled garden lawns, scented tropical flowers, all give a sense of life at its sweetest – artificial, certainly,

but irresistible. Beyond Montego Bay, around the island's north-western corner, lies Negril: traditional haunt of marijuana-hungry hippies, and presenting another face of tourist Jamaica.

The south coast is more hostile. Beautiful beaches are rarer here: the sand is dirtier and offshore currents can be dangerous. It is a dry, more thinly populated region – though not without a certain harsh appeal of its own. In places, roads become little more than rocky tracks, and car tyres kick up blinding clouds of dust. Village children scamper out to stare and shout greetings at the cars of passing strangers. Near the small resort of Treasure Beach, many people have noticeably fair complexions, with startling blue eyes and blonde-tinged curls – the traces, according to locals, of shipwrecked Scottish seamen. Inland, and farther north,

Fishermen and tourists on Tobago share a spectacular beach, backed by forest-clad hills. Fishing and small-scale farming are still important, but tourism is the economic mainstay.

The tiny Grenadines scattered between St Vincent and Grenada are a yachtsman's paradise. Seas are a brilliant turquoise, and there are many idyllic bays where you can drop anchor and row ashore for a picnic on the beach.

Girls carrying bunches of
reeds march through the
streets of Trinidad's capital
Port of Spain during its pre-
Lenten Carnival. This is the
moment when the island's
medley of traditions and
cultures – African, Hindu,
Muslim, Spanish, French and
British – come together with
particular brilliance.

The unmistakable sound of
Trinidad's steel bands
emerged after the Second
World War. To celebrate its
end, Trinidadians made music
with whatever lay most
conveniently to hand, notably
huge oil drums. Much refined
since then, steel band music
has spread to the rest of the
West Indies and to West
Indian communities in North
America and Europe.

caves. To this day, few people dare venture into its baffling maze, and in past centuries it formed a sanctuary for runaway slaves.

The slaves of the island's former Spanish settlers fled here after British forces under Admiral William Penn and General Robert Venables seized Jamaica in 1655. They formed themselves into a well-organised group known as the Maroons – from the Spanish *cimarrón*, 'wild' or 'untamed' – and were joined by escaping slaves from the British plantations. Another group (known as the Windward Maroons) established itself on the inaccessible northern slopes of the Blue Mountains. They were never conquered. Under indomitable male and female leaders, such as the Windward Maroons' Queen Nanny and the Cockpit Maroons' General Cudjoe, they defeated every British force sent against them, until in 1739 the colonial authorities decided that a peace treaty was the only answer. It gave the Maroons their own territory in the Cockpit Country

Dressing up is a key part of Trinidad's Carnival. Over the previous months, people will have formed 'camps', each with its own theme. At the end of the two days of 'jumping up' – the name given to the street festivities – the different camps are judged for the originality and flare of their costumes, floats and music.

is the 'poor white' community of Seaford Town, whose German ancestors were lured to Jamaica with promises of a rich new life, but found themselves allotted a few barren pastures.

Lying between the north and south coasts, in the western sector of the island, is a more lonely region still: the Cockpit Country. This is one of Jamaica's strangest landscapes, consisting of thousands of hummocky limestone hills. They are all covered with dense scrubby woodland and separated by round cockpit-shaped valleys which hide scores of secret and the northern Blue Mountains, their own system of justice and their own leadership – headed by an elected 'colonel' – rights which they still fiercely maintain.

Manor houses and shantytowns

Compared with many other West Indian islands, the history of Jamaica since Columbus's first landfall in 1494 has been relatively straightforward. The first Spanish settlers arrived in 1509, and slavery combined with European diseases rapidly wiped out the island's native Arawak Indians – a gentle race, living off cassava and snails. In 1655, Oliver Cromwell ordered the Penn and Venables expedition, and the Spanish were driven out, most of them escaping to Cuba. The British continued the practice of importing slaves, whose descendants now form the bulk of the population. The island remained a British colony until 1962, when it won independence within the Commonwealth.

British influence (despite a growing Americanisation in recent decades) is still noticeable: in such customs as cricket and afternoon tea, and in the architecture. The town of Mandeville, 2000 feet above sea level in the cool hills of the centre of the island, has a fine Georgian court house and parish church, and English-style cottages scattered in the hills around. Elsewhere across the island, old 'great houses', most of them colonial, still dot the countryside.

Most notable among these is the now restored Portland stone mansion Rose Hall, Jamaica's grandest

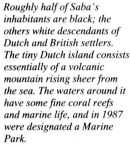

Roughly half of Saba's inhabitants are black; the others white descendants of Dutch and British settlers. The tiny Dutch island consists essentially of a volcanic mountain rising sheer from the sea. The waters around it have some fine coral reefs and marine life, and in 1987 were designated a Marine Park.

great house, near Montego Bay. Built in the 1770s by the wealthy planter John Palmer, it is also the setting for the colourful legend of a Mrs Palmer, better known as the White Witch of Rose Hall. According to the more dramatic versions of the tale, she was brought up in Haiti where she learned the arts of a Voodoo priestess; she got through four husbands, was notorious for her cruelty, enjoyed countless slave lovers and was finally murdered in bed by one of them. Sadly, there seems to be no truth to the legend; all the Mrs Palmers who ever lived at Rose Hall were eminently respectable, though one was partly brought up in Haiti.

Apart from this British influence, it is the diversity of building styles that is most striking. Inevitably, American influence is strong, as more and more old-fashioned hotels are pulled down to make way for high-rise palaces with gold mosaic floors. In downtown Kingston (the capital), modern glass and steel office blocks and condominions stud the skyline, adding to the acute social contrasts in this most divided of cities. The capital actually boasts a suburb called Beverly Hills where the villas of newly rich business people are set in sumptuous grounds, heavily protected by high walls and guard dogs. Sprawling over the hot plains at their feet are the grim slums and shantytowns of West Kingston.

Architecture thus reflects the tensions of a polarised society. For a long time, rich and poor, blacks, whites and those of mixed race, seemed to jog along together comfortably enough. But there was always a streak of violence (expressed in the old days in slave rebellions), and in recent decades this has exploded on occasions, with consequences that Jamaicans still live with.

Dutch influence is unmistakeable in the gabled houses and canals of Willemstad on Curaçao, capital of the Netherlands' West Indian territories. Although most famous for the blue liqueur that bears its name, Curaçao also brews a fine beer, Amstel – the world's only beer made with desalinated seawater. The island's economic mainstay is its oil refineries.

Painted shopfronts and a whitewashed church in Sint Maarten's capital, Philipsburg. The island is shared amicably between the French and Dutch, with no customs or frontier formalities between the two sectors. The French sector is part of the French Republic; the Dutch side belongs to the Netherlands Antilles, fully autonomous in domestic affairs, but part of the Netherlands.

A Bahamian workman peers from beneath a battered straw hat. Here, as in most of the West Indies, the majority of the population is descended from African slaves. Only a few islands, such as the French Iles des Saintes and St Barthélémy, have a white majority.

Waterfront markets are among the delights of Nassau, the Bahamian capital on the island of New Providence. Lying so close to Florida, the Bahamas have a stronger American influence than the other West Indian islands and countries. For all that, Nassau's narrow streets, wooden arcades and houses retain a British colonial charm.

The island's heyday – for the white colonists – was in the late 17th and 18th centuries. The 17th century, in particular, was the age of the Welsh-born buccaneer 'Captain' Henry Morgan, who preyed on Spanish treasure fleets, briefly captured Panama and was rewarded with a knighthood and the lieutenant-governorship of Jamaica. His base was Port Royal which, until it disappeared into the sea off modern Kingston in a catastrophic earthquake on June 7, 1692, was reputed to be the 'wickedest city in the world'. It was also one of the wealthiest, living off captured gold, silver and precious stones, where duelling, womanising, drinking and gambling were the norm.

Later, in the 18th century, the plantations became the chief sources of wealth. Ships plying the triangular trade routes between Britain, Africa and the West Indies arrived in Jamaica with cargoes of slaves and departed with sugar and rum. Planting families made huge fortunes, and often retired to England where they set up as country gentry.

From these high times (for the white minority), the island economy declined gradually, especially after slaves were freed in 1833. Independence from Britain in 1962 brought a brief boom, thanks to tourism and the export of Jamaica's large bauxite reserves. Then, in 1972, the left-wing government of Michael Manley came to power, promising much-needed reforms to create a more 'just and equitable society'. The promises proved hard to fulfil: the economy slipped disastrously; law and order broke down, and the all-important professional classes fled in droves. Inter-party violence during elections in 1980 – which returned a free-market, right-wing government – took a toll of over 500 lives (in a population of 2.6 million). A certain respite followed, though right-wing remedies seemed scarcely more successful than left-wing ones. In 1989, the socialists returned to power, avowing their previous mistakes and promising a more realistic approach.

Out of many one people

Jamaica's motto, 'Out of many one people', is notably apt. Someone of pure African descent is a Jamaican, but so too is a white, whose family may have lived on the island for 200 years or more. Between the two lie a host of nuances, which once had considerable social significance, but are now less important. Nor is it just a question of African and European descent. Jamaica has many other minorities, including Chinese, Indians (whose ancestors came from the sub-continent as indentured labourers after the end of slavery), Jews and Lebanese (including Edward Seaga, Prime Minister through most of the 1980s). Though small in numbers, many of these minorities hold considerable economic leverage, since they control a large proportion of the island's businesses.

Jamaicans are often extremely hospitable. Wealthier families often welcome chance foreign visitors with great openness, plying them with rum punches and chatting with them long into the night – as a brilliant tropical moon rises overhead and a gentle night breeze wafts the scent of flowers onto darkened verandahs.

The rich form a tiny micro-society, revolving around games of tennis and bridge, and dinner and cocktail parties – a stranger thus represents a welcome diversion from the routine. For the rest, social events and attitudes often retain a certain old-fashioned flavour. Jamaica has a strongly matriarchal tradition, and Jamaican women are often formidable businesswomen. At the same time, some girls in wealthy families are still raised to regard marriage as their chief goal in life. They are sent to local boarding schools, closely modelled on English public schools, or to England itself or increasingly the United States. Their brothers, too, will almost certainly be sent abroad to university – rather than the University of the West Indies, based in Kingston.

For the poor, things are clearly different. More and more are fleeing the countryside, and are settling instead in overcrowded slums, particularly around Kingston. With work so difficult to find, crime beckons. Tensions mount, tempers fray and violence easily erupts, often between supporters of the two main political parties, each of which has its own clearly defined working-class fiefdoms in the different slum districts. Alternatively, people can find solace in a commodity first introduced

Fish is cooked direct from the sea. The warm waters of the Gulf Stream bring an abundance of fish to the seas off the Bahamas. Places such as Bimini Island are also famous centres of sport fishing.

to the island by indentured labourers from India: marijuana or 'ganja'. Quick profits make it a tempting crop for both small country farmers and larger-scale business people; but the involvement of international drugs smugglers brings an escalation of violence.

Look to Africa

The 1930s gave birth to one of Jamaica's most unusual – and now famous – movements: Rastafarianism. It had its roots partly in the pioneering black rights' movement, the Universal Negro Improvement Association, founded by the Jamaican-born former printer, Marcus Garvey. Its avowed aim was to unite 'all the Negro peoples of the world into one great body to establish a country and government exclusively their own', and it drew its most substantial support from among millions of black Americans. The whole phenomenon aroused intense suspicion among the white-dominated American authorities, and ended in disaster in 1925 when Garvey was convicted of fraud and imprisoned.

Garvey died in poverty in England in 1940, but his teachings had left a renewed sense of identity among the 'exiled' African peoples of the New World. In his homeland, this combined with a popular 'prophecy': 'Look to Africa where a black king shall be crowned.' Whatever the prophecy's origins, it seemed for many people to be dramatically fulfilled in November 1930 when the young Ras Tafari ('Crown Prince') Makonnen was crowned Emperor of Ethiopia as Haile Selassie. Shortly afterwards, the first Rastafarian groups emerged, drawing most of their support from among the poorest black Jamaicans. For a people soaked in the Bible, Biblical imagery came most readily: Haile Selassie, for them, was a black Messiah, and their hope of redemption lay in a return, on an Old Testament scale, back home to Africa. The Ethiopian Emperor was also the 'Lion of Judah', and 'Rastas' matted their hair into 'dreadlocks', said to resemble a lion's mane.

Today, Rastafarianism has an international following among black youth, few of whom want a literal return to Africa. But in Jamaica and elsewhere, they continue to sing: 'We come from Africa, and to Africa we shall return.' It is an expression of a deep frustration and anger against the West and its values. These feelings also lie at the root of their most successful music, reggae. This was born at the end of the 1950s in the slums of Kingston, where obscure local singers used a strangely staccato beat to tell of their hopes, fears and dreams. They were songs, above all, of outcasts: provocative, often violent, longing for freedom. In the 1960s and 70s, these songs were brought to fine art by performers such as Bob Marley, now proudly claimed as the Third World's first superstar. Marley died young of cancer in 1981, but other talented stars continue to develop reggae and its various offshoots.

In Jamaica, meanwhile, it has remained inescapable. It is blared out across the hills and city streets at night; people, nonchalantly twist their hips to its rhythms as they go about their business. Indeed, for all its anger, reggae is deeply expressive of the vibrancy and even optimism of people who live with need and difficulty, yet somehow manage to survive it all.

Most West Indians are Christians – Catholic or Protestant depending on which colonial power developed the islands. But a multitude of other sects thrive alongside the mainsteam churches, often mingling African religious traditions with Christianity. Among them are the 'revivalists', clad in white for their services, who are common on some of the former British islands.

Gazetteer

Mexico

Although Mexico lost over 40 per cent of its territory to the United States in the mid-19th century, it remains a large country (after Brazil and Argentina, the third largest in Latin America). Its wide range of soil and climate, making possible a varied agriculture, and its extensive mineral resources, have freed Mexico from the economic curse of many Latin American countries – excessive dependence on a single export product. But the country shares with the rest of Latin America an explosive population growth which presses heavily on resources.

The Spanish conquest of Mexico after 1521 created a dual society of Indians, mainly poor peasants and labourers, and an upper class of creoles (whites born in Mexico), whose wealth was based on landowning and silver mining. This society, whose basic institution was the hacienda, or great estate, was drastically modified but not completely destroyed by the Revolution of 1910. Under the powerful political class which emerged out of the chaos of revolution – the so-called 'revolutionary family' – Mexico achieved stability and remarkable economic growth. Over the years, many attempts at radical reform of Mexican society have been made. But the country's social advance, though striking, has failed to reduce the gap between rich and poor.

300 years of Spanish rule
For more than 1500 years before the arrival of the Spanish conquistadores in the early 16th century, Mexico was the home of highly organised Indian 'empires' – those of the Aztecs and the Maya were the most powerful and sophisticated.

The disunity of the Indian people and their military weakness allowed a handful of Spaniards to destroy them in the years after 1521. Diseases brought by the Europeans caused a drastic fall in the population of the Indians, and the conquerors exploited the remaining population, as workers in the silver mines or as agriculture labourers on the large haciendas created out of the destruction of the Indians' communal farming system. The Catholic church as a corporation emerged as the largest single owner in the country. The importance of Mexico to Spain and Europe lay in its silver mines which by the 18th century made it the world's major producer of the metal. Spain's commercial monopoly and the exclusion of creoles from any share in political power created strong resentment among Mexicans, and by the end of the 18th century there was a growing demand for independence.

Independence: 1823
The Spanish imposed a rigid control over their lucrative Mexican colony, and it achieved independent nationhood later than the other major countries of Latin America. A rebellion led by a Catholic priest, Miguel Hidalgo y Costilla, in 1810, was a failure. Liberal guerillas fought on against Spain until, with the support of conservative creoles, they succeeded in establishing the country's independence in 1821. A new republic was officially proclaimed in 1823.

For the first 50 years of independence, Mexico was torn by violent disputes – between liberals and conservatives; between supporters of the church and its opponents. Soldier politicians exploited the chaotic state of its politics for their own ends. The most notorious of these, General Antonio López de Santa Anna, dominated the 1830s and 1840s. His rule survived Mexico's crushing defeat by the United States in the Mexican–American War of 1846–48. The immediate cause of the war was the annexation of Texas by the US government in 1845. (Texas, settled by Americans during the 1820s, had risen against Mexican control and established its independence in 1836.) Mexico lost present-day California, Arizona, New Mexico, Nevada, Utah and Texas, and parts of Wyoming and Colorado.

MEXICO AT A GLANCE
Area 761,600 square miles
Population 88,153,000
Capital Mexico City
Government Federal republic
Currency Peso = 100 centavos
Languages Spanish, Indian languages
Religion Christian (Roman Catholic)
Climate Tropical and temperate according to altitude. Average temperature in Mexico City ranges from 6-19°C (43-66°F) in January to 12-26°C (54-79°F) in May.
Main primary products Maize, sorghum, wheat, barley, rice, cotton, sugar, coffee, beans, fruits, cattle; uranium, copper, iron, coal, lead, zinc, silver, gold, oil and natural gas, aluminium, phosphates
Major industries Oil and natural gas production and refining, agriculture, mining, iron and steel, aluminium refining, vehicles, cement, machinery, textiles, pottery
Main exports Oil and gas, nonferrous ores, machinery and industrial goods, coffee, chemicals, cotton, fruit and vegetables, shrimps
Annual income per head (US$) 1820
Population growth (per thous/yr) 25
Life expectancy (yrs) Male 64
Female 68

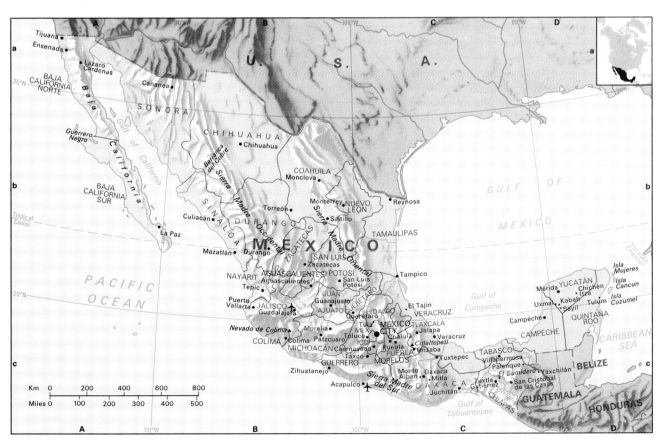

In 1855, Santa Anna was overthrown and a new government was set up under the liberal leader, Benito Juárez. Church property was confiscated and a liberal constitution proclaimed in 1857. In 1858 the conflict between liberals and conservatives erupted into Civil war. Though the conservatives were eventually defeated, France came to their aid and installed Maximilian of Austria as emperor. He was defeated and shot in 1867.

Dictatorial rule and revolution: 1876–1919

In 1876, General Porfirio Díaz seized power. He brought order to the country during his paternalistic dictatorship. In the 1890s more and more Indian land was absorbed by the great estates. The Indians became increasingly subject to the landowners, to whom they were tied by their debts. Strikes among miners and railwaymen were brutally repressed. By 1910 the Mexican economy was dominated by United States and British investment.

The Revolution of 1910, which overthrew Díaz, was sparked off by a liberal landowner, Francisco Madero, a sincere believer in political democracy as the solution to social problems. He was soon in conflict with the peasant revolutionary Emiliano Zapata, who demanded an immediate distribution of land to the peasants. Madero was deposed by the right-wing General Victoriano Huerta and, in 1913, assassinated. A period of bloody conflict followed, first between Huerta and the revolutionary leaders Zapata, Pancho Villa and Venustiano Carranza, and then, when Huerta resigned in 1914, among the revolutionaries themselves. In 1917, a constitution embodying the aims of the Revolution was framed under the victor, Carranza. The constitution provided for the separation of church and state; all mineral resources were declared national property; and land was to be restored to the Indians.

Interwar period: 1920–40

Revolutionary Mexico was dominated by two problems – the creation of a stable government, and the redistribution of the great estates among the Indian peasantry. Under President Calles (1924–29), land reform took second place to political consolidation, which included a violent attack upon the Catholic church – foreign priests were deported, church schools closed and, when the clergy retaliated by going on strike, the churches were taken over by 'citizens' committees'. The liberal president, Lázaro Cárdenas (1934–40), centralised political power in a governing party – which later became

the now dominant Institutional Revolutionary Party (PRI). His reforms included the redistribution of nearly 50 million acres of land.

Modern Mexico

After 1940, Mexico combined a large measure of political stability with economic growth. In recent years – in spite of violent outbursts of student unrest – the ruling party, the PRI, has maintained its dominance. With huge oil and natural gas reserves, the country's industrial growth has been the most rapid in Latin America. Industrial development has drawn many workers to the cities, but even so, it has not been able to absorb all the surplus rural population. One-third of the people still depend on agriculture for their living.

Mexico has long been dependent upon the United States as the major importer of Mexican products and chief foreign investor. Luis Echeverría Alvarez, elected president in 1970, tried to lessen this economic dependence. In 1976, José López Portillo was elected president of Mexico. President López Portillo declared in September 1979 that Mexico's energy needs were secure for 60 years with proven reserves of oil and natural gas.

A decline in oil prices and the worldwide recession drove Mexico into a severe economic crisis in 1982. President López Portillo nationalised Mexico's banks in September 1982, and at the same time imposed restrictions to prevent pesos from being converted into US dollars. He ordered Mexicans owning property in the US to sell it immediately and return the money to Mexico. Some $5000 million in American bank accounts was converted to pesos.

Miguel de la Madrid Hurtado became president in December 1982. De la Madrid adopted austerity economic policies in 1983 that brought some reduction from 1982's annual inflation rate of 100 per cent. Devaluation of the peso brought an influx of American tourists in 1983–84. Tourist dollars and oil exports gave Mexico a foreign exchange surplus, enabling the government to reschedule payments on its foreign debt.

The austerity programme hit the working classes hardest. Their plight was exacerbated by a devastating earthquake in Mexico City and the western part of the country in 1985. In 1988 Miguel de la Madrid was succeeded as president by Carlos Salinas who has tackled Mexico's economic problems with free market policies and debt-relief arrangements with the United States.

Guatemala

The most populous and second largest of the six mainland Central American republics, Guatemala is a country of dramatic beauty. In the north, the jungle around Lake Petén

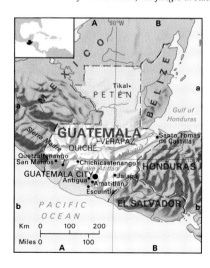

is dotted with the ruins of the civilisation of the Maya Indians. The descendants of the Maya still make up around 55 per cent of Guatemala's inhabitants, and form the largest group of Indian people in Central America.

Early History

Long before Europeans arrived in Guatemala, the area was the centre of the Maya Indian civilisation, which flourished for almost 1000 years. The indigenous people were overcome in 1523 by a Spanish force sent by Hernán Cortés and led by Pedro de Alvarado. The Spanish came in search of gold; though they found little or none, the area was soon supplying them with sugar, cocoa, indigo and other products.

In 1821 Guatemala threw off Spanish rule, first joining Mexico and then a union of the other Central American countries. In 1839, however, it became fully independent when the union was dissolved.

War and dictatorship

José Rafael Carrera, a conservative, took control of the new state and in 1854 was formally appointed president for life – the country's first dictator. Carrera used his army to suppress the liberals. In 1871 his successor, General Cerna, was overthrown, and in 1873 the liberal Justo Rufino Barrios became president. A militant advocate of Central American unity, Barrios tried to impose union on neighbouring El Salvador by force in 1885. But he was killed in battle and Guatemala quickly made peace. However tension between it and other Central American countries continued.

Guatemala has been governed through much of its history by military dictatorships, who have been unable to control the violence between political extremists and who have themselves been responsible for many atrocities. Another major cause of economic and political discontent among Guatemalans is land ownership. In 1952 the government of Jacobo Arbenz Guzmán brought in an agrarian reform law under which parts of landed estates not under cultivation were to be expropriated. But major interests were involved; in the case of one company estate 234,000 acres would have been taken. Arbenz was overthrown and the incoming regime halted the programme.

In 1956 the government provided small holdings to several thousand farmers and minor redistribution of land has continued. It has not been enough to satisfy the demands of landless peasants, cheated of land reform initiated by Arbenz.

Deprivation and political violence continue to prevail in Guatemala. Amnesty International reported in 1982 that General Rios Montt's forces had 'massacred more than 2600 Indians and peasants'. Rios Montt was toppled in a coup in 1983 by General Oscar Mejia Victores, who promised to restore civilian rule by 1985. Despite an increase in political killings by guerillas and death squads in 1984, the government reiterated its promise that elections would be held. In 1985, it duly handed over power to a civilian government. In the presidential election of January 1991 Jorge Serrano of the Movement of Solidarity Action gained some 68 per cent of the vote and formed a government of national unity.

Dominican Republic

This small republic, a mainly agricultural country whose chief export is sugar, occupies the eastern two-thirds of the Caribbean island of Hispaniola. Its people, Spanish in culture, are largely mestizos (of mixed white and black race). The west of the island is occupied by the more densely populated state of Haiti – until the beginning of the 19th century, a French colony known as Saint Domingue.

Columbus discovered Hispaniola in 1492 and claimed it for Spain. Santo Domingo became the first major European settlement in the Western Hemisphere. The French gained control of the western third of Hispaniola under the Treaty of Ryswick in 1697. In 1791, the slaves in French Saint Domingue rose against the planters, and in 1801 their black leader, Toussaint L'Ouverture, invaded the Spanish part of the island.

The invaders were later driven out, but the republic which emerged suffered constant revolts, changes of rule, and attacks by Haiti during the 19th century. Its rulers sought protection first by re-entering the Spanish Empire (1861–65), a move which was abandoned after opposition from many Dominicans, and then by proposing annexation by the United States, an

offer which the USA declined. In 1904 several powers threatened to intervene to collect their debts. From 1905 to 1941, the USA controlled the finances of the bankrupt republic, and US troops were stationed there from 1916 to 1924.

The republic experienced harsh oppression under Rafael Trujillo Molina from 1930 until his assassination in 1961. In 1962, a leftist government was voted in, but it was overthrown by a junta. In 1965 US troops supported the junta to allow the election of a moderate regime, which stayed in power through the 1970 and 1974 elections. With tacit US approval, Antonio Guzmán won the 1978 elections.

In 1979 the island was battered by Hurricanes David and Frederic, leaving 200,000 homeless and the nation and the economy in chaos. By 1982 the Dominican Republic was 'financially bankrupt' according to its newly elected president, Salvador Jorge Blanco, who implemented a programme of increased taxes and reduced government spending. In April 1984 widespread rioting broke out when the government announced price increases on food and imports to raise money for foreign debts. But the economy is still fragile: general strikes in 1990 and 1991 in protest at low pay, food shortages and the government's economic policies paralysed the country.

DOMINICAN REPUBLIC AT A GLANCE

Area 18,703 square miles
Population 7,471,000
Capital Santo Domingo
Government Parliamentary republic
Currency Peso = 100 centavos
Language Spanish
Religion Christian (95% Roman Catholic)
Climate Tropical; cooler in mountains. Average temperature in Santo Domingo ranges from 19-29°C (66-84°F) in January to 23-31°C (73-88°F) in August
Main primary products Sugar, coffee, cocoa, tobacco, rice, maize; bauxite, gold, silver, platinum, nickel, salt
Major industries Agriculture, tourism, textiles, cement, food processing (sugar, rum, molasses), tobacco products, mining and metal refining, petroleum products
Main exports Sugar, gold, silver, nickel, coffee, cocoa, bauxite, tobacco
Annual income per head (US$) 680
Population growth (per thous/yr) 27
Life expectancy (yrs) Male 60 **Female** 64

Haiti

Inspired by the liberal ideas of the French Revolution, the slaves of Haiti – then the French colony of Saint Domingue – rose against their French masters in the 1790s to form the world's first black republic. At one time Haiti dominated the whole of the island of Hispaniola, but today it occupies only the western third; the rest forms the Dominican Republic. Haiti is the only Latin American republic with French as an official language, though most of its people speak Creole, a local dialect. It is the poorest state in the Western Hemisphere.

First New World settlement
The island on which Haiti lies was discovered by Columbus in 1492. He called it Isla Española, but this name was soon corrupted to Hispaniola. There the Spanish established their first major settlement in the New World.

Gradually they colonised the eastern side of Hipaniola – which they called Santo Domingo. In the early 17th century both the British and the French tried to set up their own settlements in the western part. The French were successful and, by the Treaty of Ryswick in 1697, Spain recognised French sovereignty over Saint Domingue – the area corresponding to the Haiti of today.

French settlers imported vast numbers of African slaves to work the sugar plantations, and the colony became the richest sugar-producing area in the world.

Black rebellion
Influenced by the French Revolution, Haiti's blacks rose against the French settlers in the north in 1791. At the same time, the colony's mulatto (mixed-race) inhabitants resented the white minority's monopoly on political power. News of the black rebellion was at first welcomed by the revolutionary French government, as many of the settlers were royalists, but a wholesale massacre of the white population of the north alienated much French sympathy.

The black leader was Toussaint L'Ouverture, a self-educated freed slave. He joined the French to fight the British, who attempted to invade the island in 1793. In 1801 he proclaimed himself governor-general for life – of what was still, theoretically, a French colony – and invaded Spanish Santo Domingo.

In reply, Napoleon sent an expedition to recapture the colony and restore slavery. L'Ouverture was captured and died in prison in France. But the revolt continued. In 1803 the French were driven out and the new black leader, Jean-Jacques Dessalines, proclaimed the independence of Haiti, taking the title of Emperor Jacques I. He ruled as a despot until his assassination in 1806.

Division, reunification and division
Haiti was now divided into two states – a moderate mulatto regime under Alexandre Pétion in the south, and a black regime under Henri Christophe in the north. After Christophe's

HAITI AT A GLANCE
Area 10,714 square miles
Population 6,745,000
Capital Port-au-Prince
Government Military-dominated republic
Currency Gourde = 100 centimes
Languages French, Creole
Religion Christian (84% Roman Catholic, 14% Protestant); most also follow Voodoo
Climate Tropical; average temperature in Port-au-Prince ranges from 25°C (77°F) in January to 29°C (84°F) in July
Main primary products Bananas, cassava, maize, rice, sorghum, coffee, sugar cane, sisal, timber; bauxite, copper (unexploited)
Major industries Agriculture, mining, textiles, food processing, cement, assembly of imported parts, forestry, tourism
Main exports Coffee, light industrial products, sugar, sisal, bauxite, essential oils
Annual income per head (US$) 352
Population growth (per thous/yr) 19
Life expectancy (yrs) Male 52 **Female** 55

suicide in 1820, the Haitian states were reunited under Jean-Pierre Boyer, who annexed Santo Domingo in 1822.

When Boyer was driven from power in 1843, the former Santo Domingo – now the Dominican Republic – revolted and broke free. Haiti was torn by dissent and anarchy. A line of black 'emperors' – the last was overthrown in 1859 – attempted to seize power and reunify the island.

For the rest of the 19th century blacks and mulattos fought for power in Haiti. The blacks were deeply influenced by their African traditions, including adherence to the Voodoo religion. (Voodoo is rooted in West African religious beliefs, though mixed with some Christian elements.) The middle-class mulattos clung to traditions left behind by the French. A succession of presidents from these two rival groups brought the country into confusion, and it was burdened with ever-increasing foreign debts.

Dictatorship

In 1905 the United States took control of Haiti's customs receipts and in 1915 sent troops to occupy the republic. They withdrew in 1934. Haiti then fell under the rule of dictators. The most infamous Dr François Duvalier – 'Papa Doc' – was 'elected' president in 1957; in 1964 he became president for

life. The army brought him to power, but he soon turned against his military supporters. Increasing discontent with his regime led him to set up a police state, which used Voodoo and a private army, the tontons macoutes, as the basis of its power. Many of his opponents were murdered. On Duvalier's death in 1971, his 19-year-old son, Jean-Claude, assumed power.

'Baby Doc', like his father, became president for life and his rule continued in the family tradition. Political opponents were given long jail terms. In 1980 about 30,000 Haitians fled to the United States and were given political asylum. The island's tourist industry was badly hit in the 1980s when US health authorities named Haitians as one of the high-risk groups affected by the disease AIDS.

Political Instability

Discontent grew throughout the early 1980s culminating in the riots which precipitated Baby Doc's flight to France in February 1986.

The removal of the Duvaliers left Haiti hungry for change but popular hopes were disappointed by a series of coups, short-term presidents – including the radical priest Father Jean-Bertrand Aristide, forced into exile after seven months in office in 1991 – and continued repression.

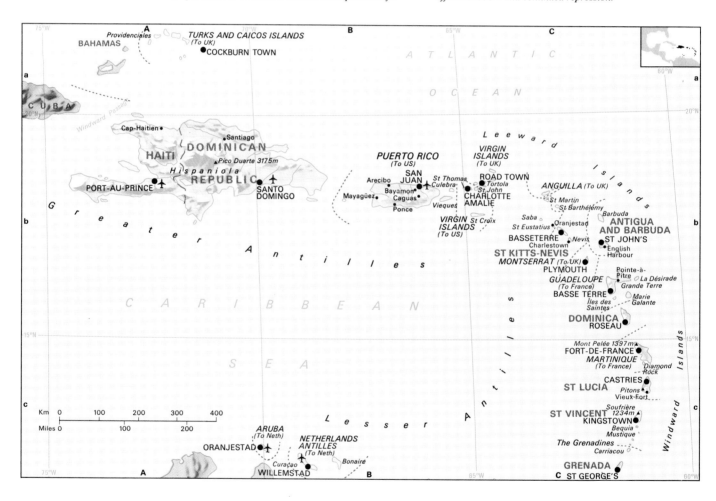

Cuba

Christopher Columbus discovered Cuba, the largest island in the Caribbean, on his first voyage to the New World in 1492. The island came under Spanish rule in the early 16th century and remained part of the Spanish empire until 1898.

Modern Cuba was created by the struggle to achieve independence from Spain, and then to preserve independence from economic and political domination by the United States. The revolution led by Fidel Castro in 1959 not only transformed Cuban society; it also made Cuba an ally of the

former Soviet Union, and the threat that this alliance posed to the United States brought the world to the brink of war in October 1962.

Colonial rule: 1500–1800

After Cuba's discovery by Columbus it became a Spanish base, first for exploration of the rest of the Americas, and then for military expeditions against anti-Spanish rebels on the mainland. During the 17th and 18th centuries Havana was the last port visited by Spanish ships carrying treasure back to Spain. As a result it was often attacked by British and French *buccaneers. In 1762 Havana was captured by the British, who were at war with Spain, but their occupation only lasted a year.*

Cuba started to prosper in the late 18th century with the cultivation of sugar cane in large plantations, which were worked by black slaves imported from Africa. Direct descendants of these slaves and mestizos *– people of mixed black and European blood – form about 25 per cent of the island's present-day population. Because of its prosperity, Cuba soon became known as the 'Pearl of the Antilles' (West Indies).*

Independence: 1901

At the beginning of the 19th century, Spain's empire in the Americas began to break up, as the peoples of such countries as Mexico and Uruguay fought for and won their independence. Cuba achieved independence late, because its wealthy slave owners, though disliking Spanish rule, needed the protection of Spanish forces against a possible slave revolt. They were haunted by the example of neighbouring Haiti, where slaves had overthrown their masters to found a black republic.

Cubans who wanted freedom from Spain at first looked for help from the United States. When this did not arrive they rose on their own against Spain in 1868 and 1895. In 1898 the United States declared war on Spain and sent an expeditionary force to Cuba. The Cubans declared themselves independent in 1898 and adopted a republican constitution in 1901. Tomás Estrada Palma became president in 1902.

Domination by USA

From its beginnings the Cuba republic was bedevilled by the problems of creating a stable government and of escaping the domination of the United States. An article of the Cuban constitution, known as the Platt Amendment, gave the United States the right to intervene in Cuban affairs. American businessmen invested heavily in the sugar industry, and this had the effect of tying Cuba to the American economy. Many Cubans resented this, raising the cry of 'Yankee imperialism'. Soon the country's politics became corrupt and chaotic. Democratic government was discredited. These conditions favoured the rise of military 'strong men' such as Gerardo Machado, who ruled as a dictator from 1925 to 1931.

Radicalism and Castro's rise

Radical, left-wing politics in Cuba date from the revolution of 1933 which overthrew Machado. After a short period of revolutionary rule, radicalism was halted by Fulgencio Batista's rise to power. He controlled politics for over 25 years and served as Cuba's president twice from 1940–44 and 1952–59.

A socialist student leader named Fidel Castro, deeply influenced by the radicals of the 1930s, denounced Batista as a tyrant. In December 1955 he and a group of supporters, including the Argentinian Ernesto (Che) Guevara, returned to Cuba from exile in Mexico. There they went into hiding in the Sierra Maestra mountains from where they launched an uprising. The rebellion spread. Although an attempt in 1957 by the 'Student Revolutionary Directorate' to take over the presidential palace and a General Strike in 1958 both failed, Castro's guerillas were aided by anti-Batista movements in the cities.

Castro rejected formal alliances with other opposition parties, relying for popular support on his own programme of social reform, the nationalisation of the sugar estates and a return to democratic government. The army deserted Batista, who fled the country, and in January 1959 Castro entered Havana in triumph.

After a brief period of informal co-operation with the democratic parties, Castro took over complete control of government in February 1959, and silenced opposition in the press and the trade unions. Many of his early sympathisers went into exile, feeling that Castro had betrayed them by becoming another dictator.

The beginnings of what was to become a socialist economy

were made with the Agrarian Reform Law of May 1959. The 'democratic' phrase of the Cuban Revolution finally ended with Castro's declaration of December 2, 1961: 'I am a Marxist-Leninist and shall be until I die.'

Breach with the United States

Castro was determined to end Cuban reliance on the United States. Most US-owned property was nationalised, without compensation, and in reprisal the USA broke off diplomatic relations with Cuba. It also halted purchase of Cuban sugar.

But these policies left Castro dependent on the former USSR, which took increasing quantities of Cuban sugar in return for Soviet oil and industrial equipment. The signing of a trade agreement with the Soviet Union in 1960 led to a boycott of Cuban goods by the USA and by many of its allies in Central and South America.

Bay of Pigs invasion: 1961

President Kennedy backed an invasion of Cuba by exiles in April 1961. But a landing at Playa Girón – the 'Bay of Pigs' – was a fiasco. The invaders were quickly overwhelmed and many were captured. Castro's position in Cuba was strengthened and he became the hero of the Left throughout South America. But he was now further committed to the USSR for support.

Missile crisis: 1962

The United States' discovery that the USSR was setting up missile bases in Cuba raised the spectre of nuclear war. The crisis was eventually settled by a dramatic confrontation between President Kennedy and the Soviet leader Nikita Khrushchev without reference to Castro, embittering Castro's relations with the Soviet Union.

Cuba extended its revolutionary efforts to Africa, training activists to fight in the Somalia–Ethiopia struggle, the Angolan war and the Angola–Zaire conflict. This hampered the resumption of trade relations with the United States. The economic crisis, precipitated by poor sugar and tobacco crops, led Castro to tighten his grip by taking control of key ministries. Since his 1959 takeover, nearly one-tenth of the population has taken refuge in the United States. In 1980, to help relieve economic pressure, Castro allowed more than 100,000 people, including released criminals, to go to the US.

The economy was further battered in 1982 when world sugar prices dropped to a record low. The US cut off the main source of American currency when it barred tourist and business travel to Cuba, demanding that Cuba stop supplying arms to Nicaragua and to guerillas in El Salvador. Relations between the two states worsened after US troops landed on the little island of Grenada in 1983 and found a Cuban 'presence'.

Cuba today

When Communism collapsed in the former Soviet Union and Eastern Europe, Cuba lost massive economic support from those countries. But Castro remained defiant, defending Communism in Cuba. The United States tried to force political change by increasing economic pressure, but despite shortages and rationing, Castro remains in power.

CUBA AT A GLANCE

Area 44,218 square miles
Population 10,808,000
Capital Havana
Government One-party Communist republic
Currency Peso = 100 centavos
Languages Spanish
Religion Christian (predominantly Roman Catholic)
Climate Tropical; average temperature in Havana ranges from 18-26°C (64-79°F) in January to 24-32°C (75-90°F) in July
Main primary products Sugar cane, rice, sweet potatoes, cassava, maize, oranges, tobacco, coffee, livestock, fish; nickel, copper, cobalt, chrome
Major industries Agriculture, mining, food processing, tobacco products, metal refining, chemicals, cement, fertilisers, textiles, fishing
Main exports Sugar, nickel, copper, fish, fruit and vegetables, tobacco, coffee, chemicals
Annual income per head (US$) 2696
Population growth (per thous/yr) 11
Life expectancy (yrs) Male 71
Female 75

Barbados

*The most densely populated island in the West Indies,
Barbados has an economy based on tourism and the export of
sugar. Sugar plantations cover much of the island, and for
centuries their owners had a monopoly of political power.*

*The island was uninhabited when it was claimed for Britain
by Captain John Powell in 1625, though there was evidence
that it had been previously inhabited by Arawak Indians.
The first settlers arrived there in 1627, later importing slaves
from Africa to work their plantations. These slaves were finally
freed in 1834, when slavery was abolished throughout the
British Empire. Today, 80 per cent of the islanders are of
African origin.*

*The plantation owners' political power was broken in 1937
by a black lawyer, Sir Grantley Adams who took up the cause
of the voteless descendants of the former slaves. Universal
suffrage was not won until 1951. In 1966 the island became an
independent state within the British Commonwealth, after the
break-up of the Federation of the West Indies.*

*The country has been politically stable. The first party to
take power was Adams' Barbados Labour Party (1954–61).
It was defeated by the Democratic Labour Party (1961–76),
before returning to government again under J.M.G. (Tom)
Adams, son of Sir Grantley. Tom Adams died unexpectedly*

*in 1985. The Democratic Labour Party returned to power in
1986, and was re-elected five years later.*

Bahamas

*Some 700 islands off the coast of Florida – only about 100 of
which are inhabited – make up the Bahamas, the first land
sighted by Christopher Columbus when he reached the New
World in 1492. Settlement did not take place there until the
17th century, when the Bahamas were reached by British
colonisers from Bermuda. Pirates used the islands as a base to
attack the Spanish, but they were expelled after 1717. Internal
self-government was granted by Britain in 1964, and
independence followed in 1973. In July 1977, the first national
election since independence, the Progressive Liberal Party*

*(PLP), led by Lynden O. Pindling, won a landslide victory.
Pindling and the PLP have remained in power ever since.*

*Today tourism is the main industry; more than 2 million
Americans visit each year and create 75 per cent of the
national income. Gambling was legalised in the Freeport area
in 1955, and many casinos and hotels were built to cater for
tourists. For many years, the Bahamas was also a popular tax-
haven. But in 1976 taxes were imposed on corporations that
were less than 60 per cent Bahamian-owned, and many foreign
companies moved their headquarters elsewhere.*

*Since the 1970s an influx of thousands of illegal immigrants
from Haiti has strained the nation's economy.*

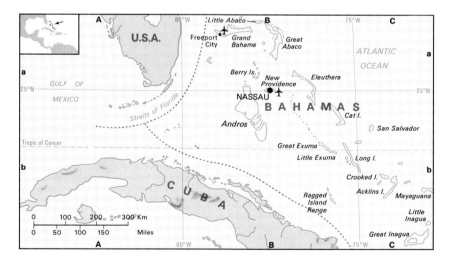

Trinidad and Tobago

Asphalt (from the Pitch lake on Trinidad) and oil form the basis of Trinidad and Tobago's wealth today – although, like the rest of Britain's former Caribbean possessions, the islands' economy was originally built on the sugar produced on its vast plantations.

Columbus discovered the two islands in 1498. The Spanish established cocoa and sugar plantations, worked largely by slave labour imported from Africa. In 1797, Trinidad was captured by a British expedition, and it became a crown colony in 1802.

Britain freed Trinidad's slaves in 1834 and joined the administration of the nearby island of Tobago with Trinidad in 1898. Under the leadership of Dr Eric Williams, the islands became independent in 1962 and a republic within the British Commonwealth in 1976. With the discovery of off-shore oil-fields in the 1970s Trinidad and Tobago enjoyed new wealth as an oil-exporting nation. Oil products made up about 85 per cent of the country's exports, but falling oil prices have dented the republic's prosperity in recent years.

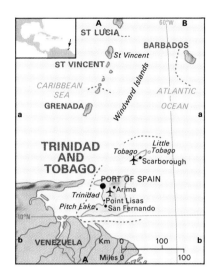

Jamaica

In the 17th century Jamaica became a haven for buccaneers, and was the original home of rum, a by-product of its sugar industry. There are two Jamaicas today: the tropical tourist paradise, and the country of shantytowns. Jamaica was one of the world's largest producers of bauxite, an aluminium ore, until the 1970s. Profits declined, however, and by the 1990s a growing economic crisis had left the island with one of the biggest foreign debts per head of population in the world.

Pirate base
When Columbus discovered Jamaica in 1494 the island was inhabited by Arawak Indians. Spaniards set up sugar cane plantations and used the Arawaks as labour; but the Indians were soon worked to death and black slaves had to be imported from Africa.

British forces occupied Jamaica in 1665, and it became a British possession in 1670. Pirates used it as a base for raids on treasure ships and settlements on the Spanish Main – the north-east coast of South America. Britain officially opposed the raids, but did little to stop them. One buccaneer, Sir Henry Morgan, even became lieutenant-governor of Jamaica.

Slaves and sugar
The island reached its greatest prosperity in the mid-18th century, when it was the biggest slave-market in the Western Hemisphere. Churchmen and liberal politicians in Britain pressed for the abolition of slavery, which eventually came – throughout the British Empire – in 1834. Many planters went bankrupt for lack of labour. Jamaica's economy was also hit when Britain, in the 1850s, stopped allowing colonial sugar to be imported at a low rate of duty. The blacks suffered severely in the economic depression that followed.

In 1866 Jamaica became a crown colony, after which a series of able governors introduced reforms. Dependence on sugar was lessened by the cultivation of bananas.

Self-government to independence
The country was badly affected in the 1930s by the world depression, and by an outbreak of banana blight. Many people emigrated: after the Second World War, the bulk of Jamaica's emigrants settled in Britain. Jamaica was granted internal self-government in 1953 with Norman Manley as chief minister. After a brief attempt to federate with other British Caribbean possessions, it achieved full independence in 1962 with a labour leader, Sir Alexander Bustamante (a first cousin of Manley's), as its prime minister. He was succeeded by another

cousin Hugh Shearer in 1967: in 1972 Shearer was replaced by Norman Manley's son, Michael.

Manley's government acquired controlling interests in the island's sugar industry in 1974 and its bauxite industry in 1975. It began a land reform programme and between 1973 and 1975 land was allocated to 11,000 small farmers and farm co-operatives. A Crash Work Programme hired thousands of unemployed people to clean the streets and generally improve the island's appearance. A minimum wage for a 40-hour week was established in 1975.

In spite of claims by the opposition that he was turning Jamaica into 'another Cuba', Manley won a big majority at the 1976 election. But the economy declined in the late 1970s and the United States and some other nations reduced their economic aid to Manley's government because of its leftist leanings. In a bitter 1980 election campaign more than 500 people were killed and the Jamaica Labour Party, under Edward Seaga, won 51 of the 60 seats in parliament.

One of Seaga's first moves was to expel the Cuban ambassador. He promised to restore Jamaica's economy by revitalising tourism and by turning from socialism to private enterprise. In December 1983 his party won all 60 seats in a general election, after the opposition refused to contest it.

A new order
In the end, Seaga's policies failed to reform the country on the scale that he had proposed. In the run-up to a fresh round of elections in 1989, Michael Manley's People's National Party was remarkably frank in avowing its mistakes during the 1970s and promised a more realistic approach if re-elected. They were rewarded with victory and duly set about deregulating the economy and establishing closer ties with the IMF. In 1992, Manley had to stand down due to ill-health and was succeeded by his colleague P.J. Patterson.

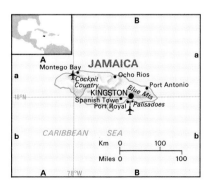

Picture Credits

p.9 Hopker-Image Bank; p.10 Boutin-Vloo; p.11 top Salmer-Cedri; bottom Jipégé-Fotogram; p.12 left S. Held; right Lochon-Gamma; p.13 Setbourn-Sipa Press; p.14 Fuisco-Magnum; p.15 top Höpker-Magnum; bottom Höpker-Magnum; p.16 top Darr-Gamma; bottom Verdon-Fotogram; p.17 Lozouet-Image Bank; p.18 S. Held; p.19 J.-P. Bégon; p.20 C. Lénars; p.21 top Höpker-Magnum; bottom J. Bottin; p.22 Hinous-Top; p.23 Sioen-Cedri; p.24 S. Held; p.25 Courau-Explorer; p.26 Bernheim-Rapho; p.27 J. Bottin; p.28 Sioen-Cedri; p.29 Gerster-Rapho; p.30 E. Guillou; p.31 top E. Guillou; bottom Obremski-Image Bank; p.32 S. Held; p.33 Barbier-Diaf; p.34 S. Held; p.35 S. Held; p.36 S. Held; p.37 top S. Chirol; bottom S. Held; p.38 Bellenand-Pix; p.39 left Barbier-Diaf; right Duchêne-Diaf; p.40 Viesti-Ana; p.41 left J. Bottin; right J. Bottin; p.42 S. Held; p.43 Glinn-Magnum; p.44 Martin-Guillou-Explorer; p.45 Hinous-Top; p.46 top Van der Hilst-Gamma; bottom J. Bottin; p.47 Pix; p.48 left Dumas-Fotogram; right Dumas-Fotogram; p.49 Duchêne-Diaf; p.50 Duchêne-Diaf; p.51 Gordon-Image Bank; p.52 Muller-Cedri; p.53 Sioen-Cedri; p.54 J. Bottin; p.55 top S. Chirol; bottom Courau-Explorer; p.56 Courau-Explorer; p.57 left Gscheidle-Image Bank; right J. Bottin; p.58 Riboud-Magnum; p.59 J. Bottin; p.60 S. Held; p.61 Moser-A. Hutchison Lby; p.62 Mangia-Vloo; p.63 top Marthelot-Scope; bottom S. Marmounier; p.64 left Jahan-Vloo; right E. Guillou; p.65 Bégon-Top; p.66 Muller-Cedri; p.67 left Van der Hilst-Gamma; right J. Bottin; p.68 Duchier-Explorer; p.70 Darr-Gamma; p.71 Darr-Gamma; p.72 J. Bottin; p.73 Arakawa-Image Bank; p.74 S. Held; p.75 A. Gaël; p.76 Roiter-Image Bank; p.77 Peress-Magnum; p.78 top Peress-Magnum; bottom Courau-Explorer; p.79 Peress-Magnum; p.80 Peress-Magnum; p.81 Marthelot-Scope; p.82 top S. Held; bottom Viesti-Ana; p.83 Reffet-Diaf; p.84 P. Frilet; p.85 left C. Lénars; right Wheeler-Rapho; p. 86 left P. Frilet; right Wheater-Image Bank; p. 87 N. Daguet; p.88 Turpault-Ana; p.89 top A. Gaël; bottom Rocha-Fotogram; p.90 Tringaud-Rapho; p.91 left Boizot-Explorer; right Reininger-Cosmos; p.92; Reffet-Diaf; p.93 Marmounier-Cedri; p.94 top J. Bottin; bottom Ducange-Top; p.95 Ducange-Top; p.96 Moisnard-Explorer; p.97 left Dannic-Diaf; right Kérébel-Diaf; p.98 L. de Selva; p.99 D. Lérault; p.100 top D. Lérault; bottom Ducange-Top; p.101 Sioen-Cedri; p.102 Quéméré-Cedri; p.103 left L. de Selva; right D. Lérault; p.104 top S. Marmounier; bottom Rives-Cedri; p.105 Régent-Diaf; p.106 Gaumy-Magnum; p.107 L. Doucet; p.108 Duplessis-Cedri; p.109 top D. Lérault; bottom L. de Selva; p.110 top D. Lérault; bottom Gaumy-Magnum; p.111 Gaumy-Magnum; p.112 Ducange-Top; p.113 Charenton-Pix; p.114 Hussenot-Top; p.115 Rogers-Cosmos; p.116 Koch-Rapho; p.117 top Moisnard-Explorer; bottom G. de Laubier; p.118 Dubois-Explorer; p.119 H. and F. de Faria Castro; p.120 Bachoffner-Diaf; p.121 G. de Laubier; p.122 top Moisnard-Explorer;

bottom Hussenot-Top; p.123 Sioen-Cedri; p.124 Rogers-Cosmos; p.125 left Rogers-Cosmos; right G. de Laubier; p.126 Detrez-Pix; p.127 Regnault-Explorer; p.128 Gallo-Rapho; p.129 Erwitt-Magnum; p.130 Montes-Gamma; p.130/1 Vogel-Rapho; p.131 Downing-Cosmos; p.132 Watriss-Cosmos; p.133; left Gorgoni-Cosmos; right Abbas-Gamma; p.134 left Gorgoni-Cosmos; right Watriss-Cosmos; p.135 Watriss-Cosmos; p.136 McCullin-Magnum; p.137 Gérard-Hoa-Qui; p.138 left Gorgoni-Cosmos; right Salgado-Magnum; p.139 Gorgoni-Cosmos; p.140 Watriss-Cosmos; p.141 Burri-Magnum; p.142 top Downing-Cosmos; bottom Lochon-Gamma; p.143 top Vogel-Rapho; bottom Gérard-Hoa-Qui; p.144 left Watriss-Cosmos; right Charliat-Rapho; p.145 Gérard-Hoa-Qui; p.146 Gérard-Hoa-Qui; p.147 Downing-Cosmos; p.148 Havanatour; p.149 Rodriguez-Top; p.150 J. Bottin; p.151 Rodriguez-Top; p.152 R.McLeod; p.153 J.-B. Sohiez; p.154 left Moisnard-Explorer; right Spiegel-Rapho; p.156 top Sioen-Cedri; bottom Funk-Rapho; p.157 Spiegel-Rapho; p.158 A. Robillard; p.159 top Spiegel-Rapho; bottom Spiegel-Rapho; p.160 top Ostrowski-Rapho; bottom Sioen-Cedri; p.161 Spiegel-Rapho; p.162 P. Frilet; p.163 Saunier-Rapho; p.164 Spiegel-Rapho; p.165 Rives-Cedri; p.166 top M.-L. Maylin; bottom M.-L. Maylin; p.167 M.-L. Maylin; p.168 M.-L. Maylin

Cover Pictures:
Top: Jake Rajs-The Image Bank
Bottom: Doug Armand-Tony Stone Worldwide

74-014-1